Formula 1 ™

THE SEASON

FOREWORD BY BERNIE
PORTRAIT PHOTOGRAPHY BY MIKAEL JANSSON

FORMULA 1 - THE SEASON. 2003 EDITION

First published in Great Britain in 2003 by Formula One Publishing, a division of Formula One Management Limited, a Formula One Group Company.

Portraits: Mikael Jansson
Principal Race Photography: Rainer and Boris Schlegelmilch
Additional Photography: Sutton Motorsport Images, Cahier Archive, Getty Images, LAT, DPPI and John Marsh.
Track Illustrations: Ulla Puggaard
Technical Illustrations: Paolo Filisetti

Reprographics by Rapida Graphics
Printed by Mohn Media with GL2

CONTENTS

Your Vision, Our Future

A PERFECT CAMERA
FOR A GREAT MOMENT

The Olympus μ[mju:] 400 DIGITAL:

Voted the best Digital Consumer Camera
in the TIPA European Photo & Imaging Awards 2003/2004.

4 million pixels in a weatherproof* metal body.

www.olympus.co.uk
0800 072 0070

*equivalent to IEC Standard publication 529 IF

FOREWORD

 I said last year that motor racing is a cyclical business. Back then we were congratulating Ferrari on doing a superb job that saw them dominate the season.

In 2003 the cycle continued. BMW Williams and McLaren Mercedes both upped their game to take the fight to Ferrari, while all of Renault's hard work over the previous two seasons began to pay off too.

In conjunction with revisions to the rules, this set the stage for one of the most gripping Formula One seasons in history.

We saw Kimi Raikkonen and Fernando Alonso win their first grands prix; and Jenson Button, Cristiano da Matta, Mark Webber, BAR Honda, Jaguar, Sauber and Toyota all lead a grand prix for the first time. And you had to go back to 1985 to find a season in which eight different drivers last won races.

There are aspects of the new rules that did not meet with universal approval, but we succeeded in creating an arena in which the contest between the greatest teams in motor racing was exciting and unpredictable, and in which there was unrivalled opportunity for everyone. All but one of the teams scored points.

As if this was not enough the battle for both World Championships - the Drivers' and the Constructors' - went down to the final race. Michael Schumacher's success in winning a record sixth crown - moving him one ahead of the legendary former joint record holder Juan Manuel Fangio - and Ferrari achieving an unprecedented fifth constructors' title in a row, were further endorsement of their greatness and confirmation that Formula One is a thriving sport that continually moves forward to set new benchmarks.

Formula 1 - The Season provides fascinating insight into an historic year that has laid the foundation for an equally stimulating 2004.
Bernie

2003 DRIVERS' CHAMPION

 The most important thing about 2003 is that Ferrari achieved both of its goals: to win the Drivers' and the Constructors' World Championships. For the team, this was particularly fantastic because they have now been champions five times in a row, which has never been done before.

I must say a big thank you to everyone at Ferrari, and I mean everyone, for the amazing job that they have done this year. They really deserve the Constructors' Championship because they have worked so hard. They are like a big family to me and I just love working with them.

As for my sixth world title, it is obviously a pretty amazing feeling to take the record. It will take quite a long time before it really sinks in and I don't want to say that it feels any different to the other five championships that I have won. They have all been unique and important to me in their own way. I don't think there are any words to describe how I feel.

As I look back through the year it's pretty obvious that every race was extremely important for us. The field was so competitive that we had to get as many points as we could at every race. That didn't always happen for us, but even though our difficult patch in the middle of the year, where I finished a lap down in Hockenheim and Hungary, I never lost faith in the team. They have done a fantastic job and I think the greatest strength of the team and all of our partners is that no-one gives up. We are all fighters and that fighting spirit really showed this year.

People keep wanting to compare my achievements to those of Juan Manuel Fangio, but all I can say is that I don't want to make that comparison. He is much higher than I see myself and there is not the slightest comparison to be made between what he achieved then and what we at Ferrari have achieved this year. They are two completely different eras of Formula One history and what Fangio achieved was unique and what we have achieved is unique.

All that is left is for me to thank all my fans around the world for their support. I hope I didn't make it too nerve-wracking for you by letting the destiny of the Championship go down to the last race!

Michael Schumacher
2003 World Drivers' Champion

2003 CONSTRUCTORS' CHAMPIONS

"**You know, I don't think you can make a comparison between** 2002 and 2003. Each year you try to achieve something different and when you achieve it, it is like a dream come true. This season there was much more competition and it was much more difficult to achieve what we did. We had to wait until the last race. It's so hard to believe, because we have been fighting so hard. It will take a few days before we truly realise it.

For the whole team I believe that we can be proud of what we have done. The drivers did an outstanding job, as did all our partners. We have been trying to push every single thing which could be pushed. We introduced a new fuel and a new oil with Shell at Monza, we were pushing each single partner to try to improve the situation. We have had to fight against very strong opposition: the rival tyre company, engine suppliers, the teams. It's something unique, but what we can be most proud of is that this team has been the same since 1997 and has achieved Constructors' Championship victories five-times in a row. Michael has won the Drivers' Championship with Ferrari four-times in a row plus the two he achieved before. He is the only driver to have won the title six-times. Even if we don't realise it yet, we should be proud of what we have achieved.

We had a tense afternoon in Suzuka. We said going in to the event that scoring one point could be harder to achieve than an outright win. Michael tried to prove that to us. That point seemed very elusive. But with Michael, you always know he is going to do it. We have so much faith in him. And Rubens did follow the team orders, because we asked him to win!

Michael is very focused and he has so much passion for his job. He is very professional and always available. He is always pushing because he wants to understand and learn. On the other hand, Ferrari has given him fantastic support: a fantastic car, fantastic engine, fantastic package. It is clear that we have not been successful all year because we have won eight races out of 16 compared with 15 out of 17 last year. And although Michael is a great guy, he needs a great car to get the job done. So it is a fantastic combination of very good people working together without any friction, each looking to do the best job they can, whilst supporting their colleagues. In the end we make the difference.

Michael felt flat after the race, but so did we. We were all drained. It was like a physical pain. I think we worked so hard and fought so hard, that we actually ached afterwards.

But I believe we are still fresh, we have respect for others, we know that we make mistakes and we know our limits, but we always keep our feet on the ground. We just do the job. I think we are all focused because we love being in Ferrari, we love being together, and the reason none of us wants to go is because it would feel, in a way, like we were betraying part of the group. And we are not ready for that yet.

Jean Todt
Scuderia Ferrari Marlboro
2003 World Constructors' Champions"

2003'S DEFINING MOMENTS

"All in all, I think Formula One is in a very good state of health." says Max Mosley, President of the FIA Motorsport Governing Body.

NEW SEASON, NEW RULES

FIA president Max Mosley on the controversial new rules introduced in 2003... and why Formula One's future has never looked so good

On Saturday 8th March 2003, FIA president Max Mosley was sitting at home wondering if Wednesday 15th January would turn out to be a day he would live to regret. That was the day when, against a background of increasing concern about the future of Formula One, he'd taken the courageous decision to force through a series of new rules and regulations designed to liven up the sport and aid cost-cutting to help the smaller teams survive.

Yet after the first final qualifying session for the opening race of the 2003 season in Melbourne, Michael Schumacher was a second ahead of his rivals, with team-mate Rubens Barrichello in the number two slot. It looked as if there would be another year of complete domination by Ferrari. "I did feel some trepidation when I saw the times and found it quite depressing – not because I was against Ferrari winning, but I just thought we couldn't have another year of complete domination by one team." Fortunately the race was different, with McLaren driver David Coulthard taking victory and Michael Schumacher not making the podium for the first time since 1999.

Mosley had had a lot to lose. He'd forced the teams to accept the huge changes, including a new qualifying format, a new points system and a new rule which kept the cars locked up in parc fermé overnight on the Saturday, the latter rule only being agreed just before the first race. Now it was his day of reckoning. In addition to this he had two teams, McLaren and BMW Williams, threatening legal action against the changes.

As it happened, Mosley had nothing to worry about. Michael Schumacher did not win the first race, or for that matter the second or

third races. A new era had been born, in which we would see some of the most varied and spectacular racing since the 1970s. "I have to say that Ferrari, who had the most to lose, made the least fuss, and of course we disarmed our opponents as they benefited the most from the new format."

Next year will see a modification to qualifying. "We have decided to run two back-to-back sessions on Saturday, in a different order. The drivers will go out in the order they finished the previous race, and in the second session they will go out in the reverse order in which they finished the first session. I think that by running the session on a Saturday it will attract people who couldn't normally watch it on Friday, and that can only be good for the sport."

The other area that Mosley is looking at is safety. With three big accidents after which the protagonists were unable to race, Formula One is still open to danger, even though Mosley has been on a crusade to improve safety standards since the fateful weekend of 1 May 1994. "One must never forget that any big accident could result in a fatality," he says. "We can reduce the probability, but it will never be zero. Compared to two or three years ago the lap times are a little too fast for the circuits, and this is something we are looking into right now."

Apart from this, Max Mosley is upbeat – and after such a great season, he has every reason to be. "I think 2003 proved that Formula One can put on a great show. Thousands of fans turned up in Indianapolis for the pit walkabout on the Thursday morning and it would be good to see more of that sort of interaction. But all in all, I think Formula One is in a very good state of health."

The all-new Jaguar XJ It's an entirely different animal.

It's the first time a luxury saloon has ever been built with a monocoque structure made
entirely from aluminium and with rivet-bonding technology found in the latest aerospace construction.
This makes for an XJ that is lightweight yet enormously strong.
Fuel efficient yet dynamic. The all-new XJ. It's an entirely different animal.

For more information call 0800 70 80 60.

JUSTIN WILSON PLC

It was brave, ingenious – and ultimately a roaring success. With aspiring Formula One drivers increasingly asked to bring money into the sport in return for a seat, Justin Wilson had a new idea: become a plc and let people invest in *him*. The public were able to buy shares in Wilson from £500 upwards, and the directors of Justin Wilson plc revealed that around 70 percent of the shares had been purchased for the minimal investment. That meant that over 1,500 investors, mainly fans, had made an investment in the talented Brit's future.

The oppportunity to give a chance to a promising young driver proved irresistible: two-and-a-half months after being launched in early March, Wilson had raised the targeted £1.2m. "I'm flattered that so many people have chosen to invest in my career," he enthused. His then boss at Minardi, Paul Stoddart, summed it up even better: "It's the best idea Formula One's seen in years."

Wilson's manager, ex-Formula One driver Jonathan Palmer, unveils the unique plc plan to raise money for the young Brit's entry into Formula One.

The race is over

The "Steinmetz Pink", created by Steinmetz. Exclusively launched at the Monaco Grand Prix 2003. A 59.60 carat, Vivid Pink, Oval cut, Internally Flawless.

JENSON CRASHES IN MONACO

Jenson Button suffered a huge accident in Saturday's free practice for the Monaco Grand Prix in June, hitting the barriers at Nouvelle Chicane at around 180mph. The sight of a Formula One car smashing sideways into those particular barriers brought back haunting memories of the horrific accident which befell Karl Wendlinger in practice for the 1994 race, an accident which put the young Austrian into a coma. It was a pertinent reminder of the dangers of Formula One, and the impact sidelined Button for the rest of the weekend.

Later on in the season, both Ralph Firman and Ralf Schumacher were involved in similarly high-speed accidents. Both walked away relatively unscathed, but were forced to sit out races as a precaution. F3000 front-runner Zsolt Baumgartner deputised for Firman, with Williams tester Marc Gene standing in superbly for Schumacher, coming in fifth at the Italian Grand Prix. These huge impacts reminded everyone how dangerous the sport could still be, but how far Formula One safety had evolved over the last decade.

SAUBER PETRONAS

Trust

Emotions

Achievements

Magnificent support

www.sauber-petronas.com

MADNESS AT SILVERSTONE

It was an image that shook the Formula One world: cars exiting Chapel corner and hurtling down Silverstone's Hangar Straight at over 160mph as a protestor, wearing an Irish dancing costume and clutching a banner, ran towards them. The scene was frighteningly reminiscent of the 1976 South African Grand Prix, at which the incredibly talented Tom Pryce collided with a track marshal who was running across the track to help a stricken car. The impact killed both men instantly.

Thankfully at Silverstone, everyone managed to avoid Father Neil Horan, who was soon rugby tackled to the ground by a marshal and spent six weeks on remand as checks were carried out on his mental state. Meanwhile, Rubens Barrichello drove one of his greatest career races that day to take victory at the British Grand Prix, ironically his second win at a race disrupted by a trespassing protester. He won his first Grand Prix at Hockenheim in 2001, after a disgruntled ex-Mercedes employee walked alongside the track.

1st Gulf Air Bahrain Grand Prix
02 - 04 April 2004

Believe it's Bahrain!

04.04.04

TICKETS & INFORMATION:

+973 406222

www.bahraingp.com

Bahrain International Circuit

With two seasons of Formula One racing behind us,
we're preparing for the future.
Building on the lessons learned to better face
the greatest motorsports challenge of all.
Watch us.

www.toyota-f1.com

THE TYRE WAR

Tyres had always been a thorny issue in Formula One, but never
more so than in 2003. The root of the problem lay in a meeting in
October 2002 between the team bosses, for it was here that they voted
unanimously to change the 2003 rules to limit wet tyres to one
specification per event. It was designed as one of many cost-cutting
measures, but the carnage of the Brazilian Grand Prix, where
intermediate tyres were chosen for what turned out to be a monsoon
weekend, caused a fairly substantial repair bill for every team.

The regulation was changed mid-season, but come the Hungarian
Grand Prix the tyre debate was back in full swing – and this time it was
war. Ferrari highlighted to the FIA their belief that the contact patch on a
used set of Michelin tyres contravened Article 77c. The FIA, rather than
declaring Michelin had broken any rules, chose to change the way they
interpreted the rule and would, from the Italian Grand Prix, check a tyre's
contact patch after the race rather than before. Michelin threatened to
boycott the Italian Grand Prix, but in the end simply modified their tyres.

The tyre war reached
new heights after the
Hungarian Grand Prix,
when Michelin were
reported to the FIA by
Ferrari. The Italians
believed the tyres didn't
comply with FIA rules.

FOSTER'S AN OFFICIAL
SPONSOR OF GRAND PRIX

NEW HORIZONS

Formula One broke new ground this year, cementing its future
in some new and exotic places. Turkey, for instance, followed Bahrain
and China by unveiling a £70 million project to build a new grand prix
track in the nation's capital, Istanbul. A deal was drawn up between
Turkish officials and Formula One Management in London at the end of
August for a seven-year deal to run the Turkish Grand Prix from 2005 to
2011. The proposed race is being marketed as a huge tourist draw to
the country and the circuit will be built on the Asian side of Istanbul.

It didn't end there. "We will be having a Formula One race in India,"
said Bernie Ecclestone in July. He didn't stipulate when, but the
complications of global tobacco advertising meant that one country's
financial loss would be another's gain. Next year will see the inaugural
Grands Prix of Bahrain and China, with the likes of India and Turkey
looking set to follow suit within the next few years. "India is moving
forward very fast," added Ecclestone, who was considering the southern
city of Hyderabad as a possible venue.

In 2003, the ever-expanding globalisation of Formula One showed no
signs of stopping.

**Turkey (above) has
confirmed its entry into the
Formula One family while
India (below) is showing
strong interest**

MOBIL 1 GRAND PRIX OF GERMANY AT THE
HOCKENHEIMRING BADEN-WÜRTTEMBERG

HOCKEN HEIM

JULY 23rd – 25th 2004

TICKETS AT:
0049(0)6205-950222
AND AT ALL GERMAN CTS BOOKING OFFICES

VILLENEUVE OUT

Even before the season had begun, the name Jacques Villeneuve filled the pages of the international motorsport media. At the launch of the BAR005 it was clear that BAR's new boy, Jenson Button, would have to win the respect of the former World Champion and this was not going to happen until he had proved his worth on the track. The two soon came to blows over a bodged pitstop at the Australian Grand Prix , but subsequently built a good rapport.

Yet with BAR looking to save money in 2004, Villeneuve always knew he would have problems retaining the salary of a champion, and so it was that in the week before the Japanese Grand Prix, BAR boss Dave Richards informed Villeneuve's manager Craig Pollock that Jacques's services would not be required in 2004. On the Thursday morning in Suzuka, Villeneuve decided he'd had enough and flew home. Once electrifying, always controversial, a former World Champion left the sport with a whimper.

MONACO®
Grand Prix

D'ÉM

épi Monaco, Tél. 97 97 61 00 - www.epi.mc   © 05077

GRAND PRIX
DE MONACO

75 ANS
OTIONS

AUTOMOBILE CLUB DE MONACO
23, boulevard Albert -1er
Boîte Postale 464
MC 98012 Monaco cedex

Tél. +377 93 15 26 00
Fax +377 93 25 80 08
E-mail : info@acm.mc
http//: www.acm.mc

The 2003-GA was hailed as the best Formula One car ever at its launch. It didn't quite dominate as its predecessor had, but still took Ferrari on to yet more glory.

THE 2003-GA

The arrival of the Ferrari 2003-GA, named after the legendary Fiat boss Gianni Agnelli who died earlier in 2003, was the point in the season where the collective groans of team bosses could literally be heard around the world. It was hailed as the best Formula One car ever made, just months after the Italians had dominated the sport in a manner not seen in years. It didn't take long to settle in, either, winning its first race in Spain.

A couple of garages along in the pitlane, there was also plenty of expectation surrounding a new car. The McLaren MP4-18 – Woking's riposte to Maranello – was on the verge of being released. Furtive test pictures were shown, work was carried out… but the new car's race debut was delayed and delayed. As Ferrari and their 2003-GA strode imperiously towards more glory, it became frustratingly clear that the MP4-18 would never race competitively.

Bridgestone and Ferrari did it!

Thank you to everyone who cheered us on!

The 2003 Formula One World Championship produced epic duels in the Drivers' and Constructors' Championships, with both titles decided in the very last race of the season, the Japanese Grand Prix.

At Suzuka, Ferrari's Michael Schumacher was crowned Formula One World Champion for the fourth season in a row. Schumacher also became the first driver ever to win six World Championships in his career, a tremendous achievement. Ferrari itself claimed a fifth consecutive Constructors' title since teaming up with Bridgestone.

Michael Schumacher and Ferrari believe in Bridgestone. They see us as more than a supplier: we are their partner. Even during a tense and fiercely competitive season, their faith in Bridgestone never wavered.

Together we battled to improve, took tyre technology to the next level, and went on to win. That's why victory this year tastes especially sweet.

Bridgestone has supported the Formula One World Champion for six straight years. With more and more customers around the world embracing Bridgestone as a partner they too can depend on, our passion and commitment will keep us focused on the road ahead.

Six for Schumacher!
The first six-time Formula One World Champion!

Our passion for the very best in technology, quality and service is at the heart of our commitment to you wherever you are in the world. Bridgestone wants to inspire and move you.

BRIDGESTONE

PASSION for EXCELLENCE

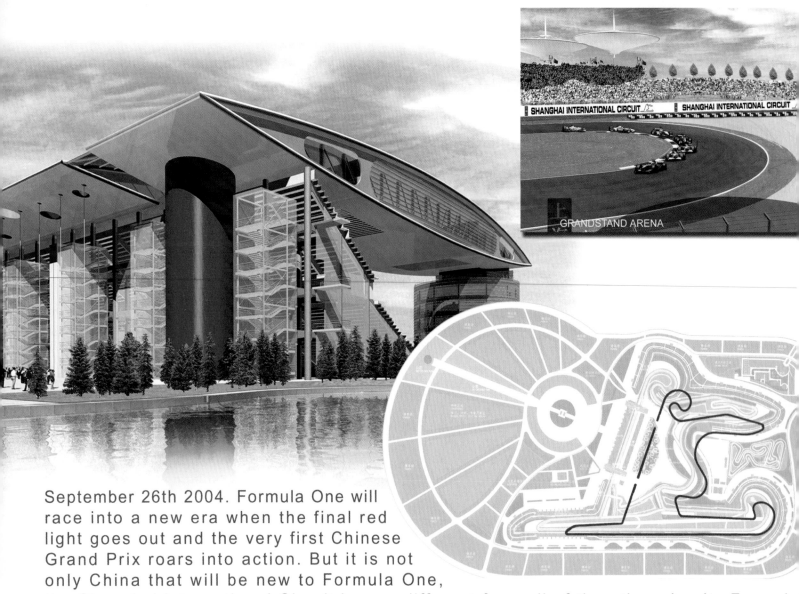

GRANDSTAND ARENA

SHANGHAI INTERNATIONAL CIRCUIT   SHANGHAI INTERNATIONAL CIRCUIT

September 26th 2004. Formula One will race into a new era when the final red light goes out and the very first Chinese Grand Prix roars into action. But it is not only China that will be new to Formula One, the Shanghai international Circuit is very different from all of the other circuits Formula One will visit in 2004. The needs of the world`s best drivers and spectators were given priority when building the 5.45km circuit. The 29,000 spectators in the main grandstand can view nearly half the circuit from their stunning vantage point. Another 20,000 fans in the arena around Turn 10 are in prime position to see the field jockey for position as the cars brake after 1.3km on full throttle. Join us in Shanghai for a new Formula One experience.

Tilke

SHANGHAI INTERNATIONAL CIRCUIT

GRANDSTAND ARENA

Shanghai, China

Shanghai is an incredible city that is attracting the world's attention with its phenomenal changes. Those who have been to Shanghai have felt the passion and pulse of this populous, dynamic city of China.

In September 2004, the world will focus its attention on Shanghai once again as the Formula One race roars into action in the city. The 16 million local residents and many more across the country will share the excitement of this high-speed sport.

Shanghai is a cosmopolitan city with excellent infrastructure and facilities, as well as Its rich experience in organizing large-scale international events and sports games, such as APEC meeting in 2001. Shanghai has already constructed a world-class auto racing circuit and is determined to make the Formula One race the most spectacular sporting event in history.

Let's meet in Shanghai in the autumn of 2004!

FIGHTING FUND

Had they known the team bosses' press conference at the
Canadian Grand Prix in June was going to be this exciting, they'd have
been selling tickets. The Fighting Fund debate had been simmering for
months, right from the point in January when McLaren boss Ron Dennis
proposed the scheme that was designed to give financial help to the
privateer teams such as Minardi who, with no manufacturer backing,
were struggling in the global economic climate of the time.

Six months later, Minardi boss Paul Stoddart sat on his own at the
press conference in Montreal awaiting the arrival of his peers, who were
having a separate meeting. As the team bosses breezed in nonchalantly,
Stoddart could contain his anger no more. "Certain commitments were
made on 15 January," he ranted. "It's time people honoured them and
stopped trying to hijack them to satisfy other agendas." Dennis'
response? "If you can't stand the heat, get out of the kitchen." Stoddart
promptly declared himself "completely disillusioned with certain people
around me". In the end the Fighting Fund issue was resolved quietly, and
Minardi survived to the end of the season.

Minardi boss Paul Stoddart
(right) is not amused over
the Fighting Fund issue at
the Canadian Grand Prix.
McLaren Team Principal
Ron Dennis (below) and
Stoddart have their say
while BAR boss David
Richards tries to bring
about a truce.

RACE STEWARDS

In what was widely seen as the most exciting Formula One
season in years, some will point to key decisions that were made off the
track that took some gloss off the sport. Towards the end of the season,
Juan Pablo Montoya's World Championship hopes were all but ended
on lap 22 of the United States Grand Prix, after race stewards ruled he
had caused an avoidable accident with Rubens Barrichello. "It is sad to
have my title hopes ended in this way," the Colombian rued afterwards.

For once, his team-mate probably sympathised. Ralf Schumacher had
been the victim of a similarly controversial stewards' decision earlier in
the season, just as his title chances were gathering momentum. He was
blamed for the first corner pile-up at the German Grand Prix and though
his 10-place grid-penalty at the following race in Hungary was replaced
with a fine, both Williams drivers will not have viewed these two key
moments of their seasons with much humour. At the last race in Suzuka,
Montoya, still seething at the manner in which his title hopes had been
dashed, called for the introduction of full-time stewards to avoid further
inconsistencies in rule application. There were many in the paddock
who agreed with his opinions.

Montoya causes what race stewards labelled an "avoidable accident" at Indianapolis. The decision effectively ended his title hopes.

IT'S NOT ONLY ABOUT ENGINES, IT'S ABOUT ENGINEERING

WWW.GAMETRAC.COM

GET TOGETHER
WITH GAMETRAC

YOUNG GUNS

There was a moment during the Hungarian Grand Prix when Michael Schumacher saw the future flash past him. A few seconds later, it was gone. He'd just been lapped by 22-year-old Renault driver Fernando Alonso, whose undoubted promise resulted in a fine victory that day. In Malaysia, Kimi Raikkonen also scored his first win in Formula One, two weeks after signalling his intent by edging the five-times World Champion off the track.

   In the long run, the title fight went down to the wire and it was Raikkonen who was snapping at Schumacher's heels all the way. If he hadn't realised it before, Schumacher now knew the threats to his dominance would be coming from all directions in 2004.

Alonso (left) and Raikkonen (below) showed Michael Schumacher they would be serious threats to his title next season

Powering Dreams Into Reality

SEPANG F1 CIRCUIT
HOME OF MOTORSPORTS

"Malaysians are practical dreamers... And through their pragmatism, they went ahead to build a circuit while negotiating the Formula One contract!"

That was how former Malaysian Prime Minister Datuk Seri Dr Mahathir Mohamad described a developing country's ambition in constructing the world's best Formula One circuit and the staging of the inaugural Malaysian Grand Prix in 1999.

Dr Mahathir retired in October leaving a dream not only already realised in the form of the Sepang F1 Circuit and a Grand Prix that has been successfully staged over the last five years, but a monument of Malaysia's determination to join the ranks of a fully industrialised nation.

Visiting the 1996 Portuguese Grand Prix at Estoril, Dr Mahathir understood the enormous gains of hosting the Formula One World Championship and immediately discussed with Bernie Ecclestone, the head of Formula One Management Ltd., the possibility of bringing Formula One to Malaysia.

Determined to transform Malaysia into a developed nation by 2020 by venturing into the automotive industry, Dr Mahathir saw Formula One as more than just a brand-building exercise for Malaysia. It would help springboard the ambition of becoming a centre for automotive research, engineering and development, and Asia's motorsports hub.

"When the Prime Minister Dr Mahathir decided to build a Grand Prix track, it was because he wanted to project the image of Malaysia in a high technology sport and he has successfully achieved that," recalled racing legend Sir Jackie Stewart.

In a whirlwind 14 months, Malaysia hosted its inaugural Grand Prix, becoming only the second Asian host country besides Japan and the first new championship venue since Hungary in 1986. Dr Mahathir's determination was a feat that had not only catapulted Malaysia on to the world's sports-entertainment map but in the process redefined standards in Formula One.

A world class facility, the 5.543km circuit set new benchmarks and was quickly acknowledged by the drivers, teams and media as the best in the world even before the circuit was officially opened.

"When I was first approached by Dr Mahathir to build a circuit, I said that Formula One was the province of rich, developed countries. But the Prime Minister was insistent. I never thought this would put Malaysia on the map, but the Prime Minister had thought about it a long time ago," said former Sepang International Circuit Chairman Tan Sri Basir Ismail.

Named *"Organiser of the Best Grand Prix for 1999"* at the annual FIA Awards after only a single race being staged, the Malaysian Grand Prix was a test that came at a critical time as the sport debated venturing further outside Europe. The Grand Prix proved that a developing country was equally worthy of staging the world's most prestigious event, if not better, and helped pave the way for other new championship venues being nominated, particularly those in Asian countries.

"Motor sports will help to put us on the world map and attract commerce and tourists to Malaysia," Dr Mahathir had once envisioned and he successfully accomplished it at only a fraction of the cost that would have been required today had his ambition come five years later.

The Malaysian Grand Prix and the Sepang F1 Circuit have empowered Malaysians with the fundamentals of that same ambition and dream.

PETRONAS MALAYSIAN GRAND PRIX 2004
19-21 March 2004

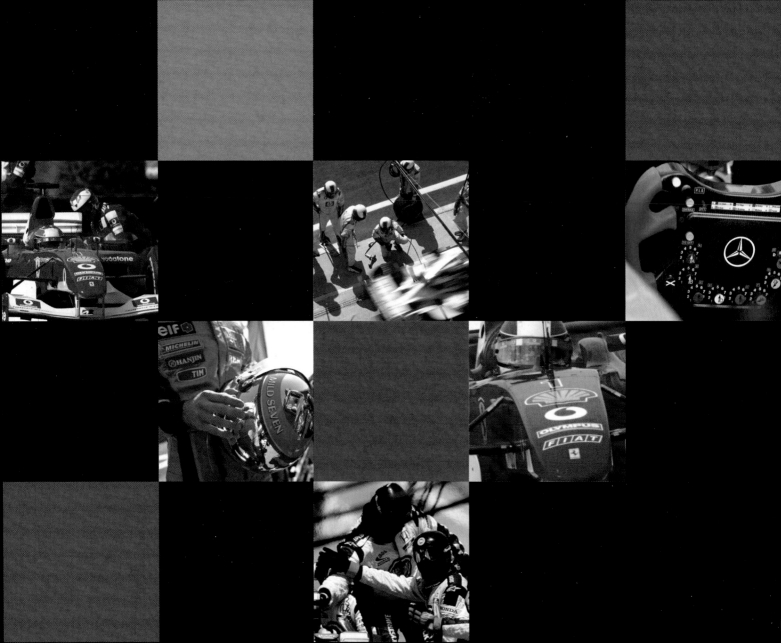

THE TEAMS

SCUDERIA FERRARI MARLBORO

"I don't think you can compare the progress we made this year with that of last year, because it was much harder for us to reach our goals in 2003. We were forced to go down to the last race, which proves how much more difficult it was. What we have achieved this year is unique, although I think it will be some time before we realise the magnitude of what we have done.

What makes our achievements even sweeter is the car that won, the F2003-GA, bore the initials of Gianni Agnelli, who died last year. He was always very supportive of the team, even in the bad times, so our championship successes this year are in memory of him.

It's fair to say that we probably didn't get the best out of the new rules at the beginning of the season. We were definitely the team that was hurt most by the rule changes last winter because we had the most to lose, but we soon learnt how to deal with one-lap qualifying. The most important thing is that we always stayed together as a team. Even when we had a difficult patch in the middle of the year, no one stopped pushing.

As for our rivals, I think everyone did a very good job this year; that's why the championship battles went down to the wire. Anyway, we are not so arrogant as to underestimate anyone.

One of the biggest advantages that we have at Ferrari is that although many of us have been together for a long time, we are still very fresh. We all love what we do and I hope that we can continue this for many years to come. **"**

45

Above: Ferrari's pit crew execute another flawless tyre change. A wasted split second can lose a race. Far right: A brace of Prancing Horses at rest.

For the first time in three seasons Ferrari didn't have a technical advantage in 2003. The F2003-GA was probably the best car, but for most of the season it was let down by the inconsistency of its Bridgestone tyres and, at several races, Michael Schumacher and Rubens Barrichello were relegated to also-rans.

But Bridgestone's deficiencies at least gave us a World Championship battle and made this the hardest-fought of Michael's four titles with the Scuderia. Schumacher faced serious opposition from Juan Pablo Montoya and Kimi Raikkonen but in the end, Michael and Ferrari were the deserved champions.

Over the course of the season, they were the most impressive and consistent driver-team combinations.

There were three areas where Ferrari held an advantage over its rivals: the tenacity of Michael Schumacher behind the wheel, their unflinching team spirit and the reliability of the F2003-GA.

Michael's driving skills, his race craft and his mentality make him the most complete driver in Formula One, but it became clear in 2003 that his closest rivals are not learning from him. Until they emulate Michael's never-say-die attitude to race driving, he will continue to reign supreme in F1. Schumacher, you see, knows that World Championships are won and lost on the bad days of the year, when the car set-up isn't quite right, and sheer bloody-mindedness sees him drag the car home in eighth place to score a single championship point as was the case in Hungary this year. He is like a pneumatic drill, always pushing week-in, week-out, and he stands out in a field of fluctuating performers.

As for team spirit, you only have to look at the united front presented by the team at their lowest points of the year in Hockenheim and Hungary to appreciate why Michael refers to everyone at Maranello as "my family". Through these bad times there was none of the internal bickering that has blighted the team's history. Mechanics went about their business in the normal way and the team's management wouldn't be drawn into blaming any of their suppliers, although the source of the problem clearly lay with Bridgestone. The only noticeable change over 2002 was the intensity of

Above: The mechanics keep a watching brief. The pressure from their rivals made the Scuderia's victories taste even sweeter. Far left: Rubens Barrichello slips on his Nomex balaclava in preparation for the US Grand Prix.

their victory celebrations as the wins became scarcer, but the atmosphere inside was never anything but serene.

Ferrari no longer have a blame culture, and they owe much of their positive outlook to Michael who, whatever the result, shakes the hand of every mechanic after each race. He is their unifying force, their leader. The team loves him.

As for reliability, the F2003-GA was peerless. Michael did not have a single technical failure all year, and Rubens had only one, which was a suspension failure in Hungary (his fuel feed problem in Brazil was in the F2002). Yet this outstanding reliability didn't come at the price of performance. In February, the team did a back-to-back test with its '02 and '03 cars and it reckoned the new car to be 0.7 seconds per lap faster than the old one. So the level of reliability was merely a reflection of the engineering excellence carried out by the team.

So the only question mark over Ferrari's season was Bridgestone and the manner in which the Japanese company was usurped by Michelin at the top of the F1 tree. Ross Brawn tried to blame the Scuderia for leading Bridgestone up a technical blind alley, but the reality is that Bridgestone took its eye off the ball last winter and, come Melbourne, they were already second best.

To make matters worse for Bridgestone, their policy of supplying only one top team hurt them further. They couldn't gather data fast enough to improve their product at a similar rate to Michelin, who had McLaren, Williams and Renault as test horses, and the gap between the two rubber giants actually grew as the season progressed.

Michelin-gate was the only thing that stopped the rot. Leading up to the team's home race at Monza, Ferrari boss Jean Todt felt the World Championship slipping away, only to strike gold after he stumbled upon a killer piece of evidence against Michelin, given to him by a Japanese photographer. He believed he had proof that Michelin's front tyres were illegal when worn down.

The FIA immediately asked Michelin to re-design their tyres, which interrupted their pre-Monza test and, when Michael then won the Italian

Perfect synchronisation as the pit crew wait for Michael Schumacher to stop on the line.

Grand Prix the following week, the advantage was back with the Scuderia. He delivered the killer blow at Indianapolis a fortnight later when his title rivals flaked away in the pressure-cooker environment of one of the world's greatest racetracks. Both titles were within touching distance.

As for the team's fifth consecutive constructors' title, the team owes much to Rubens Barrichello who, despite scoring only two wins in 2003, had his most impressive season in Formula One. He was fast and consistent and Michael publicly praised his team-mate's contribution after the race at Suzuka.

"I must say a big thank you to Rubens", said Michael. "He drove a great race and he won it in style, and he has made a big contribution to Ferrari's Constructors' Championship win this year."

More often than not, and that is no exaggeration, Michael adopted Rubens' set-up at races this year. And Rubens' impressive technical ability with the F2003-GA was matched by his speed because he was often faster than his team leader, even out-qualifying Michael in five of the last six races.

For the people at Ferrari, the extent of their achievements this year will take a few weeks to sink in. Suzuka proved to be such an emotional roller-coaster that there was more a feeling of relief than anything else.

With four races to go it looked extremely unlikely that they would win either title, such was the momentum behind Williams and, even during the Japanese Grand Prix itself, there were moments when Michael looked to have thrown it all away when he became entangled with the likes of Takuma Sato and Cristiano da Matta.

Worryingly for Ferrari's opposition, they still have an impressive desire for more next year. When Jean Todt rang chief designer Rory Byrne after the race at Suzuka (10am, Italian time), Rory was already in the wind tunnel. And engine director Paolo Martinelli was in the engine department.

Ferrari, you see, is a way of life, not a job and as long as Schumacher, Todt, Brawn, Byrne and Martinelli continue to channel everyone's enthusiasm in the right direction, they will keep on winning.

MAHLE makes Winners

Nowhere else are engines put to a tougher test than in big international races. High engine speeds above 18,000 rpm and piston head temperatures of more than 300°C call for supreme skill in development and the highest standard of perfection in technology. MAHLE has been a leading system supplier for decades to the World Champions in Formula One, to the winners of the 24 Hours of Le Mans, and to the winners of all categories in touring car, sports and racing car events.

And when the favourites set out on the next races, MAHLE pistons and engine components will once again be there on the road to victory.

So that millions of motorists the world over benefit every day from MAHLE top technology proven time and again in motor racing.

More Information: MAHLE GmbH, Pragstr. 26–46, D-70376 Stuttgart
www.mahle.com

PISTONS AND ENGINE COMPONENTS
FILTER SYSTEMS VALVE TRAIN SYSTEMS

BMW. WILLIAMSF1 TEAM

"**The 2003 season proved to be a roller coaster year for the BMW** WilliamsF1 Team. It became apparent at Melbourne that the FW25 still required a considerable amount of development work before it could contest for the podium positions. However, through hours of hard work and determination at both Grove and Munich, we started the European rounds with a more competitive racing car which eventually was able to provide a serious threat to Ferrari, McLaren and Renault for the rest of the year.

Following a much improved mid-season run, during which time we won four races, the team entered the final phase of the Championship as strong contenders in both the Drivers' and Constructors' titles. 2003 did not end the way we would have hoped, and arguably we lost both Championships as a result of our slow start to the year.

Work has already begun on the FW26 and we are dedicated to lining up a competitive car on the grid from the very first grand prix of the season. We should also profit from another season of driver continuity with Juan Pablo and Ralf also benefiting from the dedication of a blue chip portfolio of commercial and technical partners.

In 2002 we finished the Constructors' Championship in a weak second. This year we finished in a strong second. Juan and Ralf were also very competitive in the Drivers' Championship. Despite the disappointing outcome of this season, the BMW WilliamsF1 Team is aware of the challenges it faces and looks forward to 2004 with anticipation. The progress made this season highlights our potential so I have high aspirations for the year ahead. "

Above: Technical Director, Patrick Head, keeps an eye on his pit wall strategists. Far right: Ralf and Juan Pablo line up on the starting grid, poised for action.

A chest infection kept Frank Williams away from Suzuka, so when the flag dropped on the 2003 Formula One season, it was left to BMW Williams' technical director, Patrick Head, to sum up the team's season.

"It has been very, very disappointing," he said. "We simply have to do better next year." In year four of the team's partnership with BMW, nothing less than a world title will suffice. Second place in the Constructors' Championship was merely first of the losers.

What makes 2003 even more disappointing for everyone in Grove and Munich, is that both world titles were there for the taking. With four races to go, they were favourites to win the drivers' and the constructors' titles and BMW Williams even began making tentative advertising plans around the expected successes.

For the second half of the year, the BMW Williams-Michelin FW25 was the best car-engine-tyre package on the grid. There were races such as Hockenheim where Montoya literally destroyed everyone else. After that German Grand Prix, Montoya gushed praise on the car.

"It is pretty amazing what the team has done with this car," he said. "I think it is probably the best out there at the moment, although it's very close to Ferrari, depending on the tyre situation."

That was then. Now, BMW Williams have to go back to the drawing board and work out how they snatched defeat from the jaws of victory. For the sixth year in succession, the team has had to enter the winter without a world title to its name. It's the longest barren period in their history. Everyone played their part in the team's downfall. The drivers made some errors, the mechanics fluffed some pitstops and the engineers made some set-up errors. As a result, it will not be an easy fix.

Both Montoya and Ralf Schumacher had their share of unforced errors this year. Montoya spun away the lead in Melbourne, crashed in Malaysia and Brazil, spun away a potential race win in Canada and made a series of

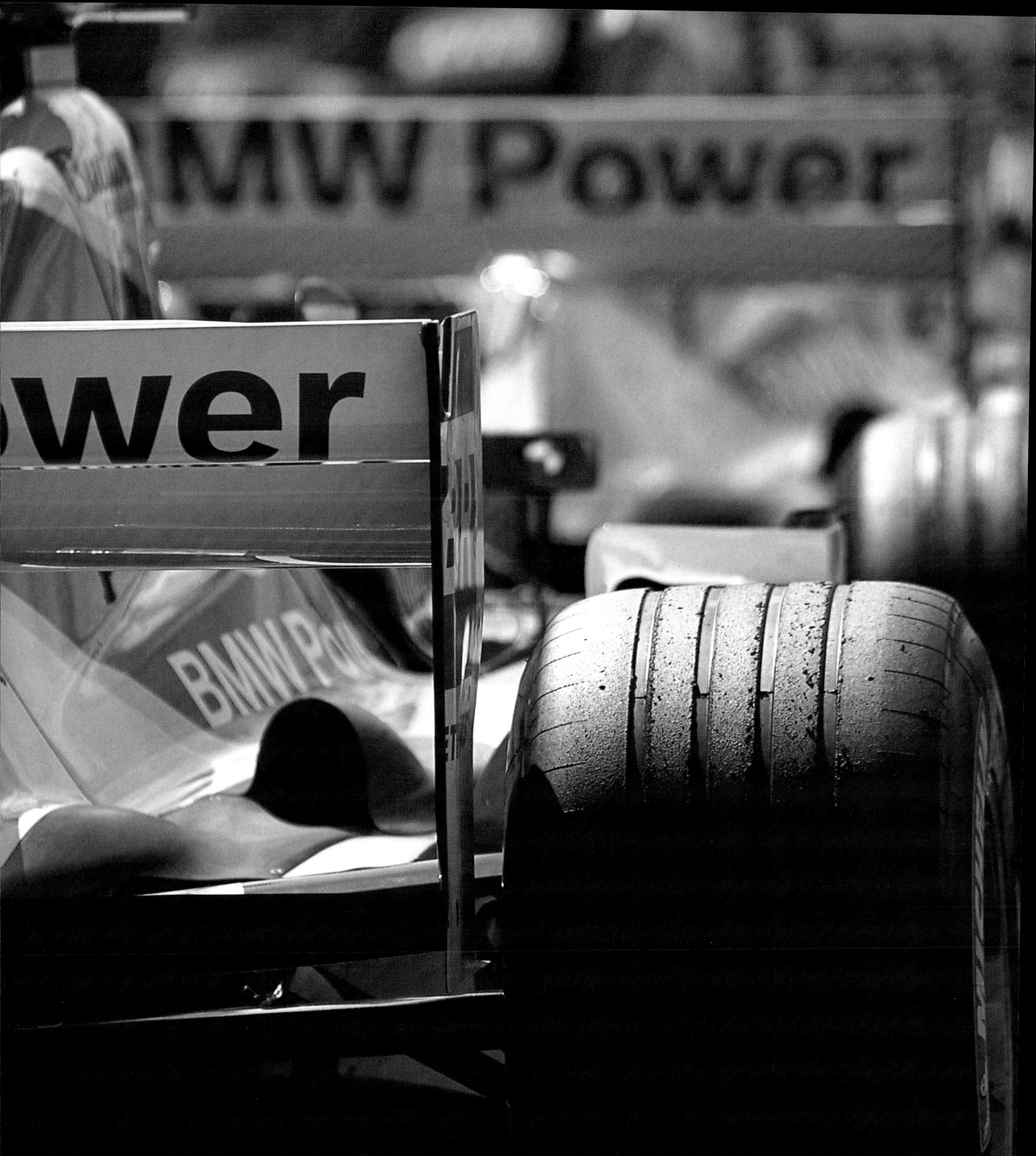
MW Power
ower
BMW Po

set-up gaffs when the pressure was on at the end of the year.

Ralf, on the other hand, was blinding at the Nurburgring and Magny-Cours (winning both races in the space of a week), yet in the last six races he scored just one point more than Marc Gene, who subbed for him at Monza, when Ralf pulled out after suffering from dizzy fits following a big accident during the previous weeks' testing.

Ralf's poor form in the second half of the year undoubtedly played a key role in the team losing the Constructors' Championship.

Early in the season the FW25 proved tricky to set-up and both drivers were guilty of overdriving in one-lap qualifying, which is why they suffered from relatively poor grid positions. But, as the season progressed, the car improved and their poor performances just when pressure for the championship was mounting were the result of poor man-management, which is not an unfamiliar story in the history of Williams Grand Prix Engineering.

The internal bickering started at the French Grand Prix, when Juan was forced by the team to change the timing of his second pitstop, thereby giving Ralf a certain victory. He was furious and exchanged expletives with Chief Operations Engineer Sam Michael over the radio.

After that Juan's relationship with the team was not as tight as it should be and of course the relationship between driver, engineers and management is always paramount to the overall success of the team. If you look at Ferrari, it is only since the internal bickering stopped that the championship titles have returned.

This situation pushed Juan into signing for McLaren in 2005, which only added to the ill-feeling between the management and its Colombian star. Again, compare that to the marriage of Schumacher to the Scuderia.

Three races later came the Hungarian Grand Prix, when Montoya qualified what turned out to be a disappointing fourth and finished third in the race. It was obvious that the cracks between team and driver were becoming even wider. After all, when it comes to wringing the neck of a

Tension mounts as the BMW WIlliams engineers carry out computerised systems checks on the car before the race.

racing car, no-one does it better than Montoya, not even Michael Schumacher. To drive any other way is complete anathema to Juan and at times it looked as if he was too busy to change his driving style, as the season headed towards its climax, so his on-track performances deteriorated as the relationship between team and driver worsened. He started to make basic set-up errors and the Montoya of old became a rudderless ship. This resulted in Juan's confused and uninspired drive at Indianapolis, where he was taken out of the running for the championship.

Ralf had fewer problems than Juan on the management side, although he has always thought himself to be a BMW man, rather than a Williams man, which isn't always conducive to there being complete harmony between the two camps inside the pit garage.

The petty politics within the team was so unfortunate this year because, as an engineering exercise, 2003 was a successful campaign for WilliamsF1. They started the year with a car that oozed potential, yet they couldn't translate that onto the track. To begin with they ran the car too stiff, then at Monaco they softened the ride for the first time and Montoya won the race. That improvement in form coincided with the arrival of veteran engineer Frank Dernie in the team. By the end of the year a relentless development programme, combined with consistently excellent tyres from Michelin, meant that the car was the fastest of all.

No one person is to blame for what happened this year and, anyway, Frank and Patrick would not want a public persecution. It's just not their style.

But the team needs to take a look at re-organising its race team because that's where most of the errors were made this year. Too much confusion, and not enough leadership.

BMW Williams have all the right ingredients for championship victory. By rights, 2004 should be their year.

Here's to the daredevils of computation.

Here's to the fearless plotters of telemetry.

Here's to the conquerors of drag coefficient.

Here's to the guys in the backroom who boldly steered

BMW WilliamsF1 Team through a brilliant season.

bmw williamsf1 team   Congratulations from their technology partner, HP.

+ hp

= *everything is possible*

RON DENNIS TEAM PRINCIPAL

61

WEST McLAREN MERCEDES

McLaren as an organisation exists to win and we didn't achieve this objective in 2003. However, it's been a great and exciting season with Kimi narrowly missing out on the Drivers' World Championship, finishing only two points behind Michael Schumacher. We have seen some tremendous races in addition to a few frustrating ones, which we dominated but didn't finish, so I very much see the 2003 season as a reflection of what could have been.

The competitiveness of McLaren, Williams and Ferrari this year definitely helped to make the races much more interesting. In addition, as we had to start the races with the fuel load with which we finished qualifying, an even greater importance was placed on strategy and I believe this was an area where we excelled and got to grips with better than anybody else.

Kimi performed well this year and I have no doubt that he will win many races and World Championships in the future. David is a fantastic racing driver who sometimes made life difficult for himself in qualifying. However, he had a strong end to the season and we are confident that our driver line up for 2004 is everything it needs to be in terms of winning.

McLaren don't spend much time looking backwards and much prefer to look forward to 2004 where we firmly believe that we will be an even stronger contender for the Formula One World Championship.

Above: The McLaren crew is among the slickest in the paddock. Far right: The complexities of the McLaren Mercedes steering-wheel is an example of the high level of engineering integrity required by modern Formula One racing.

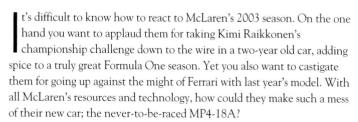

It's difficult to know how to react to McLaren's 2003 season. On the one hand you want to applaud them for taking Kimi Raikkonen's championship challenge down to the wire in a two-year old car, adding spice to a truly great Formula One season. Yet you also want to castigate them for going up against the might of Ferrari with last year's model. With all McLaren's resources and technology, how could they make such a mess of their new car; the never-to-be-raced MP4-18A?

At the start of the season, the official line was that the new car had a few reliability issues that needed to be sorted and would be introduced at Imola (race four). However, that debut was soon put back to Silverstone, which was hugely embarrassing for the team because the British Grand Prix was more than halfway through the season. Yet no-one could have predicted that, come Suzuka, Kimi Raikkonen and David Coulthard would be desperately fighting for championship scraps whilst waiting for the 18A.

The development costs of the new car have been estimated at $40 million, yet for all the team's renowned technological prowess, they never managed to solve a low speed overheating problem. Clearly, the car had a basic design flaw that the team succeeded in brushing under the carpet, but it might not be purely coincidence that technical director Adrian Newey appeared at fewer races this year than is normal for him. They might have wished to keep him away from the demanding dictaphones of the press, justifiably keen to know exactly what the problem with the 18A was. Now, it's been revealed that the MP4-18A will never be raced in a Formula One grand prix: an all new MP4-19 will be shipped to Melbourne in March '04.

The frustration for Raikkonen is not so much that the 18A never raced, because on the few occasions he tested it, the stopwatch showed no difference between the new car and the 17D. He will be more annoyed that the team continued to run a parallel development programme with the car,

long after they knew that it would never race. It was a drain on money and
man-power that might have been better-used on the old car – especially
when the World Championship battle reached its end-of-season climax.

"Although we have not raced the 18A, we have learnt a lot from it," said
McLaren boss Ron Dennis. "We are applying a lot of that knowledge into
next year's car, the MP4-19." Of course, had Schumacher and Barrichello
retired from the Japanese Grand Prix and Kimi won the 2003 world title,
Ron would be basking in the glory of perhaps McLaren's greatest drivers'
title. Never in Ron's tenure at McLaren has the team actually achieved
more in year two with a car than year one. But Kimi didn't win the title
and the team's closed-season post mortem must reflect on what more they
could have done to squeeze out increased performance from the car.

This, though, was the team's only real weak point in 2003. The race
team was as slick as ever and seemed to ride a wave of good fortune for
much of the year. First, David Coulthard won the season's first race in
Australia, then Raikkonen followed that after being gifted his first win in
Formula One in Malaysia when his nearest rivals were taken out in
accidents. Thereafter, the team – and Raikkonen in particular – were
always knocking on the door of the podium. He scored 10 top-three
finishes in total, six of which he got in the first half of the season and from
which he formed the basis of his World Championship challenge.
The race engineers even managed to eek some genuine pace from the car
when its Michelin tyres afforded it enough of an advantage over Ferrari. A
case in point was at the Nurburgring, where Kimi took the first pole
position of his Formula One career and was heading for a lights-to-flag
victory when his engine blew at just under half distance.

Kimi had already been blown away by the superior engines of Ferrari and
BMW in Canada two weeks before the 'Ring, but if there was a turning

Above: Kimi has proved he has the potential to be a future World Champion.

point in the year for him, the Nurburgring was it. On lap 26 of the European Grand Prix he was almost five seconds ahead of BMW Williams' Ralf Schumacher and looked certain to record a convincing second win of the season. But the Mercedes V10, usually so reliable, suddenly started blowing huge plumes of smoke. That retirement from the lead knocked the momentum out of Raikkonen's championship challenge and he never looked as convincing again.

David Coulthard proved a big source of frustration for the team because, after an impressive opening couple of races (winning in Australia and leading in Malaysia), his challenge disappointingly fizzled out. His races were repeatedly compromised by poor qualifying positions and, towards the end of the year, he was moved to seek help to improve his Saturday performances. Relative to the pace of his team-mate, 2003 was the weakest of David's nine full seasons in Formula One. Talk of Montoya's arrival in 2005 can't have helped ease the pressure on him either.

There is a school of thought that suggests Coulthard didn't actually get any slower in 2003; it was more a case of Raikkonen finally hitting his stride as a Formula One driver and knocking DC for six. That may be so, but David at least finished the year on an up when he out-qualified and out-raced Raikkonen at Suzuka, the most challenging track on this year's championship calendar. And he did that despite missing part of practice when he was asked to hand over his car to Raikkonen on Saturday morning.

Although Raikkonen failed to win the title this year, what the Formula One world learnt was that should McLaren turn out a good car in 2004, Kimi Raikkonen will take a lot of stopping.

Mercedes-AMG supports the Eric Clapton Crossroads Foundation

Maximum boost.
On the road and in the seat

The SL 55 AMG

▶ There are really two main factors which make up the essence of a sports car – performance and handling. And in both disciplines the SL 55 AMG has the potential for providing an unforgettable driving experience. High-performance engineering which you can feel and enjoy with all your senses. The remarkable output of the 5.5-litre V8 compressor engine, with 500 hp and no less than 700 Nm of torque, ensures intense thrust for the driver when accelerating. First-class handling and optimum contact between the car and the road is due primarily to the Roadster's specially developed AMG suspension – and of course to the downforce produced by its excellent aerodynamics. And whenever necessary the high-performance AMG braking system will bring you from high speed to a dead stop in an impressively short time. But why not see for yourself what the SL 55 AMG is like?

Your Mercedes-Benz dealer will be pleased to show you, or you can visit our website at www.mercedes-benz.com/amg

Mercedes-Benz

MILD SEVEN RENAULT F1 TEAM

"**The season was excellent. We have achieved 90 percent of our** potential and our balance sheet is in credit. We are in the black! The team worked together, with two great drivers. Alonso was the youngest driver to win a grand prix, and we brought him into Formula One, so we are very happy.

As far as the new rules are concerned, my attitude is very simple. If it's good for the spectator and good for the crowd, then I'm happy.

The high point, of course, was the victory in Hungary. We had the possibility of winning in Brazil, Barcelona and Canada and this was exactly what we had planned before the start of the season. We wanted to close the gap to the top teams. In actual fact, we achieved more than our objectives. We had many podiums, the victory, and we also closed the gap to Ferrari, McLaren and Williams, which was exactly what we wanted.

The difficult part now is next year. We didn't really have any low points in 2003. We are a very young team and we know where we are coming from. We started to build up this team just two years ago, which is not that long at all.

Everybody is talking about 2004, I think we must just work within our system and see what happens. We will be improving but then everyone else will be improving, so it will depend on how fast we are. But I'm quite confident that we will have a very good 2004 compared to the others. "

Above: Preparing an F1 car requires a lot of people power. Far right: Mike Gascoyne's detailed knowledge of aerodynamics made the R23 a highly driveable machine.

Outside the top three, Renault enjoyed an excellent year, one which saw Renault Sport win a race with a car of its own manufacture (as opposed to another manufacturers' car running one of its engines) for the first time since 1983.

This was a justification of its decision not just to hire Fernando Alonso to partner Jarno Trulli, but also to sign up to the FIA's new private testing session on Friday mornings while limiting testing away from races.

Mike Gascoyne, the team's technical director, justified the latter very convincingly by saying;

"For a start there is no limitation on testing up to the first race of the season, so pre-race testing is not affected. This means that for the bigger teams there is no disadvantage in taking up this offer pre-season. The first three races are fly-aways, so once again you have no disadvantage, as people are not testing anyway under the Suzuka Agreement. The first European race is Imola, and you don't test there. At Barcelona you've tested anyway as you've gone there pre-season. In Austria there is no pre-race testing, so again no disadvantage, and meanwhile you've had two extra hours at each circuit for free testing. At Monaco I think it would be a massive advantage to have two extra hours of track time for testing and setting the car up in conditions that are very different from most other tracks."

"Now, if you add the fact that you have the support of your tyre supplier at these Friday tests, because they want information, then it becomes clear that there might be a serious advantage in testing on a Friday morning. You have free testing so you are allowed to test all the tyres available and then choose your two types of tyre for the weekend after that session. If the tyre supplier will bring more than two types of tyre for the team then this becomes even more of an advantage."

"At this point, after Monaco, where it has all been positive for Friday testing, we are nearly mid-way through the season and you've still got the 10 days of testing you are allowed during the year. You can also take three or four cars to the session and test with a driver with grand prix experience

Above: More fuel, new boots and all executed in under 10 seconds. Far left: Jarno Trulli experimented with his helmet design this season.

such as Allan McNish, as well as with talented up and coming drivers, so it starts to look very advantageous."

"Certainly, it limits the running of the cars and it does limit the use of engines, which is great if you are a small team, but if you can pay to have more engines on the dyno doing development work and end up with 20 more horsepower because of it, then I think it would be a good thing to do."

"If you did Friday morning testing and won a couple of races, you'd probably say you'd had a good season, and we think if you're looking at it to increase competitiveness then it looks a very attractive proposition."

Renault won just the one race, but its manner was sensational as Fernando Alonso dominated the Hungaroring from the second pole of his career. And while Gascoyne's definition might have underestimated the intensity of the competition, the team could hold its head up and say that despite winning only once, it actually had a very good season.

One of the keys was the same relentless development that had driven it to success in 2002. Gascoyne and his team kept up a fantastic pace of development in 2003 and the R23 got better and better.

There were some negatives, however. Engine design guru Jean-Jacques His quit mid-season, unable to work any longer with boss Flavio Briatore. His place was taken by his former boss, Bernard Dudot, the father of the F1 V10 concept. "I think we probably focused too much on the old engine, because it was a chassis parameter," he admitted. "It gave us some new problems which were too complicated for single-race engines in 2004. But we have also learned things we would not otherwise have learned with this engine, and all of that knowledge can be used with the new engine, so we believe that it will be competitive straight away. I feel very optimistic."

There were also season-long rumours that Gascoyne had received a highly tempting offer to join Toyota as its technical director, which was confirmed in October. How badly his leaving will affect Renault remains to be seen.

LUCKY STRIKE BAR HONDA

Unfortunately our underlying performance was not always translated into race results or points but nevertheless from within the team we are confident that we are making progress.

The tyre situation clouded the issue for us, but we can't get away from the fact that we still have a significant gap that we have to make up on Ferrari who have access to the same tyres as we do. The tyre situation was a surprise to us this year!

As far as the new rules are concerned, I think we've made them work. But what really counts, are the opinions of the fans from the grandstands and from home. I think we still have to put on more entertainment over the race weekend.

I wouldn't have singled out any one event as a high point until Jenson led at Indianapolis, and of course our encouraging performance at Suzuka in which we clinched fifth place in the Constructors Championship. It's been tough, but at last we can see the light at the end of the tunnel. When you have a three or four-year plan you do get the odd boost, but basically you have to just press on and keep your mind focused on the big picture.

As for the future, we are still in a very difficult climate and there's no getting away from the fact that the commercial and economic environment isn't easy for anyone. We just have to continue to adjust to the times and be very aware of the cost associated with running the teams and ensure that we continue to deliver value to the spectators. Often we spend too much time concerned with cutting costs and not with increasing value. I think we have to be very conscious that our duty is to deliver an exciting product to the paying audience who come to race circuits and to the people who watch the races on television.

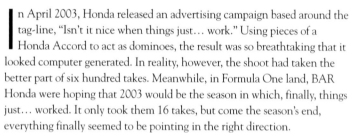

Above: Jenson Button waits impatiently as his car is fitted out with new tyres and receives a full fuel load. Far right: Jacques Villeneuve's spare nose-cones are close at hand, just in case.

In April 2003, Honda released an advertising campaign based around the tag-line, "Isn't it nice when things just… work." Using pieces of a Honda Accord to act as dominoes, the result was so breathtaking that it looked computer generated. In reality, however, the shoot had taken the better part of six hundred takes. Meanwhile, in Formula One land, BAR Honda were hoping that 2003 would be the season in which, finally, things just… worked. It only took them 16 takes, but come the season's end, everything finally seemed to be pointing in the right direction.

At the launch of the BAR005, David Richards outlined his aims for the season. "Our task must be to challenge the top three teams. To do that we need to regularly qualify in the top ten, and if we can do that we should appear on the podium and score points on a regular basis. If I look back on this season and history records and see that this was the year that BAR finally came of age and challenged the establishment, I will be very happy."

The only problem for BAR was that in 2003 the "Big Three" became the "Big Four," and the reliability of those eight cars was such that even with the introduction of the new points scoring system, BAR were left scrapping for leftovers.

Even before the F1 circus arrived for duty in Melbourne, BAR were having a tough time. In pre-season testing, the Honda engine was criticised heavily for its relative lack of power, and before the car had even run a lap, the team's drivers were embroiled in a very public war of words. Despite a fine qualifying performance at the Australian Grand Prix that saw both cars in the top ten, the contretemps came to a head in the pitstop debacle, after which the enigmatic Villeneuve eased more readily into life with Button, who he had seen as a precocious upstart. Only if the young Brit could outperform the 1997 world champion would he gain his respect, and before Jacques' premature exit from the team, Button had just edged it, holding a qualifying advantage of 8-7 and a race classification advantage of 9-6.

But this doesn't tell the whole story. BAR's season was dogged with a total of 13 retirements, the majority of which befell the Canadian. In Monaco, after a threat from PPGI - a disgruntled former sponsor - to

impound the BAR cars, Jenson Button had a massive crash, which
sidelined him for the rest of the weekend. These incidents, along with
BAR's nightmare Canadian Grand Prix weekend and PPGI's successful
impounding of the team's cars at Magny-Cours, were the obvious low
points of the season for the team.

And yet, by the time the season drew to a close in Japan, things were on
the up. Honda had made an incredible leap forward in performance terms,
utilising the many years of experience as a potent championship force at
McLaren to good use.

Negotiations for 2004 with Villeneuve's management, headed by the
charismatic Craig Pollock, finally broke down just after Indianapolis with
the result that the former champion's career came to an abrupt halt when
he decided not to participate in the last race in Japan, after BAR had
confirmed Takuma Sato as Jacques' replacement. Poised to take fifth place
in the constructors' championship, and with a resolution finally having
been reached with PPGI, Button ran home for his second fourth place
finish of the season and Sato once again had a brilliant home run to finish
sixth, ensuring BAR a final position behind only Ferrari, Williams,
McLaren and the breakthrough team of the year, Renault. All told, despite
their difficulties, BAR's objectives had been achieved. It was a season in
which the very last cobwebs of the old regime were flushed out and a new
ethos of working towards a common goal came good. The team's overall
competitiveness, however, had been held back by the disappointment of
the Bridgestone tyres, and as such it is little surprise that BAR have put in a
request to use Michelin's rubber in 2004.

While BAR did not seriously challenge the establishment in 2003, the
team certainly came of age. With the strong foundation the team
established, and with their very public problems now firmly behind them,
BAR's 2003 season should fill them with a great deal of pride, and a well-
deserved heightening in confidence for 2004.

SAUBER PETRONAS

It's been a difficult season, but don't forget that Formula One is at an extremely high level. Never before have we had seven manufacturers fighting against us. In the end it was a fantastic result to finish the world championship in sixth place ahead of Jaguar, Toyota and Ford.

Obviously our high point was Indianapolis. Prior to that race, we were only ninth in the constructors' world championship, and afterwards we were temporarily fifth. Things were not quite so bright at the start of the season, however, when we realised that our car was not competitive enough. We needed some time to find the problem on the aerodynamic side, particularly on turn-in.

The surprise of the season, for me, was what a good job Ferrari did. The common forces of BMW Williams on one side and McLaren Mercedes on the other were tremendous. This year, both these teams had the advantage of Michelin tyres. When you analyse it, it's a big deal to be world champion against BMW Williams, McLaren Mercedes, and Michelin.

Next year, I believe we will have another very interesting season, because Williams, McLaren and, I'm sure, Renault, will do everything to beat Ferrari. And also drivers like Kimi, Juan Pablo and Fernando Alonso will fight for the title. It might be even more exciting than 2003.

In the meantime we have to strengthen our technical side. We have the basis to improve the car, maybe not at the beginning of the year because the wind tunnel won't be ready then, but we have a very good tool to improve the car later on. This is essential because Toyota, Jaguar and BAR will do everything to try and beat us.

Above: The tension on the
pit wall during the race is
clear for all to see.
Far right: The Sauber
Pertronas pit crew send
their driver back out on the
track.

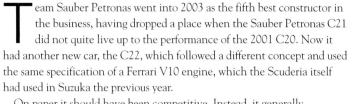

Team Sauber Petronas went into 2003 as the fifth best constructor in the business, having dropped a place when the Sauber Petronas C21 did not quite live up to the performance of the 2001 C20. Now it had another new car, the C22, which followed a different concept and used the same specification of a Ferrari V10 engine, which the Scuderia itself had used in Suzuka the previous year.

On paper it should have been competitive. Instead, it generally disappointed. What Peter Sauber needed most was a quick and reliable machine, which could pick up whatever points were dropped when Ferrari, McLaren, BMW Williams or Renault stumbled. What he got, however, was a car that was not quick enough (more of which later) and sometimes unreliable. By the end of the season, Sauber was only ninth in the constructors' points table and ready to sit alongside Minardi in the 2004 garage line-up. What Sauber needed then was a miracle, and he got one…

Initially, the C22 proved reliable enough to take new signing Heinz-Harald Frentzen to sixth place in Australia and fifth in Brazil. Between those two races, Nick Heidfeld, going into his third season with the team, took eighth in front of title sponsor Petronas in Malaysia. But then things began to tail off and the pickings were slim. Several times the car was poised to score points, but something would go wrong. In Brazil, Austria and Canada it was Heidfeld's engine.

The failure at Spielberg was particularly galling, as the young German had qualified in fourth place on the grid, which seemed to suit the car. In Spain, Frentzen's suspension broke, in Austria it was his clutch, while in Canada, it was the fault of the electrics. Meanwhile, in Monaco, he crashed after messing up the exit to the swimming pool chicane on the opening lap and walloping a wall. And in Hockenheim, he was the innocent victim when Firman tagged him after getting caught up in the Schumacher/Raikkonen/Barrichello shunt on the startline.

Gradually, however, sheer hard work by the team ironed out those problems, and a parallel programme of aerodynamic development massaged more competitive performances out of the car as the season drew to a close. At Monza, Frentzen should have finished seventh scoring two precious

points, but his transmission failed with only three laps to go. That should at least have elevated Heidfeld to eighth and a point, but he was caught on the final lap by Alonso as they were being lapped, so Sauber were denied even that consolation.

Peter Sauber made no bones about his displeasure with his team's performance, but some of the blame also had to be laid at Bridgestone's door after the poor performance of its tyres. Nevertheless, Sauber never relaxed his determination to see his cars outperform their most significant Bridgestone rival, BAR. Usually the C22 and the 005 were pretty evenly matched, but prior to the last two races BAR had amassed 18 points and lay fifth in the constructors' championship; Sauber had only nine and was ninth, behind Jaguar, Toyota and Jordan, too.

Then came the miracle of Indianapolis. In the weather-spoiled US Grand Prix an inspired tyre choice and perfect timing of the pit stop saw Frentzen opt for wet weather Bridgestone's on his first pit stop. Others did not time things as well or didn't make the right gamble, so Frentzen found himself running second to Button until Schumacher overtook on lap 33. When Button retired, Frentzen moved up to second again and a Sauber led a Grand Prix for the first time on the 48th lap when Schumacher refuelled. Subsequently Frentzen finished third with Heidfeld fifth, the 10-point haul hoisting the team to fifth place with a race to go.

Sauber has ambitious plans for 2004. Giancarlo Fisichella, a driver that the Swiss entrepreneur admits he has admired for several years, joins the team from Jordan, while Felipe Massa rejoins with Ferrari's blessing. Paddock rumour also suggests that the team's Ferrari links will be strengthened greatly to include not just using the Petronas-badged Ferrari V10 engine but also a Ferrari transmission and, possibly, a car that is based on the Ferrari F2003-GA. At the same time the state-of-the-art wind tunnel that has been taking shape at Hinwil will come on stream during the season. The result at Indianapolis was a major fillip, and the plans for the new season have created a strong spirit within the team that, at one stage this season, was weighed down by its fall from grace.

DAVID PITCHFORTH MANAGING DIRECTOR

JAGUAR RACING

One of the best things about 2003 has been the sheer dedication of everyone at Jaguar Racing, Cosworth Racing and Pi Electronics. It's been fantastic.

I think it was right for us to join the Heathrow Agreement and test on Friday mornings, although we have suffered from not having enough time to put in mileage doing extensive tyre testing. We have an excellent relationship with Michelin who have made great progress this year.

I always thought Renault would be a strong heir apparent, so their performance didn't surprise me, but I didn't think they'd do it in such amazing style.

We have two good drivers. Mark was signed up under the previous management and he is very impressive. A talented, well balanced individual with the right amount of assertiveness and a great team player.

The battle for fifth place in the Constructor's Championship was always going to be tough and in the end we lost out. However, we did hit our target of seventh place, and earned our 'respectability' although I think that morally sixth place was ours.

2004 will be very tough. We can only wait and see what the new rule changes will bring. The one engine rule will make reliability even more important. The back-to-back qualifying on the Saturday is difficult to assess. My business head says it will make good television as the reality is that the cars are now mobile bill boards. But my racing brain says it doesn't save money, it's not completely logical, and it might not be workable. We'll just have to wait and see.

Above: The Jaguar team change tyres and prepare the car for qualifying. Far right: At Monaco the famous Jaguar leaper became pink with a diamond eye to celebrate the unveiling of the 'Monaco Rose' flawless pink diamond.

2003 was a crucial year for Jaguar Racing. In his time at the helm, former IndyCar champion Bobby Rahal had spoken of the desire to generate respect, but various factors denied him that chance. Once Rahal had been ousted, Niki Lauda appeared to have a clear field, answering only to Ford's Richard Parry-Jones.

For 2003 the Austrian signed Mark Webber and Antonio Pizzonia to replace Eddie Irvine and Pedro de la Rosa, and the design team put the finishing touches to the new R4 which promised vastly improved aerodynamics and a chassis that didn't twist like a soft pretzel whenever the drivers tried to use the power of the R3's only asset, the Cosworth V10 engine.

But then the over-used revolving door to the factory at Milton Keynes spun into action again before the season had even started. This time it was Lauda himself who was being rotated out of a job. At a press conference at a London hotel, Parry-Jones and Sir Jackie Stewart introduced the new wave. The quiet man who sat alongside them was Tony Purnell, founder of Pi Research and a fellow who was rated as one of the smartest and shrewdest operators in the sport. He would answer to Parry-Jones, and in turn would be answered to by a conglomerate of engineers led by Dr Mark Gillan and David Pitchforth. Everyone got fancy and complicated job titles that everyone else immediately forgot. Then, just before the season kicked off, another appointment was made: this time the highly experienced former Marlboro man, John Hogan, came in to act as Sporting Director to handle corporate and commercial aspects of the team.

Though it seemed like a top-heavy management that might fall flat on its face, it worked. So did the car. The Jaguar R4 was far and away the best car Jaguar had ever built for Formula One. At last Jaguar Racing could hold its head up.

In the season opener in Melbourne, Webber was running in the top six, looking comfortable, when a rear suspension problem halted him. Observers dismissed the run as the product of a light fuel load, for the new regulations had introduced great confusion and people had yet to form firm opinions over car performance. This scepticism was endorsed by the cars'

failure to shine in Malaysia, where they were beset by problems and Pizzonia distinguished himself by savaging the rear end of former Williams team-mate Juan Pablo Montoya's car in the first corner.

Then came Brazil. Webber set the track alight in Friday qualifying by setting the fastest time, and continued the form on Saturday afternoon when only a small error exiting the last corner robbed him of pole position. He was still in contention for a podium finish when his accident on worn tyres on the climb from the last corner set in train the series of incidents that would produce such an extraordinary end to the race.

Jaguar never quite looked as convincing again until Hungary. But Webber scored points with seventh in Spain, Austria, Canada and Italy (Monza) and sixths in Germany (Nurburgring), France and Hungary. At the Hungaroring he qualified an excellent third and held second place against the challenge of Barrichello and Raikkonen until his first pit stop. He even led a lap in the rain at Indianapolis before falling off the road, where he admitted that he felt it worth taking a risk if not taking one merely meant finishing out of the points. His efforts won Jaguar 17 of its 18 points.

However, there was a downside. The way in which Pizzonia was treated was awkward and showed scant understanding of a racing driver's psyche. He did some silly things in the winter, but then the reliability of his car was also lamentable early on. None of this excused the pressure he came under, or the team's evident desire to dump him. By Spain, Jaguar turned its dramatic performance improvement and the first points of its season into a headache when plans to replace Pizzonia with McLaren tester Alexander Wurz backfired. The Brazilian was subsequently replaced after Silverstone by Minardi's Justin Wilson. The Briton, who beat Webber to the F3000 title in 2001, underlined suspicions that Jaguar has difficulty running two equal cars by struggling until he scored a point for a hard-won eighth in Indianapolis.

A rumoured $20m cut in Jaguar's budget may pave the way for a pay driver to join Webber in 2004. The favourites are Wurz, or Red Bull drivers Patrick Friesacher or Christian Klien.

Above: Michelin tyres helped Jaguar take home 18 points this season. Far left: Mark Webber's pace was perhaps the biggest suprise of the year. Next page: Jaguar's close relationship with Cosworth has paid dividends this year.

THE FUTURE OF ENGINEERED PLASTIC FOAMS

We provide innovative product solutions in

automotive, packaging and industrial applications

with engineered plastic foams.

JSP *International*

AUTOMOTIVE   PACKAGING   CONSUMER   INDUSTRIAL

PANASONIC TOYOTA RACING

"**Toyota could have been a lot better or a lot worse this season,** so I'm glad it isn't the latter. In basic terms we achieved the target we set ourselves. We expected to qualify in the top ten at each race, and we managed that in all but two races.

The championship points were not as forthcoming, but we are still a young team and we know that we still have a long way to go. This season I strongly believe that we demonstrated the full potential of the team.

There have been a lot of highlights in 2003. We led the British Grand Prix for 17 laps, we qualified on the second row of the grid in two successive races in Indianapolis and Suzuka, and we scored a strong double-points finish in Hockenheim.

Outside my own team, Fernando Alonso impressed me greatly this season with some outstanding performances both in qualifying and in the races. He returned to Formula One racing with considerable ease and, in my opinion, asserted himself as a potential future world champion.

The new rules and regulations had an instrumental role in improving the overall show. I still think that continuous re-evaluation is essential to maintain Formula One status as the pinnacle of motorsport. Despite my limited experience in Formula One, I feel that maybe the sport has become too clinical, hiding the drivers from the public view. We need to change this.

Looking ahead to 2004 I think we must continue the pace of development we have shown this year. We came frustratingly close to scoring good results at many races, and it's our hope to translate the competitiveness of the team into tangible results next year."

Above: A stricken TF103 is returned to its pit garage. Far right: The Toyota RVX-03 engine has proved it has the horse power to lead races.

Panasonic Toyota Racing achieved its goals in its debut Formula One season in 2002, but all the same there was an over-riding feeling in the team that things could have gone a lot better. With a completely new driver line-up, a new design approach and a year of F1 experience at their disposal, the team's goals for 2003 were comparatively high, but they managed to achieve them all and in so doing, created a steady basis on which to build future success.

An evolution, rather than a revolution, was the cliché with which the TF103 was launched, and yet behind the scenes it was clear a revolution had taken place. The car was strikingly dissimilar to the TF102, Gustav Brunner's design taking obvious inspiration from the all-conquering Ferrari F2002 that had so easily dominated the previous F1 season. Brunner explained at the launch of the TF103 that he had redesigned "Everything. Every part. Every wheel bearing, every rim, everything." An evolution or a revolution? The evidence pointed towards the latter. The new car completely disregarded the conservative approach which had dogged its predecessor.

"We have made gains in every area," Brunner continued. "I hope that we have come up with a good compromise between building a fast car and a reliable one. That is the challenge of Formula One." And it was a challenge to which Toyota raised itself majestically.

Pre-season objectives were clear – to qualify consistently in the top half of the grid and work from there. The season's results speak for themselves. Only in two races did the red and white cars not adorn a top ten qualifying position. By the end of the season, Toyota were starting races from the sharp end of the field on a regular basis; Indianapolis and Suzuka, where da Matta and Panis lined up third and fourth respectively, being the very clear highlights of the season.

Not only this, but Toyota led its very first race. In the mayhem and confusion of the British Grand Prix, many claimed the team had lucked in to their P1 and 2 on track after the mad dash of pitstops emanating from the second safety car period. Although Panis was quickly passed, da Matta held his own whilst leading the race, an achievement becoming a man who just

twelve months earlier had been used to winning races with Toyota in CART en-route to winning the American championship.

The team also enjoyed highly competitive and rewarding weekends in Spain and Germany, not to mention a wonderful Japanese homecoming in which da Matta picked up two points and cemented the team's eighth place finish in the Constructors' Championship, finishing narrowly behind Jaguar Racing in seventh.

In Panis and da Matta, the team has two drivers who not only drive with calm determination in race situations, but who also know how to draw the most from a car in testing. It is their invaluable work that has helped Toyota to develop the car throughout the season. It was the team's choice not to sign up to the Heathrow Agreement regarding limited testing, and although this may have hindered da Matta's learning time at F1 circuits, it certainly allowed him ample time away from the grands prix to get to grips with the intricacies of a Formula One car. No summary execution for Toyota's 2003 driver line up then - both drivers have been reconfirmed for 2004.

Another shot of good news for the team is the announcement that, as of December 1st 2003, highly respected designer Mike Gascoyne, who leaves his position as Technical Director of Renault, will work for Toyota as Technical Director in Charge of Chassis. His incorporation into the team will provide Toyota with 15 years worth of Formula One experience and know-how. Working alongside Gustav Brunner, and under the direction of Ove Andersson and John Howett, Toyota looks to have a very strong team in place for 2004.

So what can we expect from the team in 2004? If 2002 was a learning experience, then 2003 was a year of revision. Come Melbourne 2004, Toyota will be under examination conditions. Gone are the days when they can claim inexperience as an excuse for their performances. With a strong driver line up, a good engine and a distinguished design team in place, 2004 looks to be highly promising for Toyota. It is the year when the Cologne-based team need to prove that they are well on their way in the long climb to the top. Like Renault in 2003, they need to make that giant step forward.

EDDIE JORDAN CHIEF EXECUTIVE

JORDAN FORD

" **I don't think that many teams, maybe only Ligier, have won a race** in a season and wound up not being competitive enough in the second half of the year. From my point of view, the season seemed to be involving courts. We had to go to Paris to get the win back in Brazil, and then to court with Vodafone. It's a shame the year made me concentrate on other things.

I think as a spectacle the new rules worked. The downside is that at some circuits, one-lap is a bit boring but you can't keep everyone happy all the time. Maybe there should be more support races.

There were two high points for me - obviously the win in Brazil, which was fantastic, and the re-emergence of the competitiveness of Formula One. What we shouldn't forget is that there were eight different winners. On the down side, our car wasn't quick enough, and we had a number of engine blow-ups. The last few races were just so, so difficult too. The team, the engine, the package, just didn't gel. It's happened before, but we turned it around and we will now. Look at 1998.

I think Mark Webber has been a surprise this year. He came of age in most people's view. I'm also surprised by McLaren's performance with last year's car. Everyone thought that wasn't possible.

In the future the costs of Formula One have to come down in some way, if we are genuinely looking for a position whereby the private teams can be expected to be competitive again. Forget just surviving. "

Above: Save a surprise win in Brazil, Jordan's season was pretty much the pits. Far right: Ralph Firman speeds past the Rascasse Bar in glorious Monaco.

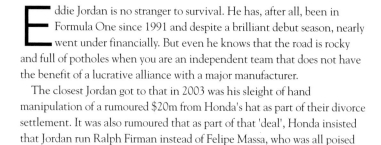

Eddie Jordan is no stranger to survival. He has, after all, been in Formula One since 1991 and despite a brilliant debut season, nearly went under financially. But even he knows that the road is rocky and full of potholes when you are an independent team that does not have the benefit of a lucrative alliance with a major manufacturer.

The closest Jordan got to that in 2003 was his sleight of hand manipulation of a rumoured $20m from Honda's hat as part of their divorce settlement. It was also rumoured that as part of that 'deal', Honda insisted that Jordan run Ralph Firman instead of Felipe Massa, who was all poised to sign. Doubtless, when he compared the season Jordan had with his time as a test driver for Ferrari, Massa figured he came out ahead.

Jordan started 2003 with customer Ford engines in a deal with Ford of Europe that had nothing to do with Detroit's involvement via Jaguar, and though Jordan spoke loftily at the beginning of the season about helping to lower the average age of Ford buyers, there was little evidence of any overt marketing of either the Ford or Jordan brands. This was a money-conscious deal from the start.

It was an odd year for the team. It began with Giancarlo Fisichella 13th and Firman 17th on the grid in Melbourne, and both retiring - the Italian with gearbox failure, the Briton after crashing (albeit having climbed to eighth place). Malaysia wasn't much better, with Fisichella 14th and Firman last on the grid. The Italian stalled at the start, but Firman drove superbly under pressure from Frentzen and only lost a point through falling fuel pressure.

It was thus clear that the EJ13 was a workmanlike (and pretty) car with a reasonable engine. You couldn't expect anything else in the financial circumstances, though insiders spoke of only 815 bhp from the customer motor, a figure that the works CR V10 series of engines exceeded comfortably from day one back in 1999.

Then came Brazil, where the luck was purely Irish. It's worth looking at what happened in detail, because while the team would take a somewhat lucky win, the way in which it made the decisions that would earn that success were testament to the fact that this is still a damn good race team,

even if it was having to get by on a ludicrously low amount of money compared with Formula One's high rollers.

First, they chose a strategy that put Fisichella eighth on the grid in mixed weather conditions, a mere 0.383 seconds off Barrichello's pole. Firman was 16th, having lost oodles of valuable track time with clutch failure on Friday morning.

On a damp race day in which the field ran the first eight laps behind the safety car because of the conditions, Firman started from the pit lane. When the safety car pulled in, he refuelled. So did Fisichella, against his wishes. Engineers Rob Smedley and Gary Anderson believed that a maximised fuel load was the way to go in what promised even at that stage to be a topsy-turvy race. That left Fisichella close to the back, and Firman only just missed him when his own front suspension broke on the 18th lap as he sped past the pits. Fisichella was desperately lucky.

As other Bridgestone runners Michael Schumacher and Jenson Button crashed in Turn 3, where a river ran across the track, Fisichella began moving up. He moved to third when Fernando Alonso served a drive-through penalty, Ralf Schumacher pitted and Barrichello stopped on the circuit. Suddenly he was closing on the Michelin-shod McLarens. He overtook both in style before the red flag incident. It would take a while before the FIA handed him his just deserts (he got the hardware at Imola), but it was a win the team thoroughly deserved.

After that the season fell apart, Firman's point in Spain notwithstanding. There was no money for development, there were clashes between some of the engineers and the aerodynamicists, and mid-season Jordan launched his ill-advised legal action against Vodafone. Then Firman crashed through rear wing failure in Hungary and had to be replaced for two races by Hungarian F3000 racer Zsolt Baumgartner. The only bright spot was two points for Fisichella in Indianapolis, which pushed the team within striking distance of Toyota.

In October, Eddie Jordan welcomed Dublin-based Stockbrokerage Merrion as his partner after it purchased Warburg Pincus's 49.9% shareholding, laying the groundwork for another of Jordan's famous reorganisations for 2004.

muermans
Group

EUROPEAN
AVIATION

. Trust

HALFORDS

BUND

COSWORTH

minardi F1 team

wilux
bathroom pleasure

muermans
groep

EUROPEAN MINARDI COSWORTH

"**We started the 2003 season on a high, with a fantastic Cosworth** engine and two good drivers. On 15th January, a meeting took place in which it was agreed that each of the small teams, such as Minardi and Jordan, would receive $8 million from a "Fighting Fund," and it finally looked as if we'd be able to compete in a season with a reasonable budget. However, our relief was short-lived, as the money was not forthcoming. The months of arguing that ensued culminated in the famous Friday 13th press conference in Montreal, which in turn had a positive result for Minardi, in that Bernie Ecclestone announced he would invest in the team.

Having said that, we have had our good moments. The Friday qualifying session in Magny-Cours, which saw Jos Verstappen in the top position, was a great morale booster. We have also enjoyed good reliability. You couldn't find a more dedicated bunch of people than those in the Minardi team, and their commitment is a major driving force for me. Other highlights in 2003 included Hungary, when we celebrated our 300th grands prix start and in Monza, when 40 per cent of the grid were either current or ex-Minardi drivers, thereby clearly demonstrating the value of the small teams as nurturers of future Formula One driving talent.

I liked the new rules and regulations for 2003. We achieved exactly what we set out to achieve, in closing up the Championships and providing better entertainment, but the rule changes for 2004 are not to my liking. We've just got it right so why go and change it?

Next year will be another challenge. The small teams are becoming an endangered species, but I'm determined we will not become extinct."

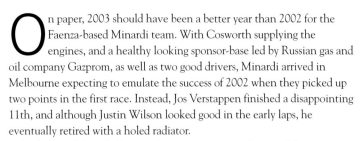

Above: Mechanics hard at work rebuilding the car before final qualifying. Far right: Out of the pits and into the foray of the Friday morning test session.

O n paper, 2003 should have been a better year than 2002 for the Faenza-based Minardi team. With Cosworth supplying the engines, and a healthy looking sponsor-base led by Russian gas and oil company Gazprom, as well as two good drivers, Minardi arrived in Melbourne expecting to emulate the success of 2002 when they picked up two points in the first race. Instead, Jos Verstappen finished a disappointing 11th, and although Justin Wilson looked good in the early laps, he eventually retired with a holed radiator.

And it wasn't long before gaps began to appear in all areas of the team from the huge hole (about 40%) in the budget caused by the loss of Gazprom, to the hole caused by the non-payment of the $8 million from the so-called Fighting Fund. To make matters even worse, Justin Wilson had to be taken to hospital after the Malaysian Grand Prix suffering from the ill effects of his HANS device, which left him unable to move his arms.

However, in spite of the lack of testing, and the constant struggle to make it on to the grid at each race, Wilson continued to impress, especially in Canada, where he sprung up the grid at the start of the race from 18th to 13th. This impressive performance helped secure him a place at Jaguar Racing from the German Grand Prix onwards as the replacement for Brazilian Antonio Pizzonia; a move which relieved the pressure on Minardi's difficult financial situation, as both Jaguar Racing and Cosworth are part of PPD (Ford's Premier Performance Division). They were then able to reduce the overall cost of the engine. Danish Formula 3000 driver Nicolas Kiesa joined Minardi.

Financially, things came to a head on Friday 13th in Montreal, when a press conference between the team bosses nearly came to blows over the Fighting Fund. It was resolved by the intervention of Bernie Ecclestone, who announced he would invest in the team. At this point Paul Stoddart had nothing to lose as he was fast running out of funds to continue the season, and if he went down then it would mean two other teams would be forced to run a third car to maintain minimum numbers, an occurrence that would not be good for the general health of Formula One.

After the showdown, Stoddart put his team back together enjoying the

SUPERFUND
Libero
MAGNETI MARELLI
Powered By COSWORTH
BRIDGESTONE
WWW.MINARDI.IT
Beta

**Above: The PS03 was originally designed to run on Michelin rubber, but when the French supplier refused to supply more than five teams, Minardi were forced to settle for Bridgestones.
Far left: Jos Verstappen takes an eight second breather.**

spotlight at Magny-Cours, when both Minardi drivers were briefly at the top of the Friday qualifying time sheet before Wilson was disqualified for his car being under weight. In Hungary, the team celebrated their 300th grand prix, and in Monza, with the substitution of Marc Gene for an unwell Ralf Schumacher, Stoddart had the satisfaction of seeing 40% of the grid made up of either current or ex-Minardi drivers, including new stars Mark Webber and Fernando Alonso.

However, this didn't take the sting away from the fact that in 2003 Minardi didn't score any points. The nearest the team got was in the rain at Interlagos. With such an unpredictable race, Minardi had their best opportunity to score points, but it wasn't to be. Both cars went out at the notorious Turn 3, which had even caught out World Champion Michael Schumacher. "This was definitely a race where there was an excellent possibility of scoring points so I'm extremely disappointed," said Verstappen. Wilson was more succinct. "I'm gutted," he said.

Reliability at the end of the season was excellent as Kiesa managed to finish in all five of his Formula One races, and Verstappen finished in the top ten at Indianapolis, but in the end Minardi finished the 2003 season on nil points and 10th in the Constructor's Championship.

Then came the hammer blow of the new rule changes for 2004, which Stoddart was not happy about. The back-to-back Saturday qualifying and the demise of the Heathrow Agreement for Friday testing has left the Minardi team boss furious.

"In Melbourne Nicolas will be last out in the first part of qualifying and if he is the slowest then that gives us precisely two minutes before we have to send him out again for the second session. In other words, we could be stuffed before the first race has even got underway."

But in spite of the dire words you can bet that Minardi will be on the grid in Melbourne in 2004. Probably last, but still in the battle. Whether Minardi survive in the long term is still very much up for debate as there is a limit to how long the sport can continue to put a sticking plaster on the problem that is the cost of running a Formula One team. The time has come for this to be resolved.

THE DRIVERS

MICHAEL SCHUMACHER

I have to say that the excitement of winning a sixth World championship took a little while to sink in. I was exhausted after the race at Suzuka because it was all so emotional. Even before the start of the race I had a very strange feeling, as though I knew it was not going to be a normal race, especially as I had to start from 14th position and just a small technical problem for me and Rubens would have given Kimi the title. There was no way we could relax until the job was done.

However, the job was done in the best possible way. Ferrari won the Constructors' Championship and I won the Drivers' Championship. We had fought a long, hard battle until the very last race. The team was just amazing, and to me the fact that Ferrari won its fifth constructors' title in a row means much more than my title.

I don't think I was surprised by the performance of our competitors. I never expected things to be as clear as they were in the end last year. We saw during the winter tests that McLaren and BMW Williams would make progress and they did, even though I honestly didn't expect BMW Williams to catch up so impressively after their start to the season.

It's good to see young drivers like Fernando Alonso and Kimi Raikkonen win races. We have had eight different winners this year, which hasn't happened since 1985, and the variety and excitement has to be good for the sport. I look forward to 2004.

A mid season lull for the reigning World Champion who finished seventh after qualifying sixth in the intense heat of Hockenheim.

117

Finally, then, Michael has done it. He has beaten Juan Manuel Fangio's tally of five world titles and entered the record books with the highest number of world championship victories after his name. It is a momentous achievement and one that puts him up there with Pele, Bjorn Borg and Tiger Woods in the pantheon of sporting greats.

Yet there were times when the challenge looked an impossible mountain to climb. Think back to Hockenheim, when Juan Pablo Montoya nearly lapped the field in what was the most dominant performance of the year by any driver. Michael must have flown back to Switzerland after the race thinking that the 2003 World Championship was a lost cause.

Yet he turned it around, as only someone of his quality can. He continued to lead the Scuderia from the front and never let the people in the team see his head drop. His break came a month later when Michelin were accused of cheating and although they were acquitted, it was enough to put them and their teams off their stride, and Michael went for the jugular. He won at Monza, and again at Indianapolis, after which the title was almost a formality.

Such were the fluctuating fortunes of Schumacher's season that this will probably go down as the greatest of his six championships. The only other one that was as closely fought was 1994, when he and Damon Hill went down to the wire at Adelaide and Michael clinched the title after a collision with Damon that put them both out of the race.

Anyway, the tragedy of Ayrton Senna's death earlier in 1994 overshadowed Michael's first championship win. But in 2003, it is the scale of Michael's record-breaking achievements that overshadow everything.

This year, Michael was as fast and tenacious as we have come to expect, but there were some chinks in his armour that were slightly unexpected, be they spinning off in Brazil or his perennial problems in setting up the F2003-GA. Team-mate Rubens Barrichello invariably made a better job of setting up the car, but it didn't seem to affect Michael, or affect his results.

Where a win was there for the taking, Michael took it. Look at his opportunist victories in Canada and Indianapolis; they were as strong as any of his 70 victories to date because his car was inferior to the Williams on both occasions. He snatched the win in Montreal after Juan Pablo Montoya made a mistake, and when the rain came down at Indy, he marched passed the stricken Michelin runners, having played second fiddle to them in the early part of the race.

The only question mark left for Michael is what next? He has beaten every rival that he has faced in 12 years of Formula One, and he has now broken virtually every record there is to break (the only one left standing is Senna's record of 65 pole positions).

The big question that remains is will he quit while he's ahead or will he push on into immortality?

Michael Schumacher re-wrote the history books in 2003 winning the Drivers' Championship for a record sixth time.

SCHUMI 2001 F1 CHAMPION

Left to right from top: Schumacher celebrates his first title in Australia in 1994; two in a row, Aida 1995; third crown but his first for Ferrari in 2000; in Hungary for his fourth world title; Jean Todt helps celebrate the record-equalling fifth in 2002; perfect six in Japan, 2003

www.olympus.com/f1

Sponsor

Scuderia
Ferrari

For once Olympus is happy to bring you a blurred, out-of-focus photo.

When Rubens Barrichello took the chequered flag at Suzuka, it was the end of a fantastic season for Scuderia Ferrari. They won their 5th consecutive constructors' title and Michael Schumacher his 6th drivers' title. Congratulations from your proud sponsor, Olympus.

OLYMPUS

Your Vision, Our Future

RUBENS BARRICHELLO

In terms of my performance I had a much better season in 2003 than 2002, which is strange as I had more points and finished higher in the Championship last year. But I think I did a good job this year.

When the rules changed at the beginning of the year, it wasn't great for us at Ferrari, but there was a new system and it worked the same for everyone. Sometimes it would work in our favour, sometimes it wouldn't. You might have two negative aspects in one part and two positive in another. You just had to accept the good with the bad, and get on with it.

I'm so proud to have helped Ferrari win four of their five titles. Winning the British and Japanese grands prix was incredibly special for me, especially the latter on what is considered a driver's circuit. Suzuka and Silverstone were the two best races of my life.

I suppose there were a few lows. Crashing in Australia; having a problem with the car in Brazil when after taking the lead and pulling away I finally thought I was going to win my home race; and the crash at the first corner at Hockenheim. But you get good and bad races in a season, and you just have to accept that.

I don't think much surprised me in 2003. We expected the opposition to be highly competitive, but maybe things like Fernando Alonso's speed and Mark Webber's performance were surprising. They both did very good jobs.

I'm really looking forward to 2004. I think we will have another very competitive car and I'm going to win more races!

RUBENS BARRICHELLO

Rubens Barrichello heading to a third place podium finish in Barcelona.

For a man who knows his place and his real role at Scuderia Ferrari, Rubens Barrichello had several days in the sun in 2003, including his victory at Suzuka which helped his team-mate Michael Schumacher to an historic sixth World Championship and Ferrari to their fifth successive Constructor's Championship.

But the year began badly with a shunt due to the greasy opening conditions of the Australian Grand Prix and then the bitter disappointment of losing the Brazilian Grand Prix. Interspersed between them was a fine second place to Kimi Raikkonen in Malaysia, but that defeat at home really hurt. With Michael Schumacher crashing out of the race after aquaplaning on the river at Turn 3, Rubinho finally seemed set to realise his destiny and give his countrymen their first home win since his mentor, Ayrton Senna in 1993. In the slippery conditions he never put a wheel wrong and gradually hauled up on to race leader David Coulthard's tail before taking the lead and instantly pulling away. But then the red car rolled to a halt. Was it fuel pressure? Had he actually run out of fuel? Only Ferrari truly knows, but whatever the reason it was a crushing blow.

Then came a string of third places, one at Imola in the trusty F2002, the other two in Spain and Austria courtesy of the new F2003. In each he was beaten not just by his team-mate (who had shouldered past him in the first corner in Barcelona) but by Fernando Alonso and Kimi Raikkonen

respectively. In Monaco he struggled home to eighth position after qualifying seventh.

The F2003-GA, it was said, was another pointy Schumacher car, and a man who could handle understeer when Schumi hates it, was in trouble at its wheel. In Canada he could finish no better than fifth. In France it was seventh place. In the team-mate stakes, only Coulthard was doing worse, and he had won a race. But then came Silverstone, and Rubens' day of all days, he won in brilliant style. It was the best of his six victories. Now, it seemed, tyre development had made the Ferrari an understeerer, and he began to do the unthinkable and start outqualifying Michael again. In Hockenheim he was the innocent victim of the first corner melee, in Hungary as he made a mistake trying to outbrake Webber for second (again running ahead of Michael), and later had his left rear suspension break in spectacular style going into Turn 1. Monza brought another third, and the US Grand Prix a superb front row starting position that was swiftly negated in his collision with Montoya.

Barrichello has long found himself in the same position that people such as Gerhard Berger and Michael Andretti did with Senna at McLaren - in one of the best cars, but alongside the best driver. Nevertheless, he has made great use of his Ferrari in the second half of 2003. Sometimes, though, you wonder if he is as appreciated as he should be.

JUAN PABLO MONTOYA

"**Overall, I think I learnt a lot as a driver this year and improved** quite a lot, so I'm happy with my performance. Of course it was disappointing not to win the World Championship, but we all tried our hardest and it was not to be. All you can do is your best and, if that isn't good enough, you come back the following year and hope that you can get the job done then.

I think BMW Williams did a good job with the FW25 this year. We developed the car a lot and it was particularly competitive in the second half of the year. We made one or two errors with set-up along the way, but we learnt from them and this will make us stronger for 2004.

There weren't many great surprises in 2003 because we all expected Ferrari, Williams and McLaren to fight for the Championship, and that is what happened. Perhaps the rate at which Michelin caught up Bridgestone surprised some people, but not those of us who work with Michelin. They are an excellent partner for the team and we could see the progress they were making throughout last winter. We knew they'd come up with something special in 2003.

I have seen what Williams have got coming up for 2004 and I am very excited about it, so let's hope we can finally realise our championship goals next year. "

aying aside the title for a moment (or the lack of it), this was the year when it all came together for Juan Pablo Montoya. Some of you might hold your hands up in horror, claiming that he threw away the 2003 world title, but he actually won races, he proved his consistency over the duration of a season and he secured his long-term future in Formula One by signing a multi-year deal with McLaren, beginning in 2005.

Juan Pablo's consistency over the season was what distinguished him from his team-mate Ralf Schumacher. Juan scored nine podiums in 16 races (as opposed to three for Ralf), which was the reason why he stayed in contact with Michael Schumacher for the title until the penultimate race. And, were it not for some harsh interference from the US GP race stewards that saw them give the Columbian a drive-through penalty, he would still have been in with a shout of the title at the season finale.

Still, the highs were very high. His win at Monaco, where he withstood huge pressure from Kimi Raikkonen and Michael Schumacher, was a mesmeric drive. Then there was the utter dominance of his win at Hockenheim where, had he not suffered a throttle problem for three-quarters of the race, he thought he could have lapped the field.

But for all these highs and perhaps because of them, Juan will think of this year as a missed opportunity. A first world championship win gone missing.

In Michelin, he had the dominant tyre company at his disposal, and, in the Williams FW25, he had the dominant car for the second half of the year. But for a few small changes in fortune, this year could have been his year.

What he will have learnt from this season is the importance of getting off to a good start in the championship. Okay, the FW25 had its set-up problems early on, but it took him until Monaco, race seven, to get his championship campaign under way. At that point in the proceedings he lay seventh in the title standings, 25 points behind then-leader Kimi Raikkonen.

He had lost two points in Melbourne, where he spun away the lead with 10 laps remaining; he was taken out of the Malaysian race by Antonio Pizzonia, losing three laps in the pits for repairs; he crashed out of the Brazilian GP; pitstop problems relegated him to seventh at Imola; and he then had an engine failure in Austria.

Then, no sooner had he got his championship on track, he fell out irreparably with his team at Magny-Cours. He still believes that he could have won that race had he not been instructed by the team on when to make his second pitstop. Efforts were made to repair the damage, but it was too late. Juan had lost faith in the team and signed for McLaren within a month.

Frank Williams has always loved Juan and, if he continues to improve at a similar rate to this year, they will miss him from 2005 onwards.

Juan Pablo Montoya finished second in the first race of the season at Melbourne.

RALF SCHUMACHER

I was in Frankfurt the Saturday after Suzuka for a marketing day on behalf of one of BMW Williams' sponsors FedEx, and not surprisingly the first question I was asked was, "Ralf, when will you be World Champion?" I smiled. To be honest, I don't know, but it was never easier than this season! I was so close to the championship - driver and constructor - and I missed both. What a shame!

It was a year full of ups and downs, one of mixed emotions with no happy end. However, I was very happy with my two wins in Germany and France and my pole position in Monaco, but only five points out at the last six races was a disappointment.

As a result, I'm sorry for the team. We were miles away from having a winning car at the beginning of the season, but the team never gave up and we came back with a vengeance in the middle of the season, which was amazing! I don't think this sort of revival has ever happened in Formula One before in such a short period of time. At the end, BMW Williams had a better package than Ferrari, and this makes me very optimistic for 2004.

Congratulations to my brother Michael, but I promise to make his life much more difficult next year. Well done also to Kimi. To be honest, I didn't believe that he could fight for the championship right until the end of the last race.

RALF SCHUMACHER

Ralf Schumacher does not make life easy for himself and having six times World Champion Michael as his brother definitely has its advantages and disadvantages. As he said "The advantage of being Michael's brother is that doors open for me, but the disadvantage is that people constantly compare us." However, six wins is not a great record for a driver who is the favoured son of BMW, engine partners of Williams, a team that has the resources to be in regular contention for the World Championship.

Ralf's main problem is his inconsistency. And 2003 has been a prime example of this. Just when you think 'aah Ralf is delivering the goods' bang off he goes again and loses it. After a disappointing performance in Monaco when he had pole position only to fade away during the race to finish fourth, and see his team mate, with whom he does not share a close relationship, win the race and end a twenty year draught for the Grove based team, he seemed to get his act together finishing second in Canada.

After two consecutive victories in the back to back races in Nurburgring and France, it looked like this year might be the Ralf Schumacher show, particularly since team mate Juan Pablo Montoya's relationship with the team was deteriorating at a rapid rate, but no sooner had the pundits started to praise him than Ralf did his snakes and ladders act and slipped down the nearest serpent.

At Silverstone Schumacher's race disappeared in the rain and the on track antics of a protester. After going off the track and damaging his car he looked lackluster and only managed a disappointing ninth.

Germany was a disaster with Schumacher being blamed for the first corner incident that took out both Kimi Raikkonen and Rubens Barrichello. As he walked across to the Steward's room after the race to face the inquisition of the three race stewards he would have glanced up at the podium and seen teammate Juan Pablo Montoya celebrating victory. In years to come he might look back on this as one of the turning points of his career. Starting from second place on the grid and with BMW Williams in strong contention for the Constructor's Championship and him fighting for the Driver's Championship he effectively threw away eight if not ten points.

After that it was downhill all the way. After a massive shunt in testing he didn't compete at Monza after feeling unwell, with test driver Marc Gene substituting him and finishing a credible fifth, when Schumacher complained of having a headache.'

In all fairness he had suffered a huge accident and in the same way that Button and Firman had time out after accidents he needed to recover. But Williams and Head are of the old school where you carry on regardless. Alan Jones a former Williams driver once drove with a broken finger.

In Indianapolis Ralf was back finishing in sixth position and at Suzuka he got caught out in the rain during the qualifying session starting from the back row, then had a difficult race nearly taking his brother out as he was fighting for the World Championship. Again in all fairness Michael was not driving his best race either.

However, at the end of yet another year when Ralf has not risen to the challenge of driving like a potential World Champion the question must be 'how long before BMW Williams decide enough is enough?'

130

Above: Having qualified in Pole Position, Ralf Schumacher faded away to finish fourth in the Monaco Grand Prix.

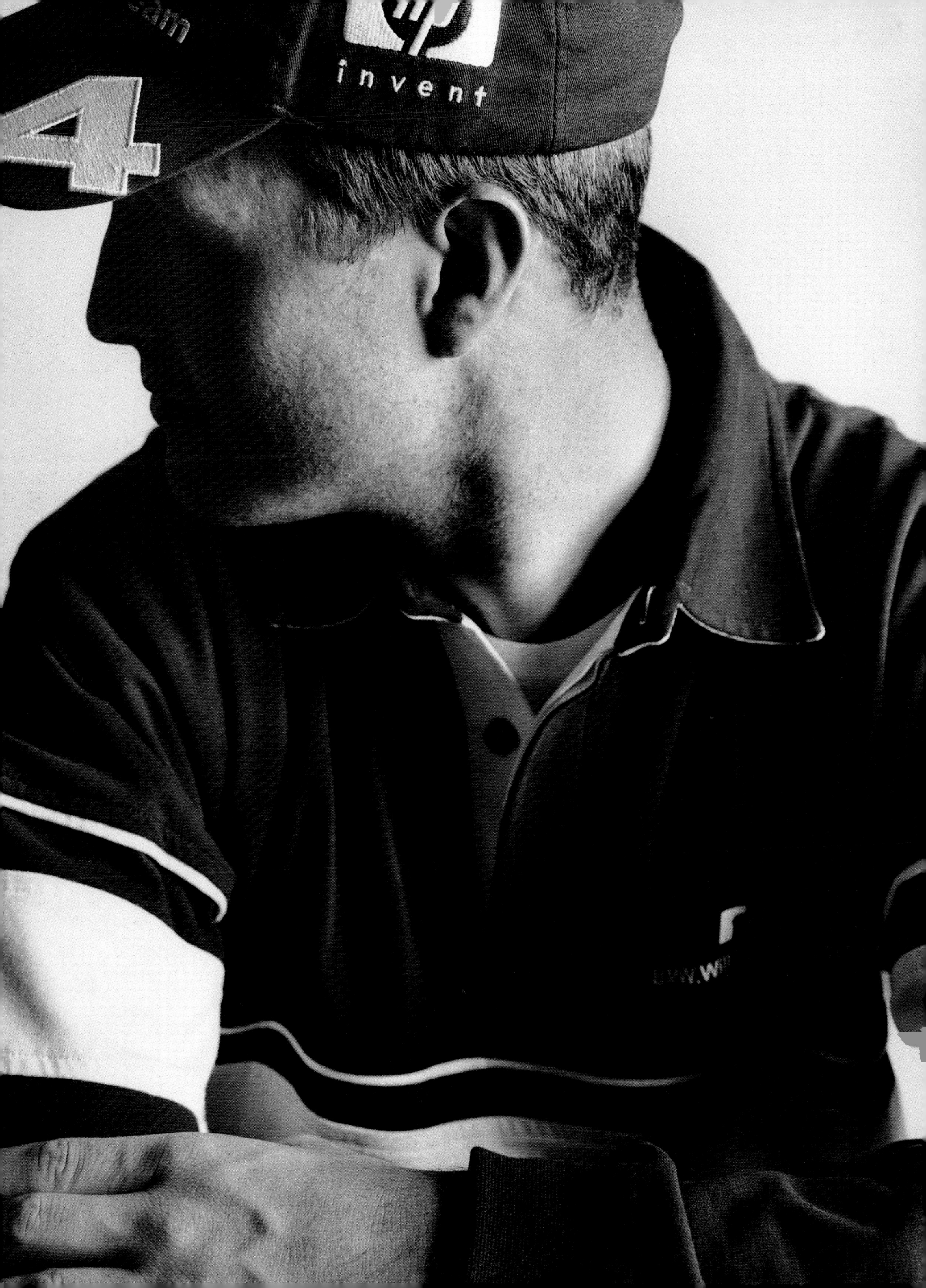
invent

I had no problems starting the season with the old car because I knew that we had improved it a lot over the course of the winter and so I thought it would be competitive. This turned out to be the case, with David winning in Australia and me winning in Malaysia.

I will look back at that first win at Sepang as the high point of my season. It was very exhilarating to stand on the top step of the podium for the first time and, while I don't think it made me any quicker as a driver, it gave me more confidence, which you need to be quick.

My first pole position at the Nurburgring was another high point, and I suppose my low points were the various retirements I had, particularly at the Nurburgring, where I retired from the lead. It was also quite disappointing not to win the world championship. I know I only had an outside chance going into the last race, but when you have a chance, you have hope, so when it didn't work out, it was a little disappointing. Still, there is always next year.

I am pleased with the work that we did at McLaren over the course of the year. We developed the MP4-17D in a good direction and the last package of updates that we had prior to Monza made us very competitive.

Overall, I don't think there were many great surprises in 2003. Everyone whom I expected to be fast was fast, although Renault got on the pace quicker than I expected and I am sure that they'll be a threat in 2004.

KIMI RAIKKONEN

Whereas most people would be terrified of driving at speeds of over 300 kilometres per hour, 24-year-old Finn Kimi Raikkonen's greatest fear appears to be the possibility of being caught with an animated expression on his face. However, the most verbally challenged driver off the track is simply divine on it. Put him in a car and he becomes the ultimate racing driver – quick, fearless and unflappable.

McLaren boss Ron Dennis spotted his potential when the Finnish youngster was in his first year of Formula One with Sauber. Many people were surprised when he chose the Finn rather than his Sauber team-mate Nick Heidfeld to fill departing ex-World Champion Mika Hakkinen's shoes in 2002. But then again Ron Dennis is not like most people – he has an uncanny knack of spotting talent and making a good deal, and in Kimi's case his instincts were spot on.

In 2002 Raikkonen nearly achieved his first victory at the French Grand Prix, but a small yet crucial error gave Michael Schumacher his fifth World Championship a race or two earlier than expected. In 2003 the tables were turned. The Finn, known as the 'Ice Man' for his cold, cool approach to life, made sure the championship battle went down to the wire by coming second in Indianapolis, making the gap between Schumacher and Raikkonen nine points going into the last race at Suzuka.

His championship potential was on show all through the season, but never more so than at Suzuka when he kept the battle going even though he had an almost insurmountable mountain to climb. In fact, in Suzuka it was World Champion Michael Schumacher who made the mistakes while the 'Ice Man' blocked out everything except the need to win.

His first appearance on the top step of the podium came in Malaysia after a first lap incident involving Michael Schumacher and Jarno Trulli, but that aside it was a perfectly executed race and a well-earned victory. He thought he'd won his second race in the chaos of Brazil, but that went to Fisichella. However, by Monaco he was leading the drivers' championship by four points from Michael Schumacher, although this was overturned in Canada when Raikkonen made a costly mistake in qualifying and ended up on the last row of the grid, from where he finished sixth in the race. The victorious Schumacher overtook him in the championship battle, 54 points to 51, and that was it. BMW Williams started their strong challenge leaving Raikkonen third in the Driver's Championship at the German Grand Prix. A fine drive in Indianapolis kept him in with a faint chance of snatching his first World Championship in only his third full year of Formula One.

Looking at the bigger picture, Kimi is still an uncut diamond. His ability to set up a car can be further refined and he drives to his limit, not the car's limit. This year the two things have not always been one and the same thing.

However, there is no doubt that one day soon Raikkonen will wear the World Champion's crown.

Kimi Raikkonen thought he had won his second grand prix but the rain-filled chaos of the Interlagos track resulted in victory going to Jordan driver Giancarlo Fisichella, with the Finn finishing second.

For me personally, it's been a disappointing season. I have found adapting to the one-lap qualifying hard, and that has affected my race results. The first race in Melbourne started off so well with a win, and Malaysia was looking good until the car broke down in the race. After a good show in Brazil, where I qualified on the front row, it was the start of a downward spiral in qualifying. But it's not really the drama that people are making it out to be. I'll get it sorted.

I have mixed feelings about the new rules and regulations. People think they have made Formula One more exciting, but I think the competitive year we've seen is more down to Michelin making progress on the tyres, and teams like Renault taking a step forward. My personal opinion is that there is a handicap system in Formula One now, as I don't believe any one of the drivers can drive 100 per cent on a single-lap going from cold. If you take Japan as an example, you see the drivers who are going for the Championship qualifying low on the grid due to the changing weather conditions, and I'm not sure this is a good thing.

People ask me whether it's been frustrating not having the MP4-18 to drive in races, but I'd say it has been more frustrating for Kimi as he was in contention for the World Championship. For me the MP4-18 has been a very positive step forward for next year. Many of the concepts we have developed on the MP4-18 will be handed over to the MP4-19. I can't wait for 2004 and a new season. My hunger to win is as strong as ever.

DAVID COULTHARD

137

DAVID COULTHARD

In a perfect world, 32-year-old David Coulthard, DC to his friends, would have been World Champion by now. Courteous, talented and above all decent, he would be a fine PR man for a sport that needs a friendly face. But, sadly, life has dictated that Coulthard will be forever in the shadows of his Finnish team-mates. The relay baton has passed from Mika Hakkinen to 24-year-old Kimi Raikkonen, who is a man of few words blessed with a huge talent.

However, at the start of the season, it really did look as if 2003 would finally be Coulthard's year. Starting his eighth season with McLaren, he qualified a poor 11th on the grid in Melbourne, but then rectified this with a truly inspirational display of keeping a cool head when all around him were losing theirs. Raikkonen and Schumacher senior had a coming together, Raikkonen incurred a pit lane speeding penalty, and Montoya indulged in one of his heart-stopping little spins whilst leading the race. DC just carried on, having changed his wet Michelins to dry, and took his first, and as it would turn out, his only victory of 2003. "We're hopefully in for an exciting season," he said. It was, but not for him.

In Malaysia it looked good until an electronics failure finished Coulthard's podium chances, and then we had the chaos of Brazil. After leading the race for some time, Coulthard went in for his pit stop as Webber had his accident, which was followed by Alonso crashing into the Australian, and causing the red flag to come out and the race to be stopped. He got fourth place instead of a win.

After this, the qualifying skill centre of DC's brain went into shut down mode, and he started to make life difficult for himself in the races. At Imola he translated 12th on the grid into a fifth place in the race, and in Austria he recorded fifth place from 14th on the grid. At Nurburgring, he had to take evading action to avoid crashing into Alonso and went off the track, officially finishing 15th.

Another fifth at Silverstone when his team-mate was on the podium did nothing to help his by now lost Championship chances. However, in Germany things looked up briefly when he secured his second podium of the season with second place. Was it a coincidence that team-mate Raikkonen had been punted out in the Barrichello-Ralf Schumacher start-line accident? "I saw the accident on the big screen as we were going round behind the safety car." Did this release the pressure of having to compete with his world championship fighting team-mate? It would seem that Coulthard races better in a Finn-free zone.

However, by Monza the news was out that Colombian Juan Pablo Montoya had signed for McLaren in 2005, so the sands of time are running out for Formula One's Mr Nice guy. 2004 is his final chance to prove he has the makings of a World Champion.

David Coulthard was on course for a podium finish in France before the problem with the refuelling rig on his third pit stop. He finished fifth.

FERNANDO ALONSO

 2003 was an amazing season for me. I'm still young and Renault have given me a fantastic opportunity. The four podiums, the two poles and the victory were a dream come true.

To begin with, having fuel on board for qualifying and having the cars in parc fermé on Saturday night with no chance to make any changes was difficult and a little bit uncomfortable for the teams and drivers, but it was the same for everybody and made the strategy more interesting. However, I soon got used to the new rules and liked them. I got into the single-lap qualifying and I think the people watching liked it too. And that definitely has to be good for Formula One.

The high point was of course winning in Hungary. So much happened in one day! The whole weekend was amazing. With pole position and then victory it was like being part of a fantastic film.

The low point was probably Brazil, where I thought I could have won. There were yellow flags everywhere because the safety car was on the track. I did one lap, no problem, then in the last corner there were pieces of Webber's Jaguar…and that was that.

I don't think anything surprised me in 2003. The only surprise I had was in Barcelona when 100,000 people came to watch the race!

I think it's going to be really competitive next year, especially for us as we are fighting with Ferrari, Williams and McLaren. These are the top teams and it's difficult to beat them. But it will be an interesting season.

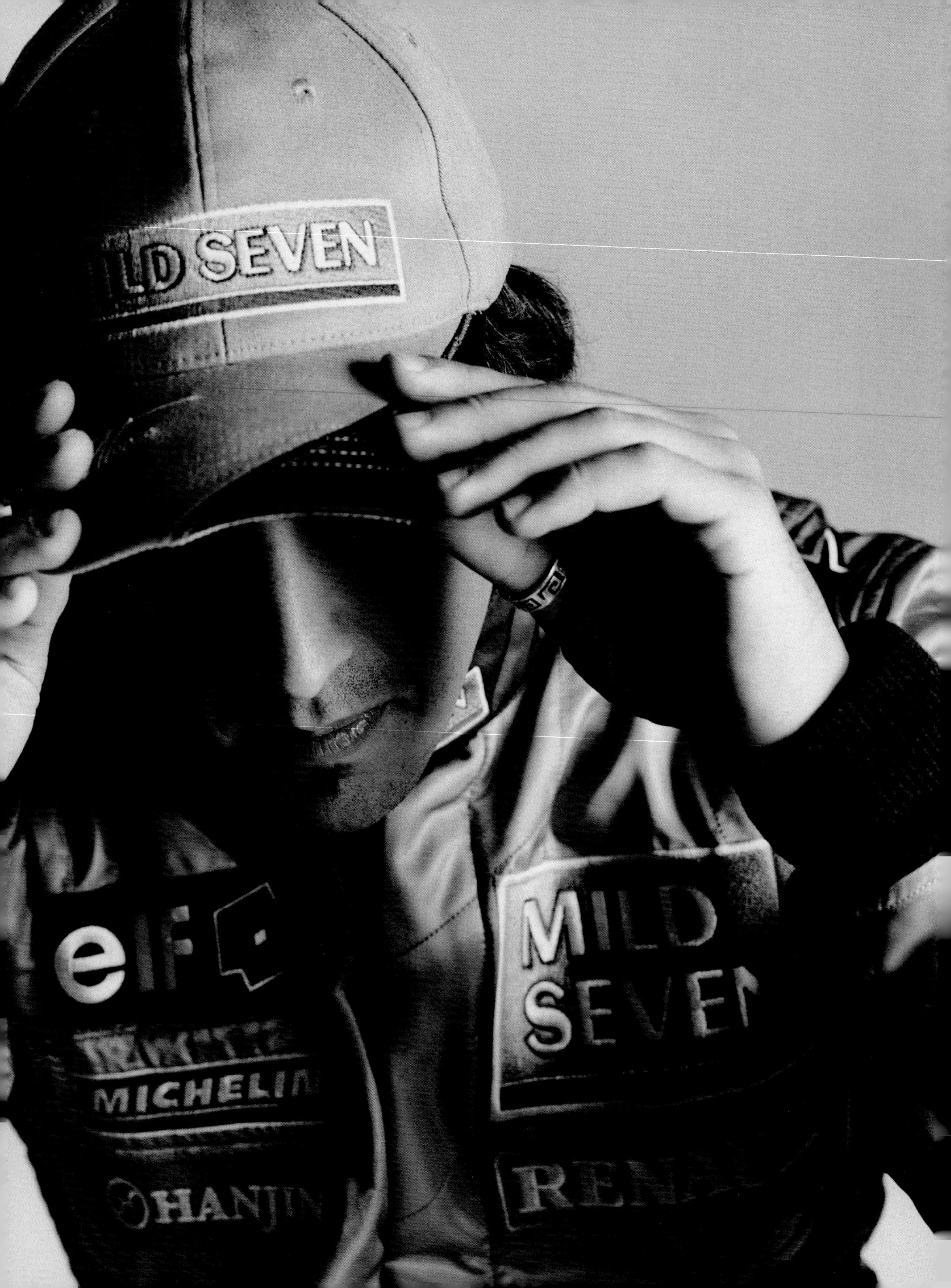
LD SEVEN
MILD
SEVE
elf
MICHELI
HANJI
REN

When he came into Formula One in 2001 with Minardi, Fernando Alonso was easy to overlook. Everyone had their eyes set on Juan Pablo Montoya and Kimi Raikkonen. But within the team, anyone you asked about the little Spaniard raved about him. That made it all the more ironic when there was no seat left for him in 2002. This forced him to sit out the year, but he was fortunate that he had a contract with Flavio Briatore and Renault Sport in his pocket.

Alonso could test for the team and amass the miles a young driver needs. And whenever he had a pukka run - as opposed to doing endurance testing on engines and transmissions - he showed that he was as fast as race drivers Jarno Trulli and Jenson Button. The latter's contract ran until the end of the season, and it was soon clear how Briatore intended to resolve his three-into-two race driver problem for 2003. At the French Grand Prix that season, Alonso was announced as Renault's second driver for the forthcoming season.

Right from the start, technical director Mike Gascoyne was excited about his new driver, and Alonso went from strength to strength delivering the goods straight away. He finished seventh in Australia, then, sensationally took pole position in Malaysia, where he went on to finish third. In Brazil he showed that Sepang was no fluke, but here his impetuosity saw him crash into the wreckage of Mark Webber's Jaguar after he ignored the yellow flags.

His shunt triggered the red flag, but despite being on his way to hospital for a check-up, he still finished on the podium there. Imola brought sixth, Spain a superb second only to Michael Schumacher, who surely took even greater note of the rookie's smooth speed for future reference. In Monaco, he was an unobtrusive but clever fifth. In Canada he was fourth - less than five seconds off victory. Nurburgring and Hockenheim brought two more fourths. Then came a second pole and that dominant win in Hungary - the first-ever for a Spaniard, making him the sport's youngest-ever winner.

It was a dream season by any standard, and underlined the threat that Alonso will pose with experience. The economy, smoothness and deceptive speed of his driving style are reminiscent of Alain Prost's, and he rarely makes mistakes. Brazil apart, he qualified only 20th at Monza owing to a traction control malfunction which tripped him into a spin.

Meanwhile, during the race, his car was never right after a collision on the start line and other sundry problems led to him vaulting hard over a chicane. Even so, he shrugged off the shortcomings there and drove the wheels off the Renault to take eighth place and the final point. Of all the top four drivers - Michael Schumacher, Kimi Raikkonen and Juan Pablo Montoya being the other three - Alonso made the least driving errors. Without doubt, he will be one of the stars of the sport's future, and possibly the biggest star.

JARNO TRULLI

This year has been a bit frustrating for me because I have had a lot of retirements from races when I have been in a good position to score points. But that has been the story of my Formula One career, and all I can do is stay motivated and keep on pushing.

On the positive side, we have had a very good car this year, which has been a big motivation for everyone back at the factory. For me personally, it has been great to go into all the races with a chance of doing well. I have been very quick, but I have lost lots of opportunities at the first corner, which is annoying.

I think I have driven some good races, so I am pleased with my overall performance. But we have to finish races if we are to move forward. That is the only way you score championship points.

There is great harmony within the team at the moment because Fernando [Alonso] and I get along very well. We are friends so everyone is able to push forward together.

From here, the goal for next year is to win races. To do that, we have to continue growing and working hard, then we can hope for some great performances.

In terms of surprises, I like to think that we have been one of the biggest ones this year. We have been fast almost everywhere, which I don't think many people expected at the start of the season.

JARNO TRULLI

Jarno Trulli finished third at Hockenheim and had to be treated for heat exhaustion after the combination of 'flu and the heat nearly finished his race.

Jarno Trulli went into 2003 on a wave of success, having generally been quicker than team-mate Jenson Button at Renault in 2002. He had his feet well under the table and was the team leader. But his season got off to a frustrating start as new boy Fernando Alonso quickly showed himself to have plenty of speed in qualifying. By Malaysia, the second race, the Spaniard had grabbed his first pole and left Trulli to be content with the other front-row position. However, one should remember that under the new rules that require drivers to race with the remains of their qualifying fuel load, team-mates can no longer qualify with exactly the same set-up. One of them must always have at least one lap's worth more fuel aboard, otherwise both would come into the pits to refuel on the same lap of the race and one would therefore inevitably lose out.

Trulli finished fifth in Australia and Malaysia (his chances in the latter spoiled in the first corner when Michael Schumacher stupidly drove into him by diving into a gap that was already closing), then eighth in Brazil, but by now people were talking about Alonso, not him. Against the remorseless onslaught of Alonso's results - seventh in Australia, third in Brazil and Malaysia, sixth at Imola - Trulli could have cracked. His critics certainly expected him to. Then came a lean spell with only two eighths and two sixths to sustain him through to a third-place podium finish at

Hockenheim. Whenever one of the Renaults broke down, it always seemed to be the Italian's. And he retired in Spain as a result of a brush with David Coulthard, and then crashed in Canada. At Monaco, having led Alonso for most of the race, he somehow lost out in the final stops and so the Spaniard sprinted ahead. Alonso finished fifth, a frustrated Trulli sixth. Seventh place in Hungary highlighted his desperate plight when his younger team-mate Alonso won.

However, Trulli kept his spirits up and his nerve intact, and in the latter half of the season began to match his team-mate regularly, regaining his reputation as a driver who is very quick over one lap. His form in races remained suspect, however. He qualified a splendid second at Silverstone and led the opening laps of the British GP in seemingly confident style until the intervention of the on-track protester, but thereafter, when he had to mix it closely with his rivals, he faded back to an unhappy sixth. Critics would say that, while he can qualify well, he doesn't push hard enough over a complete race distance. He exudes the air of a frustrated individual when things go wrong, and it's not difficult to see why. Six years after he so confidently led the Austrian Grand Prix for Prost, he is still looking for that first win. He has some way to go to prove that he can be as consistent, fast and successful as Alonso. 2004 will be his make or break year.

JENSON BUTTON

"**2003 has probably been the most satisfying season of my** career. That said, all of us at BAR were expecting a little more, but I'm satisfied because I've done the best job I can. I've been pushing myself to the limit on every lap, and been over it a couple of times.

I like the new rules - I think they're great. It's tough in single-lap qualifying when you make a mistake and then, of course, you wish the rules were different, but generally speaking, I think they make a race much more exciting.

Up until Indianapolis, qualifying third on the Thursday of Monaco was the high point of my season. Then Silverstone was pretty damn good, as was the last qualifying session at Monza. But nothing beats the feeling of leading a grand prix as I did at Indy and Japan. That was cool!

Missing Monaco when we were looking so strong was pretty tough, but mostly it was the niggling things like gearbox problems that annoyed me. You don't mind once, but it's been two or three times. The low points were really after Monaco - in Montreal and Nurburgring where we seemed to lose a bit of ground.

There were some surprises. I was amazed at how mixed up the grids were at times, and how quick certain cars were. I was also surprised at how many people have won races this year. It was the weirdest season for me. I want to win more than anything, but for some reason, if I had won this year I wouldn't have got as excited as I would have last year. I don't know why.

I think it will be another very competitive year next year, and I think BAR Honda will be a lot stronger. There are so many good things going on here, and I think we will be the team to make the most significant improvements. "

Moving to his third new Formula One team in four seasons, Jenson Button did not find the welcome mat rolled out by team-mate Jacques Villeneuve. But the Englishman did a fine job of playing down the initial unpleasantness. He chose instead, not to rise to the bait and let his driving do the talking. Though their final qualifying score was a fairly even 8-7 in Button's favour, he left the overall impression that he had done a better job than the former champion, whose points tally he doubled.

Button said nothing publicly when Villeneuve spoiled his race in Melbourne by pitting on the same lap. In Malaysia he was quicker, finishing seventh, and was running strongly in Brazil until the river at Turn 3 caught him out. It was of consolation that Michael Schumacher and Juan Pablo Montoya were also its victims. He was eighth at Imola, fourth in Austria, seventh at the Nurburgring, and eighth at Silverstone and Hockenheim. His drive in the British Grand Prix showed his determination, as he fought from the back of the grid having started there when striking a kerb on his qualifying lap broke his BAR's front suspension.

His best performance went unrewarded, however. In Indianapolis he pitted at just the right time for wet Bridgestone tyres and assumed the lead on the 23rd lap. He held it until the 38th, and it was no disgrace to lose it to Michael Schumacher, especially as the champion was headed for his 70th victory. This was the first time that Button had led a grand prix, and he did so with a smooth and economical style that matched Fernando Alonso's, the man who replaced him at Renault. He looked completely unruffled, and was able to stay in touch with Schumacher once the Ferrari had overtaken. Then his jinx struck again, as a Honda engine failure denied him his first podium finish. It was a cruel twist of fate, and as he later admitted, he was tempted to hurl his steering wheel on to the track in frustration. But he refrained, preferring instead to keep the lid on his emotions and continued to behave in the mature manner that has always been his hallmark.

What he could take away from 2003 was the knowledge that he had driven every lap to the very best of his ability and got the most out of the car. He could have been forgiven for feeling frustrated and de-tuned after having to leave Renault just as the hard work from a demoralising 2001 and a more encouraging 2002 was about to pay off. Instead, he grabbed the BAR opportunity with both hands and made a big impression on a team that he described as the most welcoming he had ever driven for. His relationship with David Richards was also very strong and they had clear mutual respect that will help both to move forwards in 2004. How he fares against Takuma Sato, his partner, now that Jacques Villeneuve has departed, will be one of the New Year's fascinating aspects.

Jenson Button led a grand prix for the first time in Indianapolis. He had to retire after 41 laps when his engine failed.

JACQUES VILLENEUVE

For me, 2003 was a lot of hard work for very little result. There were a lot of mechanical failures combined with bad luck. The few times when nothing went wrong we did a good job. So it was frustrating.

Single-lap qualifying didn't suit me partly because the car was breaking all the time, so we concentrated on race strategy, fuel and set-up all the time; it just made us look slow in qualifying, and then we made no use of it in the race. Monza was the first time it worked for us. Apart from that, though, they created a great championship which is what F1 needs.

Qualifying with racing fuel levels was hateful for qualifying but great for the race.

As for highs, I guess it was Brazil where we were very competitive in the wet. As for lows, I have many choices! I guess all the gossip that's been created and said by just a few people to discredit what I've achieved in the past. That was the lowest point, the lack of respect.

If anything surprised me in 2003, it was the lack of logic and intelligence in the paddock.

I'm not unhappy that I will not be with B.A.R. next year. We obviously have different ideas on which direction the team is taking. However, it is really disappointing how things have evolved. I gave everything I had to B.A.R. Most of my F1 career has been spent working for the team and I had built close relationships with the engineers and the mechanics and it will be a shame not to be working with them anymore.

Ever since David Richards replaced Craig Pollock as the team principal at BAR, Jacques Villeneuve's relationship with the team has been edgy. Pollock was his manager and friend, and there may have been complications when Pollock continued to act initially as the third party in Villeneuve's contractual negotiations with Richards. In this uneasy triangle, lines of communication may have become distorted.

His media manager, the delightful Jules Kulpinski has had her work cut out this year although to be fair ask Jacques a straight question and he'll answer it. However right from the start, Villeneuve seemed unsettled. Jenson Button's arrival upset him, perhaps because former team-mate, Olivier Panis, had been a quiet type who let him have his own way, possibly just because Jacques sought to lay down a marker. Whatever the cause, there were some unfriendly words spoken by the French-Canadian who made it crystal clear that Button had to earn his respect. This he most certainly did over the course of the year.

In Australia, Villeneuve further blotted his copybook by supposedly mishearing pit messages and pitting on the same lap as his new team-mate. This meant that Button, who was running faster, lost a lot of time. BAR's race was ruined.

Eventually the childish behaviour settled down, but all season Villeneuve was aware that his prospects for 2004 were not good. He simply wanted more money than Richards was prepared to pay, and regardless of the fact that he was champion of the world in 1997 with Williams, the harsh facts were that he had not delivered since. It wasn't his fault that a succession of BAR cars had been mediocre at best; his big problem now was that Button generally did a better job in qualifying and the races.

Where Villeneuve scored only six points, Button doubled that and led the US Grand Prix at Indianapolis for 15 laps to boot. Villeneuve's response was that his car was so mechanically fragile that the team usually focussed on race set-up work rather than having the opportunity to optimise it for qualifying, but that surely applied as much to Button and did not explain why the French-Canadian often looked a shadow of his former self. Continual criticism outside the team would not have helped his state of mind, but in the past he had always shown himself to be strong psychologically.

Whatever the reasons, Villeneuve had a pretty horrible time and even before the season was over it was clear that he had come to the end of the road. He and Richards had further talks in Indianapolis but left just as far apart as they had ever been. The former had wanted to pay him more, but over a three-year period; Villeneuve (or his management) at the end of 2002 had insisted on a big sum for 2003. Richards decided to pursue the economic logic of taking young racer Takuma Sato who would bring money and even further commitment from Honda. Sato was duly signed, finished sixth at Suzuka when Villeneuve declined to race, bringing home a valuable three points and helping BAR to clinch 5th place in the Constructor's Championship. Meanwhile, Villeneuve's mercurial Formula One career appears to be over,

Jacque Villeneuve's miserable season continued in Austria when he stalled in his second pit stop and eventually finished 12th.

In terms of success on the circuit, this season was definitely not as good as the financial rewards for driving! At least not until Indianapolis. Our season was not as good as I expected, especially as we were facing some very strong opposition in the midfield from manufacturers who are getting really serious. We also lost some opportunities when the car broke down when we were in a position to score points.

I have to say that, generally, I liked the qualifying system. I think it created more excitement for the audience. It was a fantastic show, especially for people who are interested in drivers' techniques.

You can question the idea of running on the fuel load you qualified with, as there's always an unknown factor. In my opinion, it made the race more exciting and carried the excitement from one day to the next.

My high point was, of course, leading the US Grand Prix at Indianapolis, and finishing on the podium there. That was fantastic! Especially as the result meant we jumped up from ninth to fifth in the Constructors' Championship. It made up for the big low after we dropped out of seventh place right at the end at Monza. The other highs came early in Australia and Brazil.

The leap forward Renault made, and also Jaguar and Mark Webber, surprised me. They had some impressive qualifying results. Next year, I think Formula One will be similar, but I think at least one team will improve dramatically, just as Renault did in 2003. It's difficult to be more precise. But it will be good.

HEINZ-HARALD FRENTZEN

An uneventful race for Heinz-Harald Frentzen at San Marino after he qualified 14th and finished 11th.

Though the man himself clearly did not think so for much of the year, many observers expected that 2003 would be Heinz-Harald Frentzen's last hurrah in Formula One. Frustrated by what he saw as Felipe Massa's youthful errors and overdriving, Peter Sauber had already made it clear in Hungary in 2002 that the Brazilian would be replaced by the experienced German, to whom he had given a first Formula One chance back in 1994. Indeed, Frentzen rejoined Sauber sooner than expected when he participated in the 2002 US Grand Prix at Indianapolis, as the team cleverly bypassed the 10-place grid penalty that had been imposed on Massa at Monza.

Back in the fold full-time, he started his year well. With the strategy that the team adopted for the Australian Grand Prix, he was able to qualify his Sauber Petronas C22 in a promising fourth position, but soon lost out when his Bridgestone tyres disliked the slippery conditions of the opening laps. Nevertheless, he held on to finish an encouraging sixth. He was ninth, just out of the points in Malaysia, but in Brazil he might even have been a contender for victory had the race not been red-flagged early.

As it was, he finished fifth, but there the story stalled. After that the C22's aerodynamic shortcomings, allied to almost universal adoption of two-stop race strategies with a low fuel load for qualifying and the first stint, the Saubers were left well down the grid and often just out of the points. Frentzen retired with suspension failure in Spain, clutch failure at the start in Austria and electrical failure in Canada, by which time he could see that his future was looking bleak. There had also been his crash driving on lap one at Monaco, when he hit a chicane kerb at the wrong angle and was flipped into the wall exiting the swimming pool.

Often he got his car better sorted than team-mate Nick Heidfeld, but there was little chance for him to showcase the ability that he still possessed. Hockenheim continued the downturn when he was an innocent victim of the first corner melee, but in Monza he upset more than a few people by apparently blocking Juan Pablo Montoya as the Colombian chased after Michael Schumacher for the lead. Frentzen was on target for a lapped seventh and two crucial points, before his transmission failed in sight of the finish.

It was thus left to Indianapolis for the sun to shine on Sauber, even though it was an overcast and wet day. Frentzen made just the right tyre choice and timed the switch to wet Bridgestones perfectly. Soon he was running second, and after Button had blown up and Schumacher refuelled on lap 48, he found himself leading until his own stop. After that there was no stopping Raikkonen from overtaking as the track dried, but third place was a fine result, which demonstrated that skill and commitment, rather than age, are the deciding factors in Formula One. Unfortunately for Frentzen, that podium finish came just too late.

"**For much of the time, 2003 was more difficult than we had** expected it to be. Our goal was to play a key role after the 'top teams', and we didn't manage to do that until Indianapolis. I wasn't happy with the number of points scored.

I haven't changed my mind about the rules since the beginning of the year. I like single-lap qualifying as a driver- it's a big challenge, which is good for Formula One. People watching on TV like it, but it's not good for spectators at the circuit. To begin with, it gave mixed grids but then everyone got used to it. What I don't like is qualifying with race fuel. Pole position and all the grid positions, no longer count from a historical perspective. The battle within the team doesn't exist anymore, and for people from outside it's difficult to judge the drivers' performances.

Nurburgring was fantastic, starting from the pits and getting a point. The worst race was in Brazil. After the safety car had gone in, I only managed three corners before I had a technical failure. That was a race where anything could have happened".

A couple of things surprised me in 2003. First, how much progress BMW made after the beginning of the season, and second, how McLaren fell back after a while. Jaguar were stronger than I expected too. But it seemed like the Michelin tyres had a big influence on their progress.

I think next year is going to be very tight again on the chassis side, and the tyres will be closer matched. The biggest issue could arise from the engine rules changing. That's because nobody knows what to expect."

NICK HEIDFELD

It was impossible not to feel sympathy for Nick Heidfeld in 2003. Two years earlier he had resurrected a career that seemed in imminent danger of being strangled by the Prost team during his rookie season in 2000, and had shone in Sauber's ultra-competitive C20. Against new sensation Kimi Raikkonen, he had held his own and both out- qualified and outraced the Finn more often than the Finn had outraced him. Yet although Heidfeld had a contract with McLaren, it was Kimi that Ron Dennis snapped up for 2002. In that season, Heidfeld had still been able to show his talent with the C21, but the 2003 C22 proved a millstone round his neck for much of the year. Where the C20 had been superb and the C21 very good, the C22 was merely good but not good enough. Without the car he needed to keep himself in the limelight, Heidfeld struggled to keep up his morale and momentum.

Suspension failure took him out in Australia. He scored his first point of the season with eighth in Malaysia, on title sponsor Petronas' home ground, but then the engine broke early in Brazil. That was the race in which he could have made a major impression on Bridgestones, and where he had finished third, his best-ever Formula One result, in 2001.

After that the results were patchy: 10th's in Imola, Spain and Hockenheim, 11th in Monaco. The fillip of fourth fastest qualifying time in Austria was instantly negated by engine failure in the race. There should

have been at least a point at Monza, where he was chasing team-mate Frentzen home in ninth place when Frentzen's transmission failed. When Heidfeld was blue-flagged as he was being lapped within sight of the flag, however, Fernando Alonso was able to nip by to deprive him of the final point. That did him no favours with Peter Sauber, who had in any case decided to replace him for 2004.

Prior to Indianapolis, the only high point was an excellent drive from the pit lane to eighth place on his home ground at the Nurburgring, where he had first started his racing career in karts. But in the US Grand Prix he recovered well from having to make an extra pit stop for wet weather tyres and ran as high as second place when Michael Schumacher and Frentzen made their final refuelling stops. He dropped back to third when he made his own, and in the latter stages on a drying track was powerless to stop Raikkonen and Jarno Trulli from overtaking. Nevertheless, his haul of four points for fifth place, when added to Frentzen's six for third, thrust the little Swiss team back into fifth place in the World Constructors Championship just in the nick of time.

The result seems unlikely to save Heidfeld's Formula One racing career. With both Sauber seats taken, Toyota retaining its drivers, and Jaguar seeking a pay driver for its second seat, the German's best chance will probably be a test drive for one of the top teams. He deserves better.

MARK WEBBER

"**I have really, really enjoyed 2003. I've spent all year wondering** when the good things were going to stop but they just kept on going. Some people might say it's not that mega, but when you look at it, we've had a steady stream of points coming in which was never going to be easy when you consider the reliability of the big guns. At Magny Cours, when Renault dropped out, we were ready to grab sixth place and three very valuable points.

I have to say that the team has made me look very good this year. We have really talented people at Jaguar such as Pete Harrison, my race engineer. For the first time I feel confident and secure. We have had some great qualifying positions, third in both Brazil and Hungary. We just have to improve in the races. But the R4 has been very good and is a solid base from which we can develop the R5 next year.

Finishing seventh in the Constructor's Championship was a bit disappointing, and we'll be looking to improve that next year. I'm not a massive fan of the new points system, which rewards drivers down to eighth position. I think the old points system had a lot of history to it. However, everything else is good. The one-lap qualifying is good and Friday testing is good.

Surprises? I thought Renault would be okay and Toyota awesome but it was the other way around. Fernando has done very well. Next year I'd like to see a podium place. After that, who knows? I hope it can only get better and better. "

Mark Webber has been one of the revelations of the season. He has shown all the hallmarks of a future World Champion: Talent, focus, opportunism, the ability to be a team player, and that very important pinch of complete ruthlessness and selfishness that all champions need.

He has taken to the complex Jaguar team like the proverbial duck to water. In Australia, he was unlucky not to repeat his miracle fifth place that he achieved in 2002 with Minardi. Only broken suspension separated Webber from his first four points of the season, but it wasn't to be.

One of his highlights has to be Hungary, in which he qualified third and eventually finished sixth, knowing he couldn't beat the big guns. But he still gave his best shot. This year, you sometimes got the impression that Webber wasn't just driving the R4, but actually picking it up by the bootstraps and forcing it to out-perform its natural ability.

But then Webber is like that. He is a down to earth Aussie. He has no pretensions. While some of his colleagues are stepping on and off private jets and settling down to home life in Monaco, he travels EasyJet, lives in Buckingham and considers a good holiday to be a week hiking through the Pyrenees as part of his relentless quest for perfect fitness.

But that doesn't mean there haven't been low moments for him in 2003. In Brazil, having qualified third, and in a manoeuvre reminiscent of Gilles Villeneuve he avoided going off at the notorious Curva do Sol, which was fast turning into a Formula One car park, but eventually had a big shunt, which Alonso ploughed into and caused the race to end. "I was pushing very hard and was in that position because I was pushing so hard. That's what happens in the heat of the battle." Silverstone was a complete washout. The new aero package didn't slot in as predicted and the team, unlike the other Michelin runners, couldn't get the right balance with their tyres. As Webber puts it, "That experience is in the bank for next year."

This is the first season we have seen the real Mark Webber. As he admits "I got a bit disheartened at Minardi towards the end as we couldn't really push hard." At Jaguar, he now has the resources to push hard.

Webber's target was to finish fifth in the Constructors' Championship so he'll be disappointed with seventh, but not down and out. There is always next year and this is a man on the move. In spite of his long-term contract with Jaguar, he will probably end up at BMW Williams or Ferrari. He has the talent and the temperament to fit into either team, and like Schumacher, he is a team man. "The team have made me look very, very good this year," said Webber. In fact, in 2003, Michael Schumacher has gone out of his way to get to know the Aussie driver. That's a good sign. World champions don't normally bother with small fry. As Gerhard Berger once said, "Ayrton only got to know me when he thought I could be a threat to him. He wanted to know my strengths and weaknesses." Clearly, Schumacher feels Webber could be the man to take his crown.

In 2003 Mark Webber proved he is a star of the future. However, at the San Marino Grand Prix he suffered a broken driveshaft.

JUSTIN WILSON

"**2003 has been an amazing year, a real roller-coaster of ups and** downs and big swings. From great races like Indianapolis, where I scored my first point, to really good races like Barcelona where I led the midfield pack for quite a few laps, to difficult races like Hungary, where I suffered an engine failure.

One of the highlights of the year was raising sponsorship through selling shares in 'Justin Wilson plc'. It was really gratifying that so many people supported me, and it gave me a tremendous boost on the track.

Silverstone was my home race and also a pivotal moment in my career. Following a midnight seat fitting on the Monday after the race, I received a call from Jaguar to say that they wanted me to join the team, and so I became a Jaguar man, which has been fantastic.

Moving from Minardi to Jaguar was a bigger change than I expected. At Minardi you only have to give feedback to a couple of people - your race engineer and your engine engineer, but at Jaguar, you have a lot more people wanting feedback, and that takes time to get used to. But by Monza I felt a lot more confident, and that was the turning point that led to the success at Indy.

Like a lot of drivers, I would like to qualify on low fuel because as a racing driver you always want to get the buzz of trying to go for the ultimate flying lap.

I think it has been a very good year for Formula One, with a hard battle for both championships and the emergence of teams like Renault and Jaguar as future contenders for the championship."

169

2003 has been a year of intense ups and downs for Sheffield-born Justin Wilson. Having won the F3000 Championship in 2001 he might have expected an easier entry into the hallowed environs of Formula One, but measuring up at 6 ft 4 was just a little too tall for most teams who need their drivers to be aerodynamically perfect for their cars.

But Wilson persisted and his persistence paid off when a touch of genius on the part of his manager, Jonathan Palmer, saw him raise over £1.2 million pounds through a share option, which resulted in over 900 people investing in Justin Wilson plc.

Wilson's father Keith put his house on the line and guaranteed the money before it was raised so Justin could start the new season with Minardi. In both Melbourne and Malaysia he was impressive early in the races, and in Malaysia he moved up to eighth position before dropping back due to the ill effects of the HANS (the head and neck support which became mandatory for all the drivers in 2003) device which resulted in him losing all feeling in his arms and having to be taken to hospital after he had been helped out of the car after 41 laps of the race.

In Brazil, the weather conditions were such that either of the Minardi drivers could have scored points, but Wilson spun in the wet and ended his race. "I'm gutted" was his brief response to a lost opportunity. Spain was one of his moments of glory where he did a fantastic job at the start in missing the stationary Jaguar of Antonio Pizzonia, while more experienced driver Kimi Raikkonen ploughed straight into the back of it. Wilson then went on to move into ninth place and lead the pack of mid-field drivers

including Jordan driver Giancarlo Fisichella. He eventually finished 11th.

Canada was the second high of Wilson's season, when he managed to get a spectacular start moving from 18th to 13th before heading up to 11th and looking good for his first points finish, but it was not to be as the gearbox broke and that was the end of his race.

However success did come at Indianapolis when the Brit finished eighth to score one Championship point. But by then he had moved on to Jaguar, earning his promotion after a series of strong races at the beginning of the season. After a midnight visit to the Jaguar factory on the Monday after Silverstone, Wilson made his Jaguar debut in Germany.

And there started a difficult second half of the season. Wilson soon found that swimming in a big pond was very different to swimming with the minnows. A big team has a different structure to a small team. It's not just a case of getting in the car and going as fast as you can, there are a whole group of people who need precise feedback. Holding the information in your head while driving at 300 kp/h takes a bit of getting used to.

In addition to that, it wasn't easy for Wilson to look good against a driver like Mark Webber, who has consistently out driven the Jaguar's capabilities all year. But in Indy it came good and he scored a precious point for the team who at that stage were still fighting for fifth place in the Constructor's Championship.

Wilson has the potential to win races. He just needs test mileage to get some more experience. Whether he realises that potential at Jaguar is another matter.

Justin Wilson switched from Minardi to Jaguar for the German Grand Prix. He scored his first Championship point here in the USA Grand Prix.

On the one hand, I am very pleased with my debut season in
Formula One, but on the other I feel that Toyota deserved much more in
terms of results. It was frustrating to have championship points within our
grasp and to see them slip away, but this was a character-building
experience which the whole team can learn from.

Personally, it was always going to be tough for me because I was
coming into F1 with no prior experience of many of the circuits, and with
only one hour of free practice to get up to speed. At tracks I was familiar
with, like Silverstone and Barcelona, I think I demonstrated my ability and
came away with solid results. Generally, our performance throughout the
season was a little bit inconsistent, but next year I will be on a level playing
field with everyone else.

In the long term, our decision not to take part in the Friday morning
testing session will pay dividends. Certainly, I would have benefited from
that extra two hours this season, but instead I was able to complete
invaluable testing kilometres over the course of the year, which helped me
get used to the intricacies of the car, and this will be a huge asset as we
develop next year's TF104.

The highlight of my 2003 season was leading the British Grand Prix. I
started the season under no illusions and knew that we would not be
challenging for victories in only Toyota's second season, so to find myself
leading the field at Silverstone was unexpected but a lot of fun. I am used
to leading races from my time in CART, but it was the first time in F1 and
in my rookie season, so it was a special feeling.

Scoring third place in Suzuka qualifying was also a fantastic
achievement. We benefited from rain late in the session, but for Olivier and
I to occupy the second row of the grid in front of Toyota's home crowd
was pleasing.

We made massive progress throughout the year, and I think we have set
very solid foundations from which we can increase our competitiveness in
2004. I thoroughly enjoyed this season's racing, but I have the feeling that
next year will be even better and even more rewarding. **"**

CRISTIANO DA MATTA

Cristiano da Matta, the guitar-thrashing Led Zeppelin fanatic, is one of the most unassuming men you could ever meet. And yet under his mask of indifference and almost childlike innocence lies a passion and determination, which is difficult to emulate and almost impossible to match, for the sport he loves. Coming to Formula One as the reigning CART champion, it seemed incredible that his advent in the highest echelon of global motor sport was not met with more fanfare, and yet after talking with him you could understand why. He lets his results do the talking, and from them he knows the plaudits and adulation will come.

His debut Formula One season was never expected to be spectacular. Joining the Toyota team in only its second F1 season, he knew he wouldn't be challenging for race wins, and as soon as the top three teams gave a hint of how strong they would all be in 2003, it became clear that every team and driver outside that top tier would be battling for the final two points below sixth place. In a season that many would have put down to one of learning and transition however, da Matta shone. Scoring two sixth and two seventh place finishes, he wound up the season in 13th position with ten points, four more than his far more experienced team-mate Olivier Panis.

His calm and mature persona saw him rack up the miles in testing and in the races, and come the end of the season he had completed the third most race laps of all the drivers, on a par with Fernando Alonso and beaten only by Michael Schumacher and Juan Pablo Montoya. Add to this his serene display whilst leading the British Grand Prix, albeit for a short while and in a race he finished in seventh place, and the overriding impression is still one of the little Brazilian having driven a highly impressive debut season.

Toyota's decision not to sign up to the Heathrow Agreement could have held da Matta back. After all, coming from a successful career in America, he would be a novice at almost every circuit the Formula One circus visited. However, the mileage he racked up in testing gave him a massive advantage in that his understanding of his steed was as good as possible. He might not have known the circuits, but he and the TF103 spent much of 2003 operating as one, retiring from just three races. Come the start of 2004, he will have experience of the tracks and his already impressive performances can be expected to be even greater still.

His debut season in Formula One, whilst as quiet and unobtrusive as the man himself, was very impressive and will have acted brilliantly as his first step on the ladder towards future greatness in the highest and most challenging motor sport formula on earth. With an impressive CV, and a maturity and determination which, when mixed with his raw ability, creates a potent force, Cristiano da Matta, when fielded with a competitive car, will be a force to be reckoned with. It may not all come together in 2004, but as his favourite band Led Zeppelin once sang, "Your time is gonna come."

Cristiano da Matta had an eventful Austrian Grand Prix when he stalled his car twice on the grid and had to start from the pit lane. He eventually finished 10th.

"**This season, we have shown that Panasonic Toyota Racing has** made big steps forward.

We qualified in the top ten on a very consistent basis, and even in the top five on three occasions. We also ran in potential points-scoring positions at many races, but ultimately we suffered from various problems during the year, which caused us to lose valuable championship points.

We finished the season eighth in the Constructor's standings, with me 15th in the Driver's, but I think we deserved much more.

We have learned a lot this year and we should be proud of what we have achieved. F1 is an ongoing learning process and step-by-step I am confident Toyota will be able to challenge the front-runners.

In general, I think that the racing spectacle was very good this season, with many different winners and mixed grid line-ups, which produced some very exciting races. I think the new points system is fair. By giving points down to eighth place, it means that there is still a chance for the midfield teams like Toyota to earn points.

I enjoyed the single lap qualifying idea. It added excitement to the Championship from the spectator's point of view and also from a driving perspective. When you have only one chance to qualify, the pressure is even greater, but so too is the fun.

One area I think we need to improve is our contact with the fans. Take Indianapolis as an example, where thousands of people turned up early on Thursday morning for the pit walkabout. You could really feel the excitement and passion for the sport and we need to encourage that.

Toyota can look ahead to next season with a lot of confidence. I continue to be impressed by the work of the entire team at both the track and back at the Cologne factory. With this sort of teamwork, we can expect to make even bigger progress in 2004."

OLIVIER PANIS

Olivier Panis has been around the block a few times. Having now competed in nine Formula One campaigns, he's got a fair level of experience. From the immense high of his first, and thus far single, grand prix victory at the 1996 Monaco Grand Prix, to the indescribable low of breaking his legs at the 1997 Canadian Grand Prix, Panis is a man who has been through everything the sport can throw at a driver. So when Toyota wanted a man they could rely on to not only develop their 2003 car, but drive it with the level-headed maturity of a seasoned veteran, they could not have asked for a better driver than the Frenchman.

He may have scored just six points this season, fewer than his young Brazilian team-mate Cristiano da Matta, but that one simple statistic does not give a true reflection of his worth to the team. Much as with the design of their debut challenger the TF102, in 2002 Toyota had also erred on the side of caution with their driver line-up. In 2003 they had the perfect balance of a young guy, full of enthusiasm and ambition following his dominance of the 2002 CART championship, and a respected, fast and hard working Formula One driver to nurture da Matta, along with the team as a whole. It is the Frenchman's achievement in this role, more than in the actual races, for which he must receive the most praise.

But that is not to say that Panis had a disappointing season race-wise. He scored Toyota's highest finish of the year with a masterful drive to fifth place at Hockenheim, and scored two more World Championship points,

one a piece in Canada and France, to raise the team to eighth place overall in the constructors standings in only their second year of competition. Without Panis' contribution, the team would have beaten only Minardi.

At 37 years-of-age, Panis will be one of Formula One's elder statesmen next season. Celebrating his tenth year of actual racing, since his debut in 1994, he will be hoping that all the hard work he has put into the Toyota team will reap its rewards. And the signs look promising. Towards the end of the season the TF103 was looking highly competitive, with Panis lining up on the second row of the grid in fourth place for the Japanese Grand Prix. But there were times, such as at the British Grand Prix, when he seemed to lack that all-important spark – Kimi Raikkonen's pass on him looked far easier than da Matta made things for the Finn.

It is as a test and development driver of almost unrivalled pedigree that Toyota value Panis' services the most, but he would not still be racing in Formula One if he didn't still possess the hunger or the talent. So, whilst his 2003 season has been spent predominantly turning Toyota into a potent force, and teaching da Matta how to play the game, in 2004 he should be able to show the world the race craft he knows he can still display. In what could be his Formula One swansong, he must hope that all his hard work in 2003 will pay off with a car that will allow him to challenge for the points and credence that his outstanding contribution over the past decade merits.

178

Olivier Panis finished fifth at Hockenheim to give his team Toyota four valuable points in their midfield battle in the Constructor's Championship.

GIANCARLO FISICHELLA

"It's not difficult to guess the highlight of my year. It has to be Brazil, even though it was hard not to be able to celebrate on the podium. I had to wait until Imola when Kimi gave the winner's trophy to me.

In actual fact, my victory at Brazil was the only highlight of what has been a very difficult year. One that was full of mechanical problems and an inability to develop the car aerodynamically. At the beginning of the year we were one and a half seconds off the pace, and by the end of it, we were three seconds off!

Having said that, I'm sad to be leaving Jordan. The guys are great and I won my first race with them, which is something you can never forget.

I'm not crazy about the new qualifying format, as I don't find doing one lap with a lot of fuel very exciting. I would get rid of Friday and have a free practice on Saturday morning and qualifying on Sunday morning.

I think Fernando Alonso has done very well, as has Mark Webber and also Kimi Raikkonen, but things weren't as easy for Michael Schumacher and Ferrari. Next year I'll be joining Sauber, which I'm very happy about, as I feel it is an important step forward in my career. I want to do well with Sauber in 2004 and then who knows? People ask me whether I'd like to drive for Ferrari. All I can say is that I'm a true Italian and so Ferrari has always been my dream team.

I hope 2004 will be a good year for Formula One and for Sauber and myself. **"**

30-year-old Giancarlo Fisichella should be with one of the top teams and next year when he joins Sauber, he'll be one step closer to his dream team - Ferrari. He has pure natural ability, speed and race craft. The only area of doubt has been his mental application, but this year he's proved he is tough enough to overcome anything that is thrown at him.

Winning Brazil in race conditions more suited to a trip up the Amazon river, wasn't just a chance victory. With Turn 3 becoming the most expensive car park in the world with driver after driver, including six times World Champion Michael Schumacher, sliding off and parking up by the barriers, Fisichella kept his head and handled the Jordan firmly on the track. "It was a race in which the driver counted a lot."

The FIA reconstructed the podium at Imola and Kimi Raikkonen officially handed the hardware over to the rightful owner. That was one brief moment of joy.

After Brazil he became very unhappy as a series of mechanical problems forced retirements in Spain and Austria, and a lowly 10th place in Monaco. A 13th place in Germany was a reflection of a very difficult car. "I had a lot of problems this weekend, the tyres, the car, the electronics, the engine." Just about everything then! Hungary was the last straw. "My engine blew up for the third time this weekend," was his short reply when he recorded yet another DNF. Cosworth take note.

It wasn't until Indy that he notched up another few points with seventh place and two valuable points which saw him finish 12th in the Driver's Championship with 12 points.

Jordan has undoubtedly had a very difficult year and Fisi has been caught in the middle. The legal action with Vodafone which Jordan lost did not help matters. Anything that takes your eye off the ball in Formula One is negative.

However, he has also had a good bunch of guys to look after him, including his race engineer Rob Smedley with whom he has a very good rapport. 2003 has been the year in which Fisichella could only look on as an observer rather than a true participant in the Formula One World Championship. Next year he is looking for a lot more. "I want to win points and win another race, although that might be difficult, but at least I want to be on the podium and in a position when I can sometimes challenge the top four teams.

He has Eddie Irvine's manager, the savvy Enrico Zanarini, to look after his interests and he'll no doubt try to edge him towards Ferrari. They are both Italians and Fisi has only ever supported one team, apart from his beloved football team AS Roma, since his childhood and that team is Ferrari. But with Rubens doing a more than adequate job as Michael Schumacher's second in command, the switch might not be as easy as it seems. But Fisichella has the talent, all he needs now is for lady luck to shine down on him in 2004.

Monza is Italian Giancarlo Fisichella's home race. Unfortunately, in 2003 he could only manage 10th place.

RALPH FIRMAN

It's the dream of every racing driver to drive in Formula One so it's been a great year for me. It has also been a steep learning curve, as, apart from Suzuka and Barcelona, I have had to learn all the circuits from scratch. Formula One is like most sports, and experience is very important, especially when you consider that split seconds can often divide the winners from the losers.

It has been a tough year for us at Jordan as we've had a series of mechanical failures including my huge accident at Hungary, but we will get it right, and I'm very much looking forward to being with the team next year and providing continuity and support. I'll take everything that I have learned this year forward into 2004, and that can only be a good thing.

As far as the rules and regulations go, I'd like to see some action on Sunday mornings. I think it would be good for the fans. Maybe we could have a half hour warm up, qualifying, and then the race.

Surprise of the season? I think David Coulthard has been unlucky. He could have won the first four races. BMW Williams have staged the biggest comeback of the year and really have done an incredible job in turning things around after having to struggle for the first two races. Renault have also done an amazing job.

I think 2004 will also be an exciting year. As well as the top three teams, I think Renault will be up there challenging for the Constructor's Championship, and I think we'll be back on track.

Fate sometimes plays a strange hand, and what could be stranger than Ralph Firman's entry into Formula One? There he was, back in January, enjoying a holiday on the Caribbean island of St. Barts when one day he popped into a shop to buy some sunglasses and there staring at him in the mirror was Eddie Jordan. Less than two months later he was sitting on the grid in Melbourne, as a fully fledged Formula One driver.

Using the male equivalent of 'I'll make you a star" Eddie Jordan seduced the young Formula Nippon Champion into his team and Firman has been grateful ever since. He has had some great moments including his drive in Spain in which he scored his first point of his career with a well deserved eighth place. A brilliant strategy decision which saw the team bring Firman into the pits when the safety car came out, gave him an advantage which he had no hesitation into translating into a hard won point.

But apart from that, life has not been easy. The Jordan has been difficult to drive and beset with mechanical failures. One of the biggest was Firman's accident during Saturday practice in Hungary, when the rear wing fell off his car launching him into the barriers with a lateral G force of 46. It is testimony to the improved safety conditions in Formula One that he survived the accident. Though he did live to tell the tale, he was substituted by young Hungarian driver Zsolt Baumgartner for two races in

Hungary and Monza as he recovered from a bad dose of vertigo and allowed his brain to settle back into its normal modus operandum. Baumgartner did a sterling job, making no mistakes and finishing 11th at Monza, just one place down from Fisichella who finished 10th.

However, to Firman's credit, the series of problems with the car did not deter him from his objective of making his mark in Formula One. "I've had a great year; tough but hard work has never frightened me." Dad, Ralph senior, and mum Angela run the famous Van Diemen racing car company, so racing is in his blood and growing up with drivers like Ayrton Senna popping in and staying in the spare room has given him a good insight into the challenges as well as the rewards of Formula One.

However, in 2004 he'll be looking for a better record than eight race finishes, only 50% of the season, and to this end he has already stated "I need more testing, it's only with testing that you really get used to the car and I lacked that at the beginning of the season."

Like Paul Stoddart, Eddie Jordan has often spotted emerging talent. He was, after all, the first man to give the opportunity of a lifetime to a certain young driver in 1991 called Michael Schumacher. Firman may not be Schumacher but he's certainly got potential. And in 2004, having completed a year's apprentice, he needs to show it to the full.

Jordan driver Ralph Firman has had a difficult first year in grand prix racing with his Jordan team. He suffered an engine failure on lap 51 at the San Marino Grand Prix.

It has been a very difficult season. We started with high hopes, but then realised we had a tough year ahead of us, as the new car was simply not as fast as expected. As a result, we were far down the grid this season. I had to do this, however, or my Formula One career would probably have been over. History will show whether the decision was the right one.

I like the way qualifying is this year – it's good. The only suggestion I would make is that the rules could allow a few small changes to be made to the car's settings for the race compared with qualifying. At the moment, your qualifying strategy is dictated by the fuel load required for your race strategy. However, we had some exciting races this year and I believe this was largely because of the rule changes.

The high point was the qualifying lap in the Friday session at Magny-Cours, when the weather helped us to take first place. That really raised morale in the garage. The low point was Brazil, in the wet, when I spun and the engine didn't keep running. I think we could have scored points, or even a podium.

In general, I think the Championship has been more exciting than in 2002, which is good for Formula One. The surprise of the season has been Michelin, who improved the effectiveness of their tyres massively compared with last year.

Renault impressed me. It was not just Fernando Alonso, who had some fantastic races, but also Jarno Trulli, who drove some great qualifying runs. All of that, however, is down to Renault and the hard work they've done.

I think there will be another closely fought battle for the World Championship next year.

JOS VERSTAPPEN

EUROPEAN AVIATION
www.verstappen.nl
muermans
Group
wilux
bathroom pleasure
puma

2003 was a year of disappointments for Dutch veteran Jos Verstappen. At Hockenheim he retired with a hydraulics failure.

It was nine years ago that Jos Verstappen first swept into Formula One. Back in '94, he was driving alongside Michael Schumacher in the mighty Benetton B194, but since then has slowly been going backwards down the grid. He was on the sidelines in 2002, but was back on the grid in 2003 with Minardi, bringing with him much needed experience and much needed sponsorship.

It would be wrong to group Verstappen with the majority of pay drivers, as his experience and stunning pace are in no doubt, and it must be frustrating for him that the only way a man of his talents can get a seat is to bring sponsorship to a tail-end team. But pre-season talk at Minardi made everything sound positively rosy. The Cosworth engine deal set the team up with easily its strongest ever power unit, and if last season's PS02 was anything to go by, the chassis wouldn't be half bad either. Unfortunately it was. The PS03 proved itself to be semi-reliable, but just wasn't fast enough to score points.

Brazil was the Dutchman's big opportunity, and he and the team were left almost inconsolable when Verstappen became one of the multitude to fall foul of Curva do Sol. If he'd managed to keep on going through the mayhem, both he and the team believed they were headed for a podium spot at the very least. "Today saw possibly the first time ever that Minardi was potentially in a genuine, race-winning position", said team principal, Paul Stoddart. "Many people may laugh, but only those of us within the

team will ever know the truth. We had the strategy, but not the luck".

And that was pretty much that, as far as decent chances went for the veteran. No such opportunities presented themselves at the San Marino GP, when Jos' cockpit filled with smoke and his engine went dead. His strategy in Spain went wrong when the Minardi ate its Bridgestone's, and Verstappen's Austrian race was over before it had even begun. Experiencing major gearbox trouble in qualifying, his race lasted three seconds after his launch control broke and he parallel parked the PS03 beside the pit wall. Fuel vaporisation forced him into retirement at Monaco.

The Canadian Grand Prix saw Jos beat Fisichella and Button in qualifying, but once again he narrowly missed out on a championship point in the race, finishing ninth. In contrast, Verstappen called the following race at the Nurburgring; "one of the worst races I have ever had". He had exhausted himself just trying to keep the Minardi from spinning.

Provisional pole position on Friday at Magny-Cours was, without doubt, the highlight of his season. The drying track had clearly helped his cause. Both he, and the team, were ecstatic. "It has taken me nine-and-a-half years in Formula One and 101 grands prix to achieve this result," he beamed. "The first 100 Formula One races are behind me, and now I have opened a new account". How long that account will remain open is still unknown, but, recognised as a man who's had more comebacks than Frank Sinatra, you can never count Verstappen out.

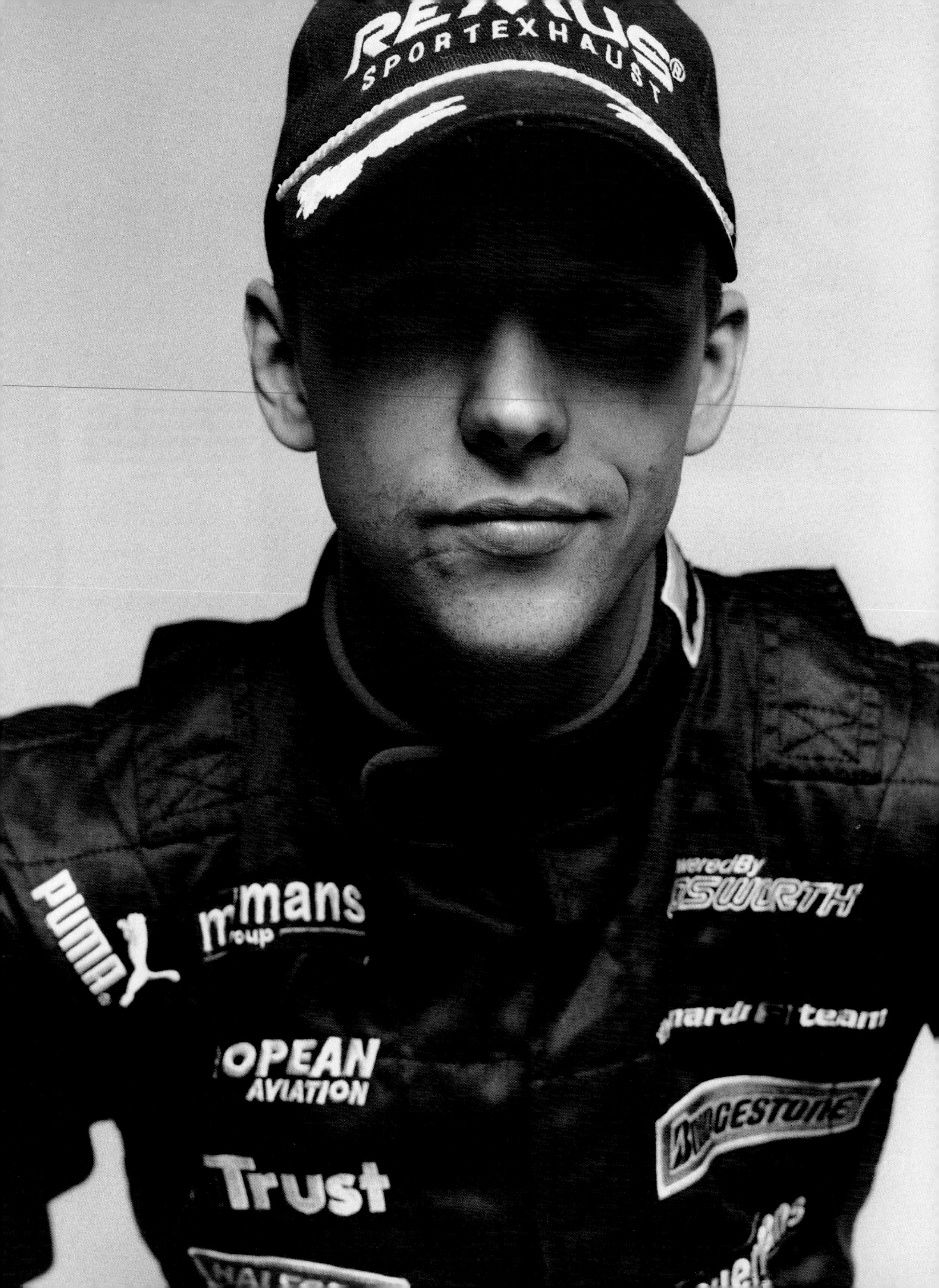
SPORTEXHAUST
PUMA
mans
OPEAN
AVIATION
Trust

It has been a rollercoaster season, which I began as an F3000 driver and ended as a Formula One driver. Faced with just five races to show what I could do, plus learn all about F1 technology and how to get the best out of my car, was always going to be a tough challenge. I'd now love to carry my experience forward into 2004.

As I was new to F1, I came into the sport without any preconceptions about the rules and have just worked with them. I don't have any particular problem with any of them.

The high point was definitely getting into F1, and realising a lifelong dream. The low point? I don't really feel like I've had one, as I knew F1 would be a huge learning experience, and to have finished five races in my five starts to date is better than I could have hoped for. If there is a low, it's not knowing if I will have an F1 drive again next year.

Perhaps the biggest surprise, though, other than my initial experience of F1, was the level of grip available in the wet, particularly under braking, which I experienced for the first time at Indianapolis.

My vote for best team goes to the whole of European Minardi Cosworth, for providing me with an ultra-reliable car in which I finished 100 percent of my races. There are a lot of far better funded teams further up the grid which couldn't have managed that.

My biggest hope for 2004 is that I'll still be a Formula One driver. ❞

NICOLAS KIESA

Nicolas Kiesa got his Formula One chance with Minardi when Justin Wilson switched to Jaguar at the German Grand Prix. He finished all of his five races, coming in 12th here at Monza.

With Justin Wilson attending a clandestine midnight seat-fitting at Jaguar Racing following the British Grand Prix, Danish F3000 driver Nicolas Kiesa received the call of his dreams. Just a month earlier, Kiesa had won in Monaco after Bjorn Wirdheim made the comical but costly error of pulling up to celebrate before he had crossed the finish line. With the phone call from Paul Stoddart, Kiesa had once again lucked in. He was to be a Formula One driver for the remainder of the year.

Friday's qualifying session at Hockenheim was a baptism of fire the Dane would probably rather forget. As he swung out of the Minardi garage and into the pitlane, the car stalled and the team failed to get it running again before his window closed. The pitlane exit light turned red, and Nicolas had missed his stage call.

What made matters worse was that Kiesa's predecessor, Justin Wilson, had just stuck his Jaguar on provisional P7 – ahead of both Ferraris. Wilson had performed well at Minardi and both Kiesa and the team had a lot to prove. Under such immense pressure, and considering he hadn't even made it out of the pitlane on Friday, his performance in second qualifying was highly commendable. He was slowest, but his far more experienced team-mate Verstappen was only 0.15 seconds ahead of him.

On race day the debutant managed to finish the race in 12th position, five laps down but ahead of Fisichella's ailing Jordan. In qualifying for the Hungarian round, Kiesa's inexperience showed as he failed to set the car up to suit the twisty and technical nature of the circuit. Still, on race day he managed to finish – again. In Italy he came home 12th, and at Indianapolis he scored his best result - 11th. His consistency continued at Suzuka when the 25-year-old brought the PS03 home in 16th and last place. He'd finished the season as the only driver with a 100 percent finishing record.

"It has been great to finish all five F1 races in which I've competed", he said. "It is incredible, with the very limited resources available to this team, how it is able to keep the cars running so reliably. I really hope to be back here again next year."

But will he? Kiesa, whilst no slouch, was never hyped up in F1 terms until he turned up at the German Grand Prix to race for Minardi. He hasn't demonstrated much in the way of speed, but in the PS03 that was always going to be tough. It's strange, because in F3000 Kiesa established a reputation for being quick but wild. His Formula One career has been the opposite thus far.

The maturity he has shown in getting to grips with Formula One has been his defining asset. Maybe he'll get a testing role in 2004, maybe he'll be back at Minardi. Regardless, given all the factors working against him in 2003, Nicolas Kiesa has handled himself very well, and won a lot of friends in the process.

CIRCUIT PAUL RICARD
HIGH TECH TEST TRACK

Circuit Paul Ricard
HIGH TECH TEST TRACK

The Paul Ricard High Tech Test Track is the test circuit for the 3rd millennium, dedicated to Formula One teams and manufacturers providing the highest standards of safety and technological innovation found no where else in the world.

2760 Rte Hauts du Camp • F-83330 Le Castellet
T : + 33(0)494 983 666 • F : + 33(0)494 983 667

Aéroport du Castellet

Immediately next to the Paul Ricard HTTT, the airport is offering a full range of passenger and business aviation facilities, including control tower, passenger terminal and a 3-star hotel La Résidence des Equipages providing accommodation for teams and aircrew.

3100 Rte Hauts du Camp • F-83330 Le Castellet
T : + 33(0)494 983 999 • F : + 33(0)494 983 998

HÔTEL DU CASTELLET

Hôtel du Castellet

Across the High Tech Test Track and the Castellet Airport, the Hôtel du Castellet ****L, member of The Leading Hotels of the World, offers the highest standards in service and accommodation. 47 bedrooms, fitness centre, swimming pools, golf course, tennis courts, walking track and an exquisite gourmet restaurant.

3001 Rte Hauts du Camp • F-83330 Le Castellet
T : + 33(0)494 983 777 • F : + 33(0)494 983 778

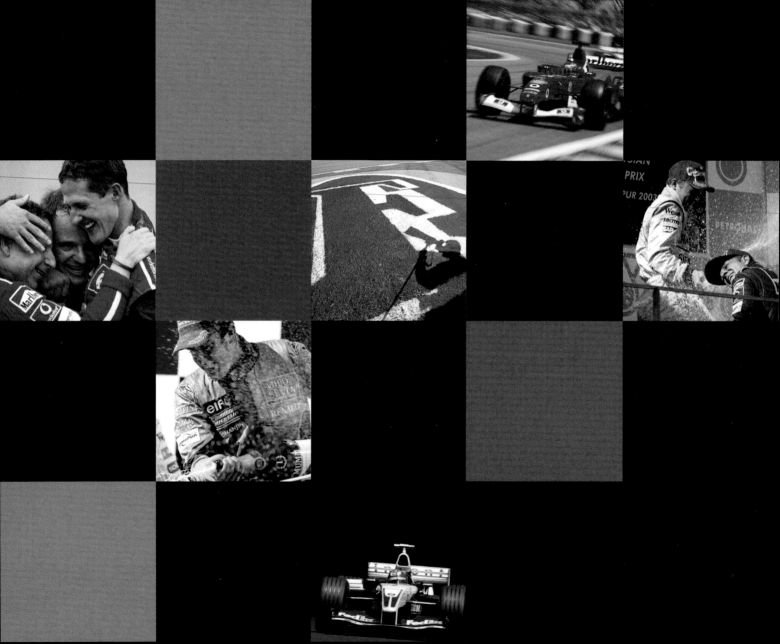

THE RACES

ROUND 01 MARCH 09 **AUSTRALIAN GRAND PRIX**

MELBOURNE

As the Formula One circus arrived in Australia, the paddock had a 'back to school' feel about it, and, as usual, nobody really knew who would perform. Would Ferrari pick up where they had left off in 2002? How would the midfield pan out? Would the new rules shake things up and would they actually work? By the time the race was over, the new format had a promising feel to it. One of the best season openers in recent times had seen incident and racing aplenty, with David Coulthard bringing his McLaren home in first place. Was 2003 finally to be his season? Only time would tell…

BARRICHELLO OUT 5/58
On a quickly drying track, Ferrari had taken the gamble to start on Bridgestone's intermediate tyres. Rubens Barrichello lost traction on his fifth lap and slammed into the wall at Turn Five. Ralph Firman did the same on the next lap. The Michelin runners, meanwhile, had no problems.

KIMI V MICHAEL 38/58
Side-by-side along the start-finish straight, the Ferrari and McLaren entered Turn One together. Having lost out on his first F1 win to the German at the French Grand Prix in 2002, Kimi was going to be hard to pass. The Finn held his nerve and edged the world champion onto the grass.

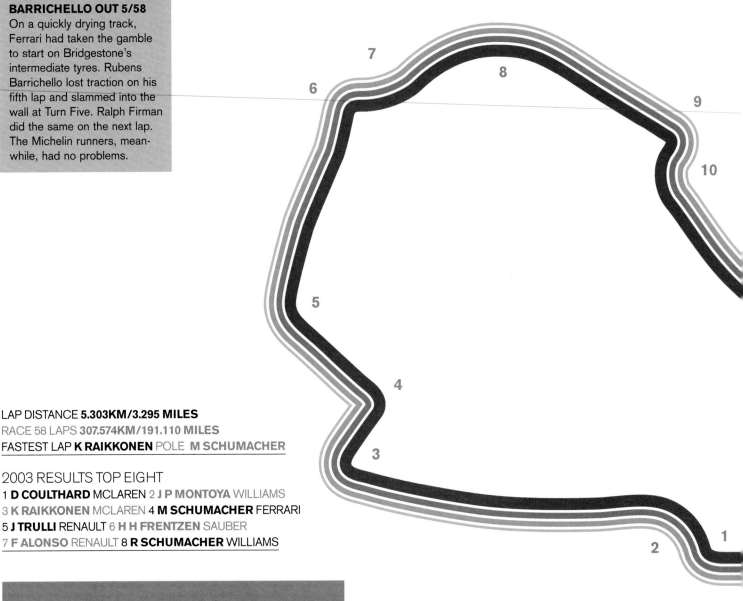

202

LAP DISTANCE **5.303KM/3.295 MILES**
RACE 58 LAPS **307.574KM/191.110 MILES**
FASTEST LAP **K RAIKKONEN** POLE **M SCHUMACHER**

2003 RESULTS TOP EIGHT
1 **D COULTHARD** MCLAREN 2 **J P MONTOYA** WILLIAMS
3 **K RAIKKONEN** MCLAREN 4 **M SCHUMACHER** FERRARI
5 **J TRULLI** RENAULT 6 **H H FRENTZEN** SAUBER
7 **F ALONSO** RENAULT 8 **R SCHUMACHER** WILLIAMS

TRACK DESCRIPTION

One of the most popular circuits on the calendar, Melbourne's Albert Park track provides the perfect season opener. The track itself has all the characteristics of a street circuit, including a 'green' surface, which reduces grip in the early sessions. The combination of long straights, sweeping curves and tight chicanes make it a tough challenge, but one that every Formula One driver relishes. Melbourne itself turns into Formula One party central for the duration of the grand prix weekend, making it one of the most enjoyable races, as well as one of the most exciting. As the promotional hype states, it is indeed a "great place for a race."

MONTY IN A SPIN 48/58
After an action packed race, Juan Pablo Montoya looked to have things sewn up for only his second Formula One career victory. Then, with just a few laps remaining, he spun his BMW Williams on the exit of Turn One and threw it all away. He would have to wait for victory number two.

FALLIBLE FERRARI 46/58
Ferrari may have the most reliable car in F1, but at the Australian GP it was shown to be mildly fallible. Towards the end of the race, having run over some kerbs and the grass, the champ's bargeboards started to fall off and he was called in to the pits to have them removed.

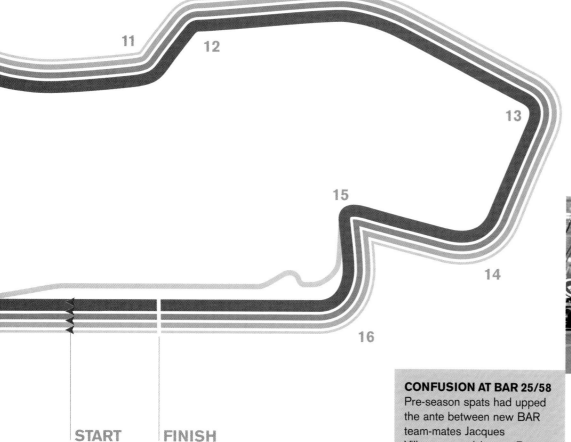

11
12
13
15
14
16

START   FINISH

CONFUSION AT BAR 25/58
Pre-season spats had upped the ante between new BAR team-mates Jacques Villeneuve and Jenson Button. When they pitted on the same lap, Jenson was furious with the '97 champ, and claimed he'd ruined both their races. Villeneuve argued he hadn't heard his radio properly.

Left: Nick Heidfeld got off to a bumpy start in what would be a trying season, exiting the Australian GP with suspension failure. Above right: The class of 2003 line up for a photocall. Below right: A Jordan disappears into the trees of Albert Park. Next Page: David Coulthard celebrates victory.

David Coulthard won the Australian GP with Kimi Raikkonen third, but only a dramatic salvage job by McLaren made up for their mistake of starting both cars on wet Michelins on a track that dried quickly. It was a gripping race, and for the first time since Nurburgring 1999 there wasn't a Ferrari on the podium.

Michael Schumacher took pole position, running low fuel, but brother Ralf and both McLaren drivers made errors, lining up in respective ninth, 11th and 15th positions. Heinz Harald Frentzen ran low fuel to take fourth, and with Olivier Panis' Toyota fifth, things looked different from 2002.

The opening laps were exciting. The Michelin runners could run dry tyres on a damp track, in the expectation that it would soon dry out. But the Bridgestone runners could not. Even Michael Schumacher ran intermediates rather than dries.

McLaren realised their mistake in opting for wets even before the grid formation lap was over. Raikkonen decided to come in and change to dries, as McLaren got their strategy back on track, and the team threw in enough fuel to allow the Finn, who started from the pit lane, to go with one stop. Coulthard had his doubts too late. The Ferraris surged into the lead, followed by the Saubers and the BAR Hondas, and the Scot was only eighth. But at the end of lap two McLaren made its second tactical correction as Coulthard came in for fuel and dry Michelins.

Michael Schumacher led from Barrichello and Montoya, but Barrichello, who lost traction on a quickly drying track, crashed at Turn Five on lap five, followed by rookie Ralph Firman, who had driven well on his dry Bridgestones to climb to eighth by lap seven. Schumacher dropped to eighth, pitting for dry tyres.

The first intervention of the safety car, during lap eight, dealt Raikkonen - sixth, Schumacher- seventh, and Coulthard- a remarkable eighth, fresh hands. Before that, Montoya had been looking good for BMW Williams, holding a 5.7second lead over Fernando Alonso's Renault.

Setting a series of fastest laps, Montoya opened his lead over Jarno Trulli's Renault, (Alonso having refuelled on lap 10) as racing resumed on lap 12. But then Mark Webber's Jaguar, lying an impressive sixth, broke its rear suspension and stopped in an awkward place, so out came the safety car again on laps 19 and 20. This time Montoya benefited, having made his first refuelling stop on lap 17. Now Raikkonen led from M Schumacher and Coulthard. When Schumacher pitted on lap 29 Montoya moved up to third behind the two McLarens, which were on one-stop strategies, but Raikkonen's resistance to Schumacher had ruined Ferrari's aggressive splash 'n' dash refuelling strategy. Coulthard and Raikkonen refuelled on laps 32 and 33, resuming second (Raikkonen) and fifth (Coulthard). Five laps later, Schumacher's heavy attack on Raikkonen came to grief at Turn One when the Finn held his line and his nerve, the German falling back afterwards. But Raikkonen's race also went wrong. He incurred a pit lane speeding penalty after a systems malfunction allowed him to go 1.1 km/h over the limit on lap 33.

Now Montoya had an 8.3 second lead after his final pit stop on lap 42. But then he spun exiting Turn One on lap 48. Coulthard was home and dry, well ahead of a great scrap for second between the recovered Montoya, Raikkonen and Schumacher. They finished 8.6 seconds adrift of the Scot.

The Australian Grand Prix provided some of the best racing in years, although the jury was still out on the new regulations.

26 reasons to visit the Foster's Australian Formula One Grand Prix.

26 °C

Great weather, great attractions and a great city. There's no better way to kick off the next Formula One season than with the 2004 Foster's Australian Grand Prix.

Melbourne 4-7 March

Corporate Hospitality, Grandstand and General Admission Tickets
-day Corporate Hospitality Packages, reserved Grandstand seating and General Admission
ickets are available. Book online at www.grandprix.com.au

Travel Packages
For accommodation packages including a range of GP ticket options call the Grand Prix
ravel Office on +61 3 9676 2144 or book online at www.grandprix.com.au

GRA 0018/FPC

FOSTER'S AUSTRALIAN
GRAND PRIX 2004

ROUND 02 MARCH 23 MALAYSIAN GRAND PRIX

SEPANG

The youngest driver ever to achieve a pole position, a new race winner and a nightmare weekend for the world champion - the 2003 Malaysian Grand Prix had it all. The first all-Renault front row in almost 20 years heralded the dawning of a new age with Fernando Alonso just edging out team-mate Trulli to get P1. Michael Schumacher made an uncharacteristic error in his haste to get after the rampant French cars, and through all the commotion sailed the ever-cool Kimi Raikkonen to take his first Formula One victory. McLaren were starting to look like real contenders.

UNDER PRESSURE 1/56
Taking a wide line around Turn One to set himself up for the sharp left hand Turn Two, Schumacher had not reckoned on Jarno Trulli getting there first. The world champion hit the side of the Renault, ruining both of their races. The German was later awarded a drive-through penalty for his part in the crash.

MORE MAYHEM 1/56
As Schumacher collected Jarno Trulli, the rest of the field had to take evasive action. Unfortunately for Juan Pablo Montoya, Antonio Pizzonia was flying, literally, and the leaping Jaguar took a huge bite out of the Colombian's rear wing, forcing him to pit for a new one and ruining his race.

LAP DISTANCE **5.543KM/3.444 MILES**
RACE 56 LAPS **310.408KM/192.878 MILES**
FASTEST LAP **M SCHUMACHER** POLE **F ALONSO**

2003 RESULTS TOP EIGHT
1 **K RAIKKONEN** MCLAREN 2 **R BARRICHELLO** FERRARI
3 **F ALONSO** RENAULT 4 **R SCHUMACHER** WILLIAMS
5 **J TRULLI** RENAULT 6 **M SCHUMACHER** FERRARI
7 **J BUTTON** BAR 8 **N HEIDFELD** SAUBER

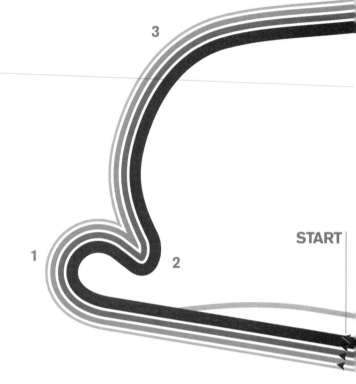

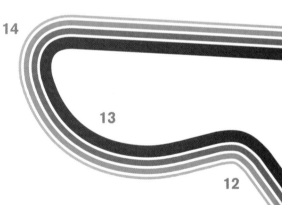

TRACK DESCRIPTION

The Sepang circuit, which lies just south of Malaysia's capital city Kuala Lumpur, is the very definition of a modern grand prix track. The 3.444 miles of winding asphalt is blessed with a backdrop of palm trees and an enormous grandstand whose focal point is a sprouting canopy resembling a flowering hibiscus plant. With long, wide straights plunging almost immediately into slow, tight corners, the track has been designed with one thing in mind – that most hallowed of Formula One manoeuvres, overtaking. With the race being run early in the season, Malaysia's tropical weather can often play a part, making this race both scintillating and unpredictable.

THREE WAY SCRAP

A titanic battle in the last third of the race had everyone enthralled. Button's BAR was sick, Trulli spun his Renault and Michael Schumacher was on a mission. After an enticing duel, Trulli came home fifth, followed by Schumacher and the luckless Button who lost two places on the last lap.

CONFUSED GIANCARLO

Giancarlo Fisichella seems to have a habit of doing this at the Malaysian Grand Prix. Mirroring the images of his Sepang experience with Benetton, the Italian missed his grid slot and had to reverse around the start-finish straight until he was slotted into his corrrect qualifying position on the grid.

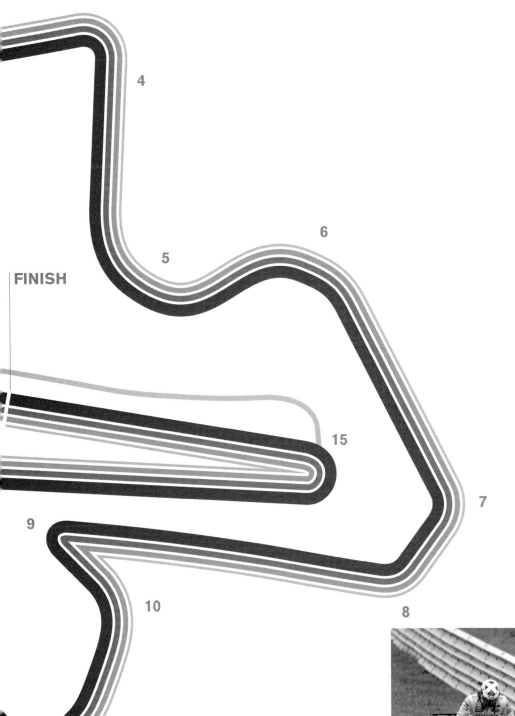

4

6

5

FINISH

15

7

9

10

8

11

BROKEN DOWN 2/56

Having won the season opening race in Australia, David Coulthard had serious hopes that 2003 could be his season for the taking. But when electrical gremlins struck on just the second lap in Malaysia, Coulthard was furious. After all, this should have been a reliable version of the 2002 McLaren.

Left: The Malaysian grid girls have a certain level of class about them. Above right: Joined by Rubens Barrichello, Kimi Raikkonen tastes success for the first time in F1 on the Malaysian podium. Below right: Slick pitwork from McLaren helped the Finn to his maiden grand prix victory.

Two wins from two races gave McLaren Mercedes a dream start to 2003, as Kimi Raikkonen scored a maiden grand prix victory which again highlighted cracks in Ferrari's hitherto impenetrable armour.

Renault created a stir by qualifying both of its cars on the front row, Fernando Alonso becoming the first Spaniard and, at 21, the youngest driver ever to achieve pole position. But McLaren Mercedes were quietly confident all weekend. Ferrari and Bridgestone put a brave face on things, but knew they were going to have to be mighty lucky to win.

Formula One had become a forensic science with its new rules, and Renault's performance had everyone trying to predict their strategy. It turned out to be a short first stint and a long middle stint in a two-stop race. Some liked this cloak and dagger stuff, others didn't.

Alonso made a great getaway, but David Coulthard's even better momentum was hurt when he came up behind the Spaniard and got boxed in by Schumacher who was trying to go the long way round the outside of Jarno Trulli. In the left-handed Turn Two the Italian turned in, and Schumacher rashly went for a gap that wasn't there. Trulli spun, and Schumacher had to pit for a new nose, later receiving a pit lane drive-through penalty for causing an avoidable accident. Montoya was also involved, an innocent victim for the second year in succession.

So Coulthard was second, ahead of Nick Heidfeld, who had qualified with low-fuel, followed by Raikkonen. McLaren were Renault's biggest threat. But only two laps later electrical failure stopped Coulthard, in a foretaste of the season that lay ahead for him.

Once Raikkonen had disposed of former team-mate Heidfeld on lap three, he only had to wait for Alonso's early stop on lap 14 to take the lead.

From that point on the race belonged to the Finn. The only time he was not in the lead was between laps 20 and 22 as he made his own first refuelling stop and Barrichello, who had taken over second spot by lap 15, went ahead.

The Brazilian was struggling to make his tyres last, and while he could beat Alonso, Raikkonen remained so far ahead that the Finn could make his own second stop on lap 40 and resume his race before the red car even appeared. Another excellent performance by McLaren Mercedes.

Alonso was happy to become the only Spaniard apart from the Marquis Fon de Portago to score a podium finish (British GP, 1956), surviving some gear selection problems along the way and shifting manually by the finish. Before the race, Renault technical director Mike Gascoyne had expressed the view that a win was asking too much, but that he'd be angry to miss a podium, so Renault were happy. However, Ralf Schumacher wasn't after finishing a lacklustre fourth for BMW Williams after starting 17th following another driving error in qualifying, and Jenson Button was disappointed to lose out on fifth place on the final lap when his worn Bridgestone tyres simply didn't have enough grip left to keep the recovering Trulli and Michael Schumacher behind.

Ralph Firman was also unlucky. After a strong drive that earned him his spurs, he lost ninth place to Heinz Harald Frentzen on the last lap after his engine hiccuped due to a marginal fuel load. Justin Wilson also had a tough day, retiring when he lost the feeling in one of his arms.

Two races in a row with Michael Schumacher not winning had certainly given 2003 a dramatically different complexion and it was clear that there would be some interesting racing ahead.

ROUND 03 APRIL 06 **BRAZILIAN GRAND PRIX**

INTERLAGOS

With just two grands prix of the season gone, pundits were already claiming that 2003 was going to be one of the most exhilarating seasons in living memory. But even the most open-minded could not have envisaged what would happen at the Brazilian Grand Prix. The rain came, and with it excitement, action and some great racing. In the end it was the weather which was the deciding factor. In a race of high attrition, Kimi Raikkonen took to the rostrum and celebrated his second win in two races… but he hadn't actually won the race - Fisichella had. Confusing? It certainly was.

CURVA DO SOL
Curva do Sol was the corner which caught everyone out. When the rain came, a river flowed over what is normally an almost flat-out corner. On intermediate tyres, the damp conditions even caught out Schumacher, the rain-master himself. Webber had a spin here but held it brilliantly.

RED FLAG DAY
The incident which brought a premature end to the race. Webber was running well until he put his Jaguar into the wall on the uphill section before the start-finish straight. Alonso, himself on a charge, smashed into the Jaguar's debris and had a massive shunt, which brought out the red flags.

FINISH

START

CURVA 1

LAP DISTANCE **4.309KM/2.677 MILES**
RACE 54 LAPS **232.656KM/144.565 MILES**
FASTEST LAP **R BARRICHELLO** POLE **R BARRICHELLO**

2003 RESULTS TOP EIGHT
1 **G FISICHELLA** JORDAN 2 **K RAIKKONEN** MCLAREN
3 **F ALONSO** RENAULT 4 **D COULTHARD** MCLAREN
5 **H H FRENTZEN** SAUBER 6 **J VILLENEUVE** BAR
7 **R SCHUMACHER** WILLIAMS 8 **J TRULLI** RENAULT

SENNA S

CURVA DO SOL

TRACK DESCRIPTION

Interlagos is a notoriously difficult track on which to create the perfect car set-up as it consists of two very distinct parts. The circuit has three incredibly long straights separated by numerous challenging corners, before entering the undulating, hilly, technical section where grip is essential. The question is always whether to set up for straight line speed, or cornering efficiency as improving one will always lead to problems with the other. As such, a compromise will always have to be made. To add to this, the circuit is remarkably bumpy, and as the drivers discovered in 2003, even more challenging when it rains and all you have are intermediates!

FIRMAN'S EXIT 17/54
At the end of the start-finish straight the front suspension collapsed on Ralph Firman's Jordan Ford. The rookie Brit was left powerless to avoid an accident with the Toyota of Olivier Panis, which turned into the first corner in the path of the out-of-control yellow car. Both were out.

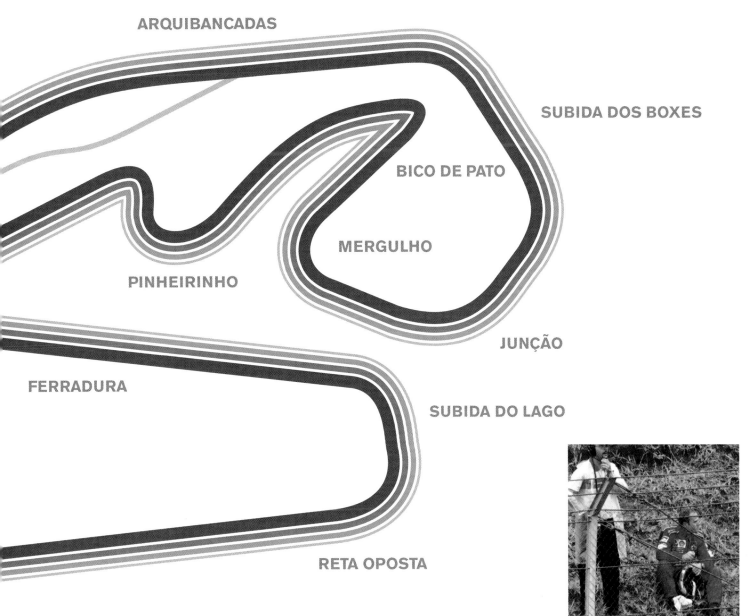

ARQUIBANCADAS

SUBIDA DOS BOXES

BICO DE PATO

MERGULHO

PINHEIRINHO

JUNÇÃO

FERRADURA

SUBIDA DO LAGO

RETA OPOSTA

KIMI ON A CHARGE
Despite many older and more experienced drivers losing it in the treacherous conditions, Kimi Raikkonen drove a super race full of panache, pulling off some breathtaking overtaking manoeuvres not only on his team mate David Coulthard, but also on the BMW Williams of Ralf Schumacher.

BRAZILIAN LUCK 46/54
What does this guy have to do? Holding his nerve in tough conditions the race looked to be Barrichello's for the taking. The plucky Brazilian has never scored points at his home grand prix and a 'fuel feed' problem saw him retire yet again in 2003. Cynics claimed he'd run out of fuel.

Left: The track was damp before the race began, and with only intermediate tyres on hand, everyone prayed the rain wouldn't continue. Above right: But the rain came and with it crashes and safety cars. Below right: Fisichella thought he'd won his first race, but had to wait a week for his confirmation.

There had never been a more confused Grand Prix since Canada in 1973. This time, they picked the wrong winner. Kimi Raikkonen and McLaren got the laurels, but five days later the FIA ruled that Giancarlo Fisichella and Jordan Ford had really won. It was one of those weekends.

It began when heavy rain on Friday highlighted the folly of the single wet tyre rule. Michelin and Bridgestone only brought intermediates, and there was so much aquaplaning there was talk of drivers seeking cancellation of the day's qualifying session.

Things improved on Saturday, but mistakes in the dry cost Montoya, Raikkonen and Schumacher their chances. Barrichello took pole from Coulthard, but only after a tiny error had cost Mark Webber and Jaguar their first pole. It was a stunning display by the Australian.

Then, just like Spa in 2001, more rain forced the race to be started behind Bernd Maylander in the Mercedes-Benz safety car. He would cover more laps than Heidfeld, Wilson, Firman and Panis. When conditions were deemed suitable after eight laps, Maylander peeled in and Coulthard slipped into the lead from Raikkonen and Montoya. Then out came the safety car again as Firman's front suspension broke at 190 mph down the pit straight, as he was shaping up to have a go at team-mate Fisichella, whom Jordan had pulled in on the seventh lap to top it up with fuel. That would prove to be the most crucial decision of the race.

Raikkonen resumed the lead when the race went green again on lap 23, but rivals such as Coulthard, Schumacher, Montoya, Barrichello and Alonso had all refuelled under the safety car. Schumacher and Barrichello attacked, but then the next batch of incidents began on lap 25 when

Montoya crashed in Turn 3, where water was running across the track. Next came Pizzonia, then Schumacher on lap 27. Six laps later Button went in front-end first. There were only 11 cars left.

The safety car came out yet again, allowing Raikkonen to refuel.

Coulthard was back ahead on lap 37, chased by Barrichello, Ralf Schumacher and Alonso who was penalised for passing under yellow flags. Raikkonen was fifth, Fisichella an excellent sixth. Barrichello passed Coulthard on lap 45, but on lap 47 the Ferrari died with a 'fuel feed' problem. McLaren Mercedes were 1-2 again, but most of the Michelin men were now struggling on the drying surface. Then came more drama. Coulthard refuelled on lap 52, dropping behind Raikkonen, Fisichella and Alonso. Then on lap 54 Kimi slid wide and up the inside went Fisichella in the key move of the race. But on that lap Webber also crashed his gripless Jaguar in the last corner. Out came Maylander again.

Fisichella picked though the debris, so did Raikkonen, who headed for his fuel stop, both on their 55th lap. But Alonso, unaccountably, hammered through yellow flags and crashed heavily into Webber's wreckage. Out came the red flag.

Jordan thought they had won. Fisichella threw his helmet skywards as the back end of his car caught fire momentarily just to add to the chaotic climax. But the spoils went to Raikkonen as the race was backdated two laps. But that wasn't the end, it was actually just the beginning.

It wasn't until Wednesday that the FIA confirmed that since Fisichella was on his 56th lap at the time of the red flag, the countback had him crossing the finish line in the lead on laps 54 and 55, and ruled that Jordan had indeed won on their 200th Grand Prix outing.

ROUND 04 APRIL 20 **SAN MARINO GRAND PRIX**

IMOLA

With Michael Schumacher and Ferrari under fire from the press, and Ralf also having to fend off the media, the brothers arrived at Imola in the knowledge that their mother was gravely ill. Sadly, she passed away shortly before the race, but both Michael and Ralf took to the track as she would have wished. The elder dominated proceedings and put his and Ferrari's season back on track with a brilliant win. But as the German national anthem played on the rostrum, and the champion choked down his emotions, the whole world sympathised that his thoughts were naturally elsewhere.

SCHUMACHER SCRAP
For the first 16 laps the world witnessed a brilliant duel for the lead between the Schumacher brothers, just hours after their mother had passed away. Michael's determination set him up for a brilliant and timely victory and silenced all the doubters in the international motorsport media.

TEST OF FRIENDSHIP 1/62
As the lights went out and the 20 cars belted down towards Tamburello, two friends were testing the limits of their loyalties. David Coulthard and Jacques Villeneuve were side by side all the way to the first corner – it was a close call, with JV forced onto the grass, but both stayed in the race.

LAP DISTANCE **4.933KM/3.065 MILES**
RACE 62 LAPS **305.609KM/189.896 MILES**
FASTEST LAP **M SCHUMACHER** POLE **M SCHUMACHER**

2003 RESULTS TOP EIGHT
1 **M SCHUMACHER** FERRARI 2 **K RAIKKONEN** MCLAREN
3 **R BARRICHELLO** FERRARI 4 **R SCHUMACHER** WILLIAMS
5 **D COULTHARD** MCLAREN 6 **F ALONSO** RENAULT
7 **J P MONTOYA** WILLIAMS 8 **J BUTTON** BAR

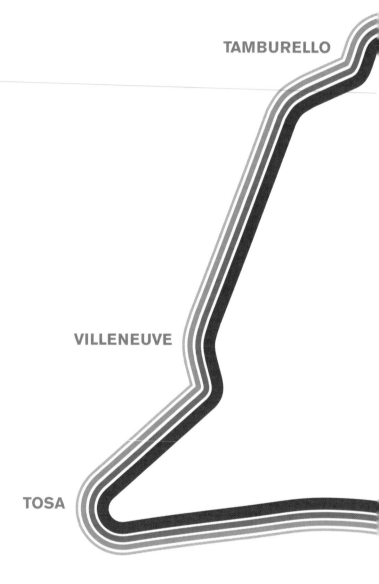

TAMBURELLO

VILLENEUVE

TOSA

TRACK DESCRIPTION

The Imola circuit may not be as technologically and architecturally advanced as many of the newer Formula One circuits, but with a history of triumph and tragedy it has a completely unique atmosphere. Since the dark weekend of 1994 the track itself has been modified severely, but despite the once mighty Tamburello corner now existing as a chicane, there are still some areas of excitement, Acque Minerale and Variente Alta being just two. Imola is not the easiest of tracks on which to overtake – it is fairly narrow and there are no really long straights along which to receive a slipstream – but in the heart of Ferrari country, the Tifosi just love it.

START | FINISH

RIVAZZA

VARIANTE BASSA

TRAGUARDO

ACQUE MINERALI

VARIANTE ALTA

PIRATELLA

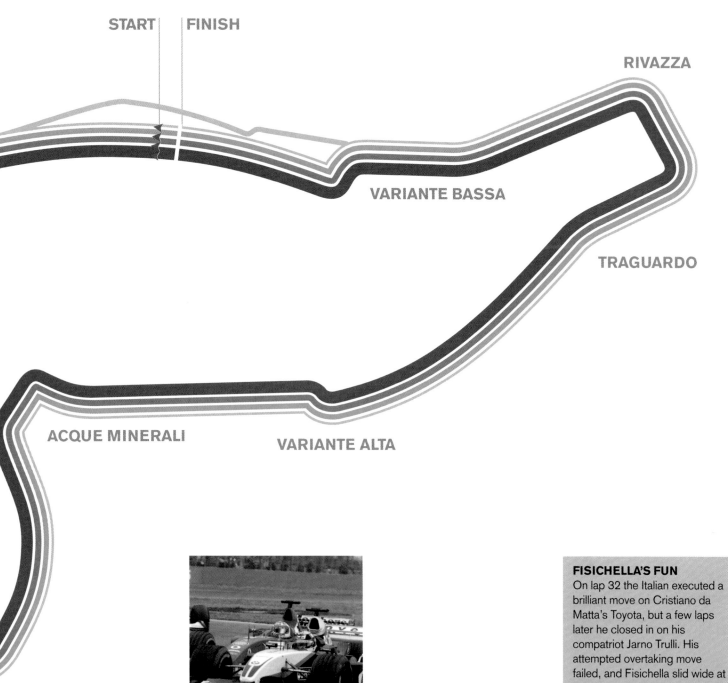

RUBENS GETS RALF
The Ferraris were both highly competitive in San Marino and at the end of the 52nd lap, Rubens Barrichello could stand the sight of Ralf Schumacher's BMW Williams rear wing no more. Getting the better run through the final chicane, he sailed past the blue and white car on the home straight.

FISICHELLA'S FUN
On lap 32 the Italian executed a brilliant move on Cristiano da Matta's Toyota, but a few laps later he closed in on his compatriot Jarno Trulli. His attempted overtaking move failed, and Fisichella slid wide at Rivazza undoing his hard work and allowing the Brazilian back through again.

Michael Schumacher didn't have to race, but he and brother Ralf participated in the San Marino Grand Prix because they wanted to. And, perhaps, because each needed to, following the death of their mother Elisabeth the previous evening. Both drivers' teams gave them the option to withdraw, but each elected to participate. Elisabeth Schumacher had been a steadfast supporter of her sons' careers ever since they took their first tentative steps at the family-run kart track in Kerpen.

It turned out to be an emotional 65th Grand Prix victory for the world champion, and his first in a troubled season. And, the emotional side apart, it was easy.

Ralf Schumacher surged into the lead for BMW Williams, but Michael, on a three-stop strategy, dogged him until Ralf refuelled on lap 16. Michael stopped two laps later, and emerged in the lead. Rubens Barrichello's failure to beat Ralf on the stops cost Ferrari a 1-2.

It was a crucial result for the team, with their 'old' car, which Schumacher described as "A good farewell to this incredible car." Rivals were wary that the F2003-GA was ready in the wings, yet the old car was still a winner. Its success brought Formula One back down to earth after the three sensational opening races, but both McLaren Mercedes and BMW Williams left Italy buoyed by their performance. The former retained their lead in both the drivers' and constructors' world championships, thanks to Kimi Raikkonen driving home a strong second despite a fierce challenge from Barrichello in the closing laps, and David Coulthard taking a disappointed fifth. And McLaren, like Ferrari, at that stage harboured high hopes for their own new car, the MP4/18A that was taking shape in Woking.

Ralf Schumacher lost out to McLaren's two-stop strategy, and then later to a scrap with Barrichello, who shoved inside him in the final corner on the 52nd lap to snatch away third place to the delight of the tifosi. His BMW Williams team-mate Juan Pablo Montoya was seventh after a problem with his refuelling rig during his second stop on lap 30, which prompted another, unscheduled one, two laps later. Fernando Alonso drove his Renault extremely well to sixth, and Jenson Button took the final point for BAR Honda.

"It was a good fight with Kimi, but obviously my race was hampered by BMW Williams' strategy and the fact that I could not overtake Ralf during the first stops, the way that Michael managed to," Barrichello said. "It seemed like there were only three or four laps in this race in which I was not fighting somebody and had a clean lap. I spent my entire race pushing the car to the maximum."

So, too, did Raikkkonen, who did the perfect damage limitation job for McLaren Mercedes on an afternoon when the old Ferrari still had more than enough up its sleeve too see off its Anglo-German rivals. "Our two-stop strategy worked quite well," Raikkonen said. "My only problem all afternoon was too much oversteer on my second set of tyres. It's always good to get points while we are waiting for our new car, and once we get that I hope that we can start to fight again for the wins."

McLaren's new challenger was at that point of the season most likely to appear in Austria at the end of May. While the MP4/17D was doing the winning, the team had the luxury of racing the old car while honing the new one in testing. But after Ferrari's demonstration that Sunday afternoon in Imola, it was beginning to look like the MP4/18A might be a necessity.

ROUND 05 MAY 04 SPANISH GRAND PRIX

CATALUNYA

An all Ferrari front row signalled that life was getting back to normal at the Spanish Grand Prix. Perhaps what was more worrying was that this weekend saw the debut of the F2003-GA, Ferrari's new and frighteningly beautiful car – which claimed to be even better than that which had set new levels of reliability in Formula One the year before. It wasn't quite the whitewash that most were expecting, however. Local boy Fernando Alonso put in a masterful drive to take second place. Ferrari might have been back to winning ways, but the Spanish fans had eyes for only one man – Alonso.

KIMI'S SHOCKER 1/65

A qualifying mistake which saw Raikkonen run onto the gravel, ended in him lining up at the rear of the grid. At the start, Pizzonia was desperately slow away and Raikkonen, with nowhere to go, slammed into the Brazilian's gearbox. With both cars stranded on the grid, the safety car came out.

TRULLI V DC 1/65

A terrific start saw the Renaults battling hard at the front. On the exit of Turn Two however, David Coulthard's McLaren and the French car of Trulli came to blows. Both blamed the other, but as Coulthard carried on, Trulli was left to trudge back to the pits, out of the race.

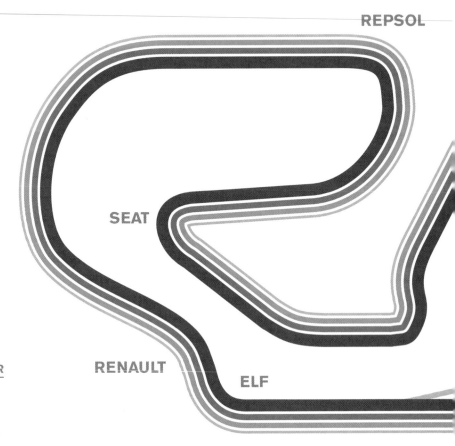

REPSOL

SEAT

RENAULT

ELF

228

LAP DISTANCE **4.730KM/2.047 MILES**
RACE 65 LAPS **307.324KM/190.961 MILES**
FASTEST LAP **R BARRICHELLO** POLE M SCHUMACHER

2003 RESULTS TOP EIGHT
1 **M SCHUMACHER** FERRARI 2 **F ALONSO** RENAULT
3 **R BARRICHELLO** FERRARI 4 **J P MONTOYA** WILLIAMS
5 **R SCHUMACHER** WILLIAMS 6 **C DA MATTA** TOYOTA
7 **M WEBBER** JAGUAR 8 **R FIRMAN** JORDAN

TRACK DESCRIPTION

The teams arrive at Barcelona with their first realistic ideas of how competitive their rivals will be. Used as a testing venue in the off-season, there is perhaps no other track on the calendar where the teams will have so much data or be better prepared. The bumpy and harsh surface can make this race really tough on both driver and car however, and the huge g-forces exerted on the driver in the many high-speed corners make this a ruthless event. Heat is also a factor in performance. Drivers and car set-up must be at an optimum here, as a small mistake in one corner will lead to a big mistake at the next, so crucial is the optimum line at the track.

FIRST WIN FOR 2003-GA
It was not the obliteration that most had expected, but few could deny that Ferrari's new car was anything but very impressive. With the car taking pole position, race win and fastest lap, the signs looked ominous for the rest of 2003. Alonso, in second place, gave a glimmer of hope though.

A CLOSE CALL 1/65
With Alonso fighting the Ferrari of Michael Schumacher hard into Turns One and Two, Rubens Barrichello saw a way through and attempted a graceful pass. Schumacher edged ever closer to his team-mate however, and Rubens had to edge onto the grass to avoid a coming together.

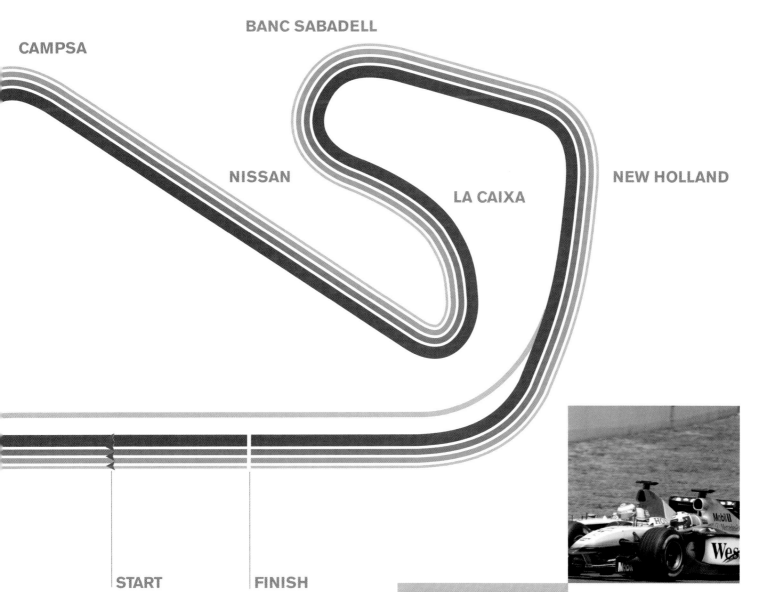

CAMPSA

BANC SABADELL

NISSAN

LA CAIXA

NEW HOLLAND

START

FINISH

BATTLE OF BRITAIN 18/65
With Coulthard having survived his first lap contretemps with Jarno Trulli, he was on a mission to make up lost places. On the 18th lap however he was dumped out of the race by Jenson Button in the BAR Honda. With Raikkonen out on the first lap, McLaren were left far from amused.

If Ferrari could not have come up with a better script for the Spanish GP, McLaren Mercedes could not have penned a more nightmare scenario than the one which befell Kimi Raikkonen in Barcelona.

Ferrari's brand new F2003-GA was just as quick as everyone had feared it would be, but a lot more reliable than they had secretly hoped. After rumours of breakages in testing, it performed faultlessly and took Michael Schumacher to a victory that came with the same insouciant ease that most of his 2002 triumphs had demonstrated.

Raikkonen, meanwhile, screwed up his qualifying lap and was obliged to start from the back of the grid. As Schumacher fled from the startline, the series leader slammed into the back of Antonio Pizzonia's stricken Jaguar and became an instant retirement. At virtually the same time, David Coulthard was being bundled off the road in the second corner by an over-enthusiastic Jarno Trulli.

Schumacher's only problem, by contrast, was team-mate Rubens Barrichello. Battling with local star Fernando Alonso on the run to the first corner, Barrichello had the outside line which then gave him the inside line for Turn Two. Momentarily he was ahead of Schumacher, but then the world champion rubbed wheels with him and edged his number two on to the dirt to confirm his lead.

Soon Schumacher simply drove away, leaving Barrichello with his hands full with upstart Alonso. All were on three-stop refuelling strategies, and after his first stop Alonso was able to move into second place. After that the 21 year-old Spaniard thrilled his countrymen with a superbly mature performance that kept the pressure on Schumacher, albeit from a distance. Alonso's only problems were being delayed in a fight with Ralf

Schumacher after his second stop, which saw the BMW Williams driver eventually sliding into the dirt, and another encounter with the German when he was lapping him on the 63rd lap. It was not an edifying afternoon for the champion's younger brother, as he struggled with his car's hard compound Michelin tyres and an early change from three to two-stop refuelling strategy. He also lost out in a fight with team-mate Juan Pablo Montoya, which momentarily saw them running wheel to wheel until the Colombian moved ahead to finish fourth. In the closing stages the battle for fifth between a defensive Schumacher Jnr and the challenging Brazilian Cristiano da Matta was one of the race's highlights.

The final points fell to Jaguar's Mark Webber, after a steady two-stop run, and Jordan's Ralph Firman, who once again staked his claim to a grand prix seat with a spirited drive to eighth place and his first-ever championship point.

For a while Firman had fended off Jenson Button, who delayed himself on the 18th lap after hitting Coulthard in Turn One. The two were due to party together after the race as their boats were moored in the local marina, and remained cordial despite the tangle.

"I thought you were my mate," Coulthard smiled, hands spread, as Button approached.

Schumacher said the result was "a perfect day for the championship and for the new car." The result put him only four points behind Raikkonen, with Alonso third another three adrift of Schumacher. McLaren Mercedes were three points ahead of Ferrari in the constructors' points table, but the writing was on the wall: Ferrari's challenge was now firmly back on track. The title fight was really hotting up.

Formula 1 ™

48 GRAN PREMIO DE ESPAÑA

CIRCUIT DE CATALUNYA
7-8-9 MAY 2004*

Barcelona

ticket service

Circuit de Catalunya

www.circuitcat.com

International Hotline +34 93 571 97 71

ROUND 06 MAY 18 AUSTRIAN GRAND PRIX

A1-RING

Three wins out of three for Michael Schumacher and Ferrari, and suddenly 2003 was looking a lot brighter for the Scuderia. But it could all have been so different. Montoya was looking good for his first win of the season until his engine got rather over-excited and blew its lid, and Schumacher had a big moment in the pits. As the Ferrari mechanics pulled the fuel hose away from the champion's car, a fireball erupted. But Schumacher being Schumacher he just sat there, waited for his mechanics to put the fire out, wiped the foam from his visor and set off to win the race.

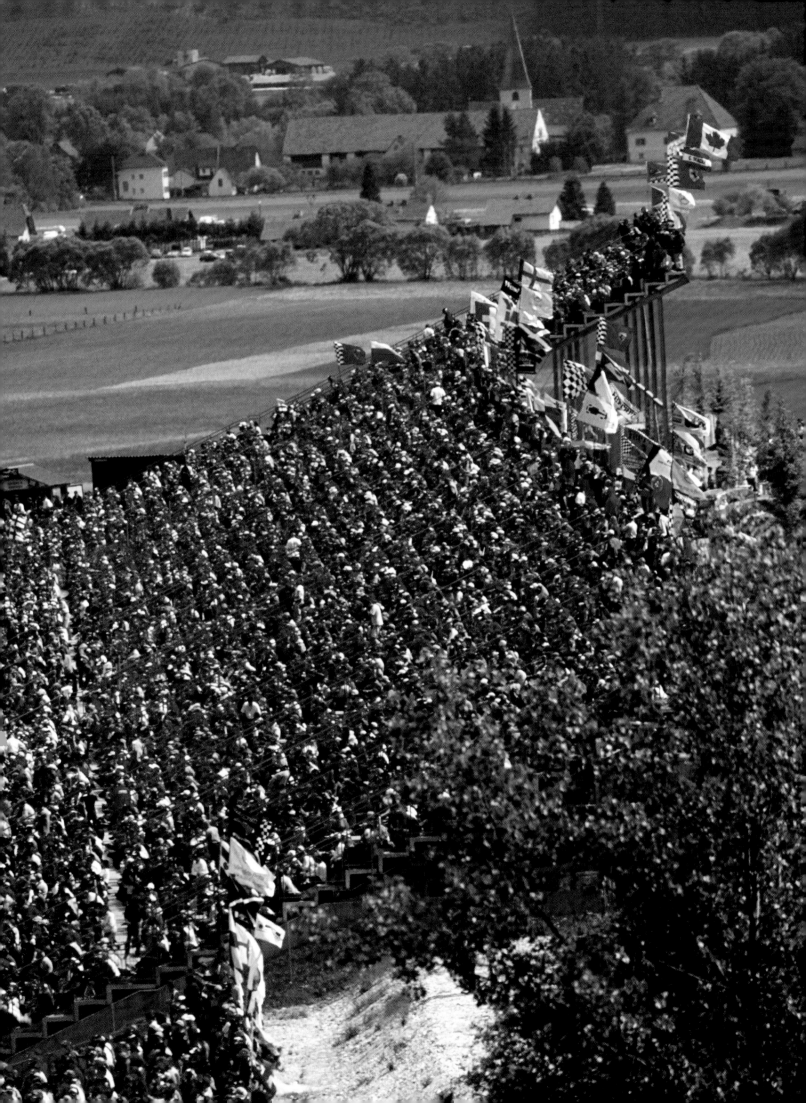

FINISH STRAIGHT 1/69
Cristiano da Matta stalled his Toyota twice on the grid and on the third attempt he was moved to avoid a fourth start. Once the race finally got underway Jos Verstappen's Minardi broke down on the start-finish straight and the safety car was deployed while it was moved from a dangerous position.

SCHUEY ON FIRE 23/69
At his pitstop Barrichello's refuelling machine had not worked, so both he and Schumacher were forced to use the same one. When Michael came in, residual fuel in the nozzle sparked a fire. The champion stayed calm and drove away, wiping fire extinguisher foam from his visor.

LAP DISTANCE **4.326KM/2.688 MILES**
RACE 69 LAPS **298.494KM/185.475 MILES**
FASTEST LAP **M SCHUMACHER** POLE **M SCHUMACHER**

2003 RESULTS TOP EIGHT
1 **M SCHUMACHER** FERRARI 2 **K RAIKKONEN** MCLAREN
3 **R BARRICHELLO** FERRARI 4 **J BUTTON** BAR
5 **D COULTHARD** MCLAREN 6 **R SCHUMACHER** WILLIAMS
7 **M WEBBER** JAGUAR 8 **J TRULLI** RENAULT

TRACK DESCRIPTION

The picturesque A1-Ring lies in a natural bowl in the Styrian mountains, in the heart of 'Sound of Music' country. The circuit itself is smooth and flowing, and although appearing somewhat simple due to its long straights, corners such as Lauda and Berger do provide a challenge. The track is one of the slowest on the calendar, despite having one of the quickest lap times, and overtaking opportunities are never at a premium. Grid position is therefore crucial, as is a good start, because collisions at turns 1 and 2 are commonplace.

REMUS KURVE

NIKI LAUDA KURVE

GERHARD BERGER KURVE

CASTROL KURVE

GÖSSER KURVE

MICHAEL V KIMI 32/69
Setting a blistering pace following his incident in the pits, Michael Schumacher had caught up with Kimi Raikkonen. Into the Remus Kurve, the German carried greater speed and a better line, and snatched second place from the Finn. Moments later he would be in the lead.

BLOWN CHANCES 32/69
No sooner had Schumacher taken second position from Kimi Raikkonen than he inherited the lead. As Juan Pablo Montoya's Williams left the Remus Kurve just ahead of the second place battle behind, its BMW engine let go in a huge plume of smoke and Montoya's race was well and truly over.

JOCHEN RINDT KURVE

A1 KURVE

START | **FINISH**

ALONSO'S OFF DAY 45/69
The impressive youngster was having an nightmare day. Having started at the back of the grid, he'd made his way up to fifth before a pitstop saw him fall back to eighth. He might have scored some points had his engine not expired on the 45th lap. He spun on his own oil and was out of the race.

238

Michael Schumacher underwent trial by flood and fire in Austria
to win his 67th Grand Prix victory and move Ferrari into the lead of the
Constructors' Championship.

It took two attempts to start the race after Cristiano da Matta twice
stalled his Toyota on the grid due to a problem with the electronics. But
then Schumacher rocketed past Juan Pablo Montoya. After 15 sensational
laps he had built a lead of 10.6s, but almost as quickly he lost it as rain
momentarily fell on parts of the track. Michelin's grooved rubber had the
advantage now, and Montoya quickly reeled in the Ferrari and was only
three seconds behind when the Colombian made his first refuelling stop on
lap 20.

Schumacher and second-placed Kimi Raikkonen pitted on lap 23. The
Finn's stop went smoothly, but the German met with near disaster. During
Rubens Barrichello's stop there had been a problem with his refuelling rig
so the crew used Schumacher's. On Schumacher's stop, there was still some
fuel in the nozzle, and as it dripped on to the car there was a sudden fire.
Flames licked round the side of the cockpit and the end of the fuel hose,
but Schumacher calmly resisted any temptation to bale out and the Ferrari
crew quickly had things under control.

"I could see the fire," Schumacher said. "Maybe the mechanics thought
I was cold and wanted to warm me up! But the team did a good job to
control the situation, reacting quickly with the fire extinguishers." He
remained calm and only lost 10 seconds before rejoining, nonchalantly
wiping extinguisher foam from his visor as he left the pit lane.

Now Montoya had a three-second lead over Raikkonen. The previous
evening, McLaren Mercedes had successfully appealed to the race stewards

for permission to replace two valves on Raikkonen's engine, and he was
unable to use full revs. Schumacher quickly closed in, but it was Montoya's
car that faltered. Just as BMW Williams' fortunes seemed about to change,
a water leak caused the Colombian's engine to blow up on lap 32.

On that same lap, Schumacher got a good run on Raikkonen as they
swept down to the Remus corner, and slipped by into second place. By the
end of the lap he found himself back in the lead, and stayed there until the
race was shortened from 71 to 69 laps after the two aborted starts.

Rubens Barrichello drove a hard race to push Raikkonen all the way
home. Schumacher had chosen harder tyres, but the Brazilian had opted
for softer Bridgestones yet was unable to exploit any potential advantage.
He nosed momentarily ahead of Raikkonen on the 67th lap, but the Finn
had the inside line for the next corner and moved back ahead. At the flag
they were 3.3 seconds behind Schumacher, and only 0.589 seconds apart.

Jenson Button was in contention for a strong finish throughout, and
duly came home fourth for BAR Honda, but team-mate Jacques Villeneuve
lost his chance of points after his car suffered electronics problems and
stalled during his second stop.

"I had a great race; I really enjoyed it," Button said with a broad smile.
"I matched my best race finish today so it's great to be back up there getting
the points again. We earned our result today; it wasn't just a fluke." David
Coulthard was fifth, Schumacher Jnr sixth and Webber seventh.

So now Ferrari were in the lead of the Constructors' Championship for
the first time, a point clear of McLaren, and in the drivers' table
Schumacher's triumph had brought him within a two-point striking
distance of Raikkonen.

ROUND 07 JUNE 01 MONACO GRAND PRIX

MONTE CARLO

BMW Williams celebrated their first victory in Formula One for over 12 months at the Monaco Grand Prix, and their first in the Principality for 20 years. Juan Pablo Montoya drove the perfect race to take the spoils of victory, becoming only the second man in history, after the legendary Graham Hill, to win both the Monaco Grand Prix and the Indy 500. There wasn't much overtaking around the narrow streets, but that didn't mean it wasn't an exciting race. By the time they reached the podium, the top three were physically and emotionally exhausted - as were most of the fans.

BIG ONE FOR BUTTON
Button was on for a fantastic Monaco Grand Prix until a big accident in Saturday's free practice session left the Brit hospitalised. He lost control of his BAR on the exit of the tunnel and slammed sideways into the barriers at Nouvelle Chicane, sidelining him with concussion for the rest of the weekend.

MONTY'S MAGIC START
The start of the Monaco Grand Prix is possibly one of the most important of the year, so difficult is it to pass on the streets of the principality. Montoya made a great getaway and passed Kimi Raikkonen's McLaren into the first corner. The Finn was never able to get back past the fast Colombian who went on to win.

LAP DISTANCE **3.340KM/2.075 MILES**
RACE 78 LAPS **260.520KM/161.879 MILES**
FASTEST LAP **K RAIKKONEN** POLE **R SCHUMACHER**

2003 RESULTS TOP EIGHT
1 **J P MONTOYA** WILLIAMS 2 **K RAIKKONEN** MCLAREN
3 **M SCHUMACHER** FERRARI 4 **R SCHUMACHER** WILLIAMS
5 **F ALONSO** RENAULT 6 **J TRULLI** RENAULT
7 **D COULTHARD** MCLAREN 8 **R BARRICHELLO** FERRARI

TRACK DESCRIPTION

The most glamorous race of the year, the tight and twisting street course around the Principality is the one race that every driver wants to win. Precision driving is not just important at Monaco, it is essential. No other track on the F1 calendar is so unforgiving, and as such no other circuit demands so much concentration. Maximum downforce settings mean that the cars are almost bolted to the track, and with barely enough room for two cars to drive side-by-side, overtaking is a luxury rarely afforded. Despite all this, or maybe because of this, however, the winner's trophy remains one of the most coveted prizes in global motorsport.

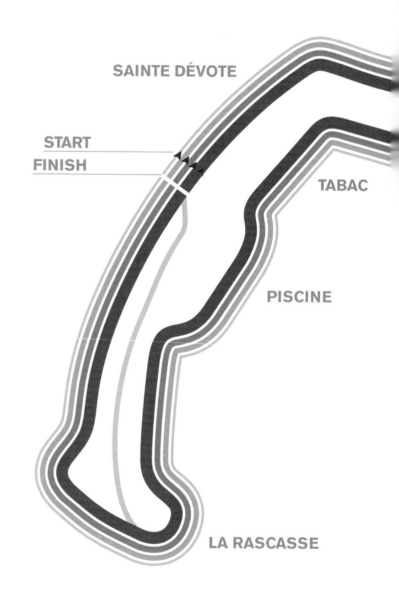

SAINTE DÉVOTE

START
FINISH

TABAC

PISCINE

LA RASCASSE

ALONSO'S BLINDER

Fernando Alonso made a brilliant start at the Monaco Grand Prix, getting ahead of both Barrichello and Coulthard. However, he became stuck behind Trulli and DC after the first pit stops. Taking his second stop late, Alonso vaulted past both and went on to score fifth place after a great drive.

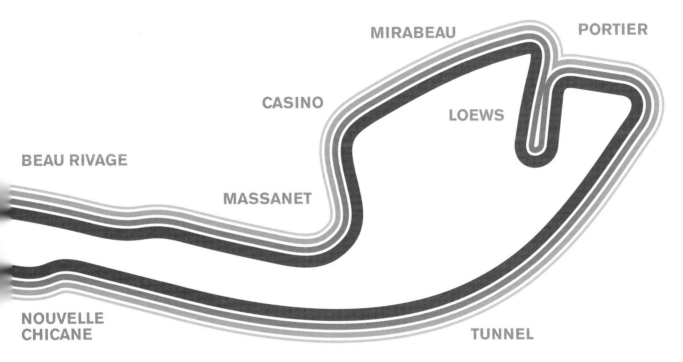

MIRABEAU

PORTIER

CASINO

LOEWS

BEAU RIVAGE

MASSANET

NOUVELLE CHICANE

TUNNEL

GONE SWIMMING 1/78

The Monte Carlo track had a bit of a different feel to it for 2003. The Swimming Pool section had been changed since 2002 and provided a very different challenge to previous years. Unlucky Sauber driver Heinz-Harald Frentzen slammed into the barriers here in the race on the very first lap.

Juan Pablo Montoya emerged an emotional victor of a Monaco Grand Prix that could have gone the way of the pursuing Kimi Raikkonen or Michael Schumacher. After 78 gruelling laps that left even the super-fit Schumacher looking drained, only 1.720s separated the three of them.

The win could not have come at a better time for BMW Williams, amid political backbiting that delayed renewal of their contractual alliance beyond 2004. It not only prevented Michael Schumacher from equalling the late Ayrton Senna's record of six victories in the Principality, but made the Colombian the only man other than the late Graham Hill to have won the Monaco Grand Prix and the equally prestigious Indianapolis 500.

Team-mate Ralf Schumacher and rival Raikkonen had the upper hand in qualifying, but Montoya passed the Finn in the first corner. There was a brief interlude when the safety car was deployed between the second and fourth laps to scrape away the wreckage of Heinz-Harald Frentzen's Sauber Petronas, and then Schumacher Jnr pulled away. But Montoya wasn't worried and kept ahead of Raikkonen and Trulli, whose presence in fourth place was distinctly hurtful to Schumacher Snr who was bottled up behind the Renault and struggling on his Bridgestone tyres.

Schumacher Jnr led the first 21 laps, at which point he took his first refuelling stop, handing the lead to Montoya, who himself stopped on lap 23. Raikkonen had two laps in front before his stop on lap 25. Schumacher did not stop until lap 31, but although falling behind Montoya and Raikkonen when he rejoined, moved up to third place. Another heavy fuel load in his second stint did not allow him to make much headway.

Raikkonen went four laps longer than Montoya on the second stops - lap 53 against lap 49 - and again Schumacher did a long stint, running until 59. Thus the stage was set for a gripping confrontation in the closing laps as Raikkonen put Montoya under massive pressure and Schumacher played catch-up. As their individual strategies played out, it created the most genuinely fascinating race so far under the new regulations that were introduced for the 2003 season. Overtaking is relatively impossible at Monaco, however. Montoya readily admitted that he made a few small errors in the closing laps, as Raikkonen pushed really hard and brought the deficit down to below a second, but none of them was sufficient to jeopardise his success. When the chequered flag finally fell, he still had 0.6s in hand over Raikkonen, who was 1.1s ahead of Schumacher. "Everybody at BMW Williams really needed this win so much," Montoya said.

Overshadowed by the fight ahead of him, Ralf Schumacher yet again faded and could only finish fourth, but at least he was clear of the fight between David Coulthard and the Renaults for fifth place. The Scot, like Schumacher Snr before him, found himself bottled up behind the unpassable Trulli for much of the race, but stopping as late as possible allowed Fernando Alonso to vault ahead of both of them with 17 laps to run. Rubens Barrichello, in the second Ferrari, had a quiet race and was never able to challenge them.

Montoya's victory took him into equal fifth place in the championship chase as Raikkonen stemmed the recent tide and extended his lead over Schumacher to four points. Meanwhile, Williams' first win in Monte Carlo since Keke Rosberg triumphed back in 1983, moved them up to third place in the constructors' table as McLaren moved back ahead of Ferrari, who had lacked their usual strength. Nobody knew it at the time, but the BMW Williams onslaught had begun.

ROUND 08 JUNE 15 CANADIAN GRAND PRIX

MONTREAL

BMW Williams came to Canada in high spirits after their success at Monaco a fortnight earlier. By the time the team packed up to go home however, they were left wondering how an all-Williams front row had turned into a Ferrari victory. Juan Pablo Montoya's speed in recovering the places he lost when he spun out of second place suggested he might have challenged the winning Ferrari of Michael Schumacher, but in the end it was academic. The world champion drove with such majesty that his scarlet steed looked as wide as the track, making any attempt at overtaking him impossible.

QUALIFIED MISTAKE

McLaren as a team seemed to be finding it harder than their rivals to master one-shot qualifying. In Canada, Kimi Raikkonen made another mistake, this time in the wet, and after slamming into the barriers would once again start from the back of the grid when the lights went out on Sunday.

DEFLATED CHANCES

Following a big smack in the rear by Antonio Pizzonia at the hairpin, Jarno Trulli's Renault suffered a puncture. But his was not the only flat of the race. On the fast final straight, one of Kimi Raikkonen's rear tyres also let go, but he was well placed to dive into the pits for replacements while refuelling.

LAP DISTANCE **4.361KM/2.709 MILES**
RACE 70 LAPS **305.270KM/189.685 MILES**
FASTEST LAP **F ALONSO** POLE **R SCHUMACHER**

2003 RESULTS TOP EIGHT
1 **M SCHUMACHER** FERRARI 2 **R SCHUMACHER** WILLIAMS
3 **J P MONTOYA** WILLIAMS 4 **F ALONSO** RENAULT
5 **R BARRICHELLO** FERRARI 6 **K RAIKKONEN** MCLAREN
7 **M WEBBER** JAGUAR 8 **O PANIS** TOYOTA

VIRAGE SENNA   **FINISH**
                START

TRACK DESCRIPTION

The Isle de Notre Dame was built to house the 1967 Expo, but today it is the home of the Circuit Gilles Villeneuve, a tricky little track that offers few overtaking opportunities. The cars run close to the barriers at certain points, the most exhilarating of which being the exit of the final chicane onto the start-finish straight. Get it wrong here and it's race over. Traction is always crucial in Montreal as a good exit speed from the slower corners will ensure a fast lap and will keep pursuing drivers behind for that little while longer. But this circuit is a real car breaker. With long straights followed by hairpins and tight corners the brakes take a real hammering.

STRESS CONFERENCE

As if the on-track action wasn't hot enough at the Canadian Grand Prix, the pre-race press conference for team bosses was pretty spicy too. A huge debate erupted between Minardi boss Paul Stoddart and McLaren supremo Ron Dennis over the fighting fund for the smaller teams.

PONT DE LA CONCORDE

VIRAGE DU CASINO

L'EPINGLE

DROIT DU CASINO

FIRST LAP ANTICS

The first corner at the Circuit Gilles Villeneuve is almost always the scene of some commotion. In 2003 it was no different as a slight coming together between Fernando Alonso and Rubens Barrichello left the Ferrari's front wing broken and trailing underneath the Brazilian on the first lap.

RACING REPUTATION

In his rookie season, Justin Wilson was making quite a name for himself driving for Minardi. Although in qualifying, the inadequacies of the car were highlighted, in the races Justin was drawing praise from every quarter with his instinctive and gutsy performances, and Canada was no exception.

MONTRÉAL 2003

Left: Michael Schumacher may have won the race, but BMW Williams were on a roll following their triumph in Monaco. Above right: The field enters Turn One at the Circuit Gilles Villeneuve. Below right: David Coulthard passed da Matta early on but retired with gearbox problems.

Michael Schumacher's brilliant victory in the Canadian GP saw the points lead of the world championship see-saw once again in his favour, and former leader Kimi Raikkonen played little part as the world champion led his brother, Juan Pablo Montoya and Fernando Alonso across the finish line with less than five seconds covering them.

The BMW Williams duo wrapped up qualifying, but once again Raikkonen gave himself a mountain to climb by spinning on his crucial lap. Schumacher Jnr grabbed the lead from Montoya and his brother at the start of the race, but on the second lap Montoya made his second unforced error of the season, spinning down to fifth exiting the last corner. That was where Schumacher won the race.

First Michael played a waiting game until Ralf pitted on lap 20, and in his usual fashion he just managed to grab the lead going into the first corner after his own stop a lap later. Ralf kept his brother honest for the ensuing 26 laps, with a repentant Montoya closing to within 7.8 seconds of them. Schumacher Jnr stopped again on lap 46, and Schumacher Snr came in two laps later, resuming easily in the lead. But the Ferrari had brake problems, and Michael was dictating a minimal pace. Ralf and Montoya closed in, bringing Alonso with them. The Spaniard had enjoyed a spell in the lead during the first stops with a Renault that, for once, was running a lot of fuel for its first stint. Now he was flying. By lap 57 the three leaders were all less than two and a half seconds apart, by lap 60 a second covered them. And Alonso was catching them. What had seemed dull suddenly had become potentially explosive.

Meanwhile, Raikkonen was also flying. After starting from the pit lane with a full tank of fuel he was unable to make much progress initially,

running in a bunch with Jacques Villeneuve, Justin Wilson, who was having yet another brilliant race, Nick Heidfeld, Giancarlo Fisichella and Jenson Button, all fighting for ninth place. As others stopped for fuel Raikkonen was fifth by lap 30.

Jarno Trulli's Renault had thrown a right rear tyre tread on lap four, and on lap 33 Michelin's second failure of the race forced the Finn to pit on with a similar problem. He was lucky that the failure occurred just as he was on the final straight before the pits, so McLaren were able to alter their refuelling strategy slightly to get him going with minimal delay. He resumed quickly, chasing after fifth-placed Barrichello who had been delayed earlier by a brush with Alonso which had seen the Brazilian needing to pit for a new front wing.

Up front, it was the sort of pressure that Schumacher Snr was weaned on, but though it made great television there was little chance of the World Champion making the costly sort of error that his pursuers needed. As the chequered flag came out he was still 0.7 seconds clear of his brother, and had moved three points ahead of Raikkonen in the title chase. Just to make it a great day for Ferrari, they moved nine points clear of McLaren.

"It doesn't get much better than today," Schumacher said in the post race press conference, incidentally having scored the 999th championship point of his career. "It was a tight race and a tough race, and I had to be very careful on the brake side so I wasn't pushing and was just driving to the pace I needed to, and opened the gap a little bit on the pit stops. 999 points is a good number - in Germany that means giving a free drink to everyone, so let's see what happens tonight!"

BMW Williams meanwhile, already had a hangover to contend with.

ROUND 09 JUNE 29 **EUROPEAN GRAND PRIX**

NURBURGRING

A BMW Williams one-two made local hero Ralf Schumacher extremely happy at the European Grand Prix. The race had looked to be going Kimi Raikkonen's way until an engine failure robbed him of his shot at victory. The Ferraris could not continue their winning ways, but Michael Schumacher looked good for second place… until Montoya decided he'd had enough of seeing the red car's rear wing and made a magnificent pass at the Dunlop Kurve. Schumacher, after a push out of the gravel, admitted it had been a fair move, but Ferrari's Ross Brawn was less than impressed.

JACQUES AND JOS
A bad day for Jacques Villeneuve or a great day for Jos Verstappen? Which ever way you look at it, the 1997 champ had a mammoth tussle with the Dutchman which was eventually resolved when the French-Canadian ran into the new bollards at the NGK chicane and broke his wing.

CHICANE CHANGE
The Nurburgring seems to change every year that Formula One comes to visit, and 2003 was no exception. The NGK chicane was changed this year. Some liked it, some did not. What most agreed on was their dislike of the new mini bollards which took great pleasure in smashing front wings to pieces.

BIT-KURVE

RTL-KURVE

SHELL-KURVE

FORD-KURVE

DUNLOP-KURVE

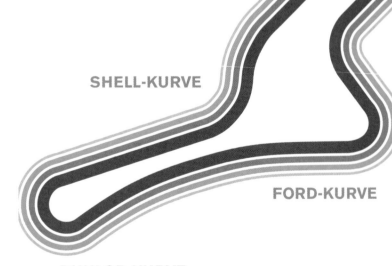

LAP DISTANCE **5.148KM/3.198 MILES**
RACE 60 LAPS **308.863KM/191.918 MILES**
FASTEST LAP **K RAIKKONEN** POLE **K RAIKKONEN**

2003 RESULTS TOP EIGHT
1 **R SCHUMACHER** WILLIAMS 2 **J P MONTOYA** WILLIAMS
3 **R BARRICHELLO** FERRARI 4 **F ALONSO** RENAULT
5 **M SCHUMACHER** FERRARI 6 **M WEBBER** JAGUAR
7 **J BUTTON** BAR 8 **N HEIDFELD** SAUBER

TRACK DESCRIPTION

In 2003, the NGK chicane was modified and the new Mercedes Arena loop from 2002 remained in place to provide a tight, and tricky, first sector of the lap. Atmosphere at the European Grand Prix is always superb, with the legions of Schumacher fans making it one of the noisiest races of the year. The circuit is a shadow of the old Nordschleife, but in its distilled form it provides a unique challenge to cars and drivers alike. The hilly nature of the track and the long, flowing corners and flat-out straights mean that this track suits those teams with the most horsepower, and as Raikkonen would discover, the best reliability.

BRAKE TEST 57/60
Coulthard had started the race back in ninth place, and was having a miserable afternoon when he came up to try and overtake Alonso's Renault. Whether Alonso braked early, or the Scot misjudged things, his move went wrong and he spun out of the grand prix.

ITT-BOGEN

NGK SCHIKANE

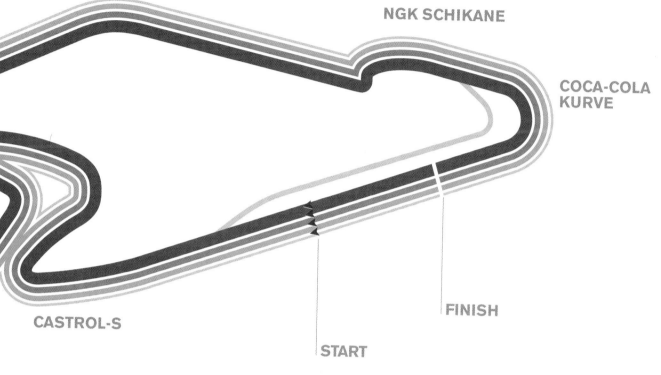

COCA-COLA KURVE

FINISH

START

CASTROL-S

VALVOLINE-KURVE

MONTY'S MUSCLE 43/60
Down into the Dunlop hairpin, Juan Pablo Montoya attempted, and pulled off, a brilliant overtaking move around the outside of Michael Schumacher which resulted in the champ spinning off. Ross Brawn said Montoya lacked class, but Schumacher admitted that the Colombian's pass was good.

KIMI'S ENGINE 26/60
Pole sitter, Kimi Raikkonen, looked to have set himself up for his second F1 career victory with a sensational drive at the European GP. Then, on lap 26, his engine let go and his race was over. His pace had been so hot in the early laps that despite not reaching half distance, he set fastest lap.

256

For 25 laps of the European Grand Prix , Kimi Raikkonen looked set to score a fabulous victory from his first-ever pole position and regain his championship lead. Then his McLaren Mercedes' engine broke, and instead it was Ralf Schumacher who came through to redeem himself with his first win of the year. But after the closeness of qualifying, it wasn't quite the incredible race that everyone had expected.

Having recovered well after his Canadian GP qualifying gaffe by taking pole, Raikkonen soon built a lead over Ralf Schumacher. He was nine seconds clear when he made his first refuelling stop on the 16th lap, with Schumacher Snr another 10 seconds further back. Ralf led briefly for BMW Williams and ran until lap 21 before refuelling, but this was still insufficient to keep Raikkonen out of the lead. Schumacher Jnr was still 4.8 seconds behind when the Mercedes engine blew up. Somewhat remarkably, Raikkonen was the first retirement of the race.

His demise lit a slow-burning fuse that led to further explosions of drama. On the 43rd lap Montoya and Schumacher Snr collided while fighting for second place. Montoya had gradually reeled in Schumacher until they were side-by-side on the run down to the Dunlop Kurve. In a moment that reminded some of his controversial clash with Jacques Villeneuve at Jerez in 1997, Schumacher ran up the kerb and tagged Montoya's BMW Williams as it moved into second place. As Schumacher spun and sat stranded, his Ferrari's rear wheels spinning helplessly in the gravel, Montoya continued unabashed. By the time three marshals and a fireman pushed the Ferrari from its dangerous spot on the corner's apex, Schumacher was down to sixth.

"Michael was quick on the straights, but in the corners he was very

slow," said Montoya. "He was on the inside and I was on the outside. I thought I gave him plenty of room. I wasn't going to give him all the track, but I thought it was all right."

Even Schumacher believed that Montoya had given him sufficient room, and after a stewards' enquiry, no action was taken. Ferrari's Ross Brawn was far from amused with the situation, but BMW Williams technical director Patrick Head remarked trenchantly that, had Montoya been penalised, it would effectively have been a declaration that overtaking was no longer allowed in Formula One.

Then, on the 57th lap, Coulthard suddenly had to swerve round Alonso approaching the chicane, and spun spectacularly into retirement in yet another dramatic incident.

"Alonso braked 10 metres earlier than he had the lap before," said Coulthard. "He was dealing inconsistently with problems, as his rear tyres looked completely worn out. But I just got caught out." The Spaniard continued, and was very nearly caught on the final lap by the recovering World Champion.

BMW Williams' haul of points from a race in which McLaren went home with none moved them up into second place in the Constructors' Championship and first sparked speculation of a late challenge for the title. Ever cautious, Sir Frank Williams, who never likes to reveal his cards in public, was careful to play down such talk. But with Ferrari only 13 points ahead, everyone within the team was seriously motivated and firmly believed that they had a genuine chance of challenging long before the season was over. The third phase of the 2003 World Championship, the Williams phase, was now well under way.

ROUND 10 JULY 06 FRENCH GRAND PRIX

MAGNY-COURS

Minardi took provisional pole on Friday – a shot in the arm for all those who'd said the new rules wouldn't shake things up. However, in the race it was a second installment of the Ralf and Juan Pablo show, with the German taking his second win in a row. The Michelin tyres looked fantastic, while the Bridgestones were once again shown to be lacking the grip demanded of them by Ferrari. This time last year Michael Schumacher was celebrating his fifth world championship. In 2003, the French Grand Prix served not to settle the championship, but to blow it wide open.

SPIN SPIN SUGAR 1/70
Rubens Barrichello had started down in eighth place, but a mistake at the final chicane spun him out of contention for a decent result. Waiting until the field passed him, he spun the car round the right way and went off in search of a points finish - which he achieved.

MICHAEL V DC 1/70
At the start of the race the two BMW Williams cars flew off into the distance. Michael Schumacher might have thought about trying to catch up, had he not had David Coulthard to contend with. The two went side-by-side through the first two corners.

LAP DISTANCE **4.411KM/2.740 MILES**
RACE 70 LAPS **308.586KM/191.746 MILES**
FASTEST LAP **J P MONTOYA** POLE **R SCHUMACHER**

2003 RESULTS TOP EIGHT
1 **R SCHUMACHER** WILLIAMS 2 **J P MONTOYA** WILLIAMS
3 **M SCHUMACHER** FERRARI 4 **K RAIKKONEN** MCLAREN
5 **D COULTHARD** MCLAREN 6 **M WEBBER** JAGUAR
7 **R BARRICHELLO** FERRARI 8 **O PANIS** TOYOTA

TRACK DESCRIPTION

One of the most heavily revised circuits of 2003, Magny-Cours had undergone many changes in the off-season in the hope of improving overtaking opportunities. The circuit, however, remained overtly technical, combining long straights, medium speed corners, hairpins and slow chicanes. Chateau d'Eau, one of the key corners of the track, was lengthened and tightened to allow more overtaking, whilst the run down to Lycee was lengthened and drawn out before pulling into a hard right hander, a short straight and a brand new chicane just before the start-finish line.

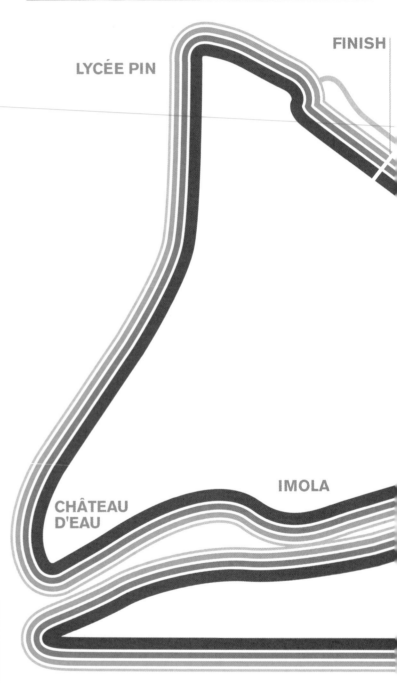

LYCÉE PIN

FINISH

CHÂTEAU D'EAU

IMOLA

ADELAIDE

MINARDI ON POLE

It was the kind of result the new rules had been designed to throw up. On a drying track, Jos Verstappen put his Minardi on provisional pole position. Wilson would have been up there too but his car was underweight, and his brilliant time was taken away from him.

PIT LANE CONFUSION 48/70

Hoping to take advantage of other drivers' misfortunes, Coulthard came in for his third stop hoping to get out ahead of the pack. In his haste to get away however, he dragged fuel man Steve Morrow along with him, before his passenger fell over the McLaren's rear tyre.

START

GRANDE COURBE

ESTORIL

180°

NURBURGRING

GOLF

VA VA BOOM 44-46/70

This was not what the French wanted to see at all. Renault had been the surprise of the season, and on Michelin rubber were expected to do well at Magny-Cours. On lap 44 Fernando Alonso's engine went bang, and then two laps later, so did Jarno Trulli's.

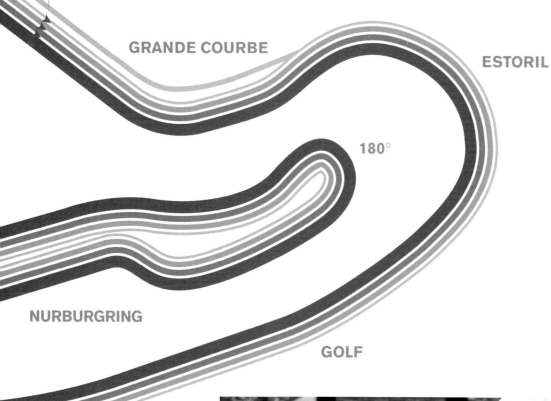

262

With his second victory on the trot, Ralf Schumacher staked his claim to his brother's World Championship crown in France, and in beating team-mate Montoya, led another crushing 1-2 for BMW Williams.

The result confirmed Michael Schumacher's worst misgivings about the performance of his Bridgestone tyres. Such was the dominance of the revitalised BMW Williams cars that even when Montoya backed off in the closing stages, angered that a change of Ralf's refuelling schedule had enabled the German to maintain the lead when Montoya had been fighting tooth and nail to steal it, he still finished well ahead of the Ferrari. Some hard driving and clever racecraft, however, allowed him to jump ahead of the McLaren Mercedes of Kimi Raikkonen and David Coulthard, which had run ahead of him in the early stages.

Ralf Schumacher's sole 'problem' came on the 52nd lap when, having made his final pit stop the previous lap, Juan Pablo Montoya closed to within 1.2 seconds of him. But the German kept his head and simply opened up the gap again.

"The car was very good from the start and I was able to disappear after the first stop," said Ralf. "Maybe we got the pressures wrong with the second set of tyres because the car felt bad and Juan was able to get closer while we were lapping guys. I came in a little early for my final stop, because I knew that he would have caught me if I'd stayed out longer. Near the end I got a bit wide in Turn 7 when I braked a bit late, but nothing special. You know, I really can't believe that I have won two in a row! It's fantastic!"

Montoya was philosophical in defeat. He said that his FW25 did not feel particularly comfortable to begin with, and then he lost time with a problem with a wheelnut in his first stop. After that he pushed very hard and was right with Ralf before their last stops, being notably more aggressive in traffic. But when he stopped two laps earlier than scheduled, Ralf came in a lap sooner, nullifying any advantage. Furious with his team, Montoya backed off. That may have been the moment in which he began to seriously consider a switch to McLaren for 2005.

Raikkonen only just made the flag after a rear brake disc shattered three laps from the finish. Coulthard had trouble too and lost a much-needed podium place with a misunderstanding during his final pit stop on lap 48. First the original refuelling hose developed a problem and Raikkonen's had to be substituted. Then Coulthard mistakenly believed he had been signalled to leave the pit as the pit stop controller raised his lollipop prematurely while refueller Steve Morrow was still in the process of disconnecting his hose. Morrow was dragged along the ground and fell over the left rear wheel as the McLaren Mercedes surged forward. Fortunately he was unharmed.

Before the French GP weekend, Ferrari and Bridgestone representatives had met for a crisis meeting in a local restaurant, and planned an intensive test session prior to the British Grand Prix. But Ralf Schumacher, who had now closed to within a mere 11 points of his big brother's championship lead and was only three behind Raikkonen, sounded cautiously optimistic as BMW Williams moved to within three points of Ferrari in the constructors' chase.

"If we keep working like this we can keep this going," he said, referring to the team's newfound momentum. "There will be circuits that are tough for us, but we are very encouraged." Battle was now fully engaged.

ROUND 11 JULY 20 BRITISH GRAND PRIX

SILVERSTONE

As if the 2003 season wasn't already exciting enough, the British Grand Prix saw yet another different visitor to the top step of the podium, more overtaking manoeuvres than one could normally expect in a season… and a protester invading the track. All this played rather brilliantly into Rubens Barrichello's hands, and the Ferrari number two swept home for an emotional and thoroughly deserved victory, the second of his career at a race temporarily held up by a track invader. Truly, this was one of the most exciting, if fairly random, races in recent memory.

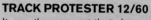

TRACK PROTESTER 12/60
It was the moment that changed the course of the 2003 British Grand Prix. A religious protester ran onto Hanger Straight - one of the fastest parts of the Silverstone circuit - but somehow everyone avoided him. As the safety car came out and the protester was removed, most cars jumped into the pits.

DC FALLS TO BITS 5/60
The incident that brought out the first safety car of the day involved David Coulthard's McLaren. Starting back on the grid, he was driving well until his cockpit restraint system came loose and had to be held in place by the Scot. After a while he got fed up and simply ripped it off at Copse corner.

LAP DISTANCE **5.141KM/3.194 MILES**
RACE 60 LAPS **308.355KM/191.602 MILES**
FASTEST LAP **R BARRICHELLO** POLE **R BARRICHELLO**

2003 RESULTS TOP EIGHT
1 **R BARRICHELLO** FERRARI 2 **J P MONTOYA** WILLIAMS
3 **K RAIKKONEN** MCLAREN 4 **M SCHUMACHER** FERRARI
5 **D COULTHARD** MCLAREN 6 **J TRULLI** RENAULT
7 **C DA MATTA** TOYOTA 8 **J BUTTON** BAR

TRACK DESCRIPTION

Silverstone is a heady mix of fast and slow corners and high speed straights. It is a punishing track for both car and driver and the prospects of the notoriously bad British weather always ensure that nobody is ever really sure what the British Grand Prix will throw up. Car set-up is clearly crucial to a good lap and good race, as the track contains many quick corners which all require lots of grip. This used to be one of the fastest circuits on the calendar, and despite having a very slow final complex, built since the track first opened in 1950, it has lost none of its charm or excitement for the drivers who absolutely love this place.

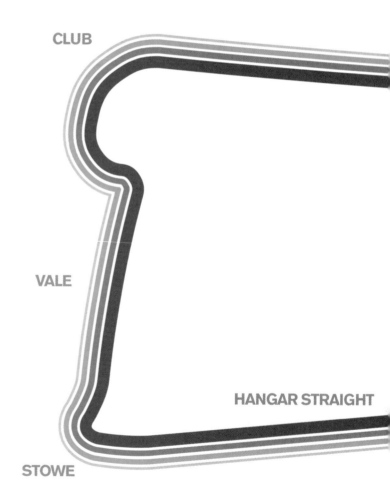

CLUB

VALE

HANGAR STRAIGHT

STOWE

THE CAR IN FRONT...
... is a Toyota. Following the intervention of the protester and the sudden rush of cars into the pits, the two Toyotas were left leading the race for the very first time in the team's short F1 history. They made a good account of themselves although they were eventually passed by the bigger teams' cars.

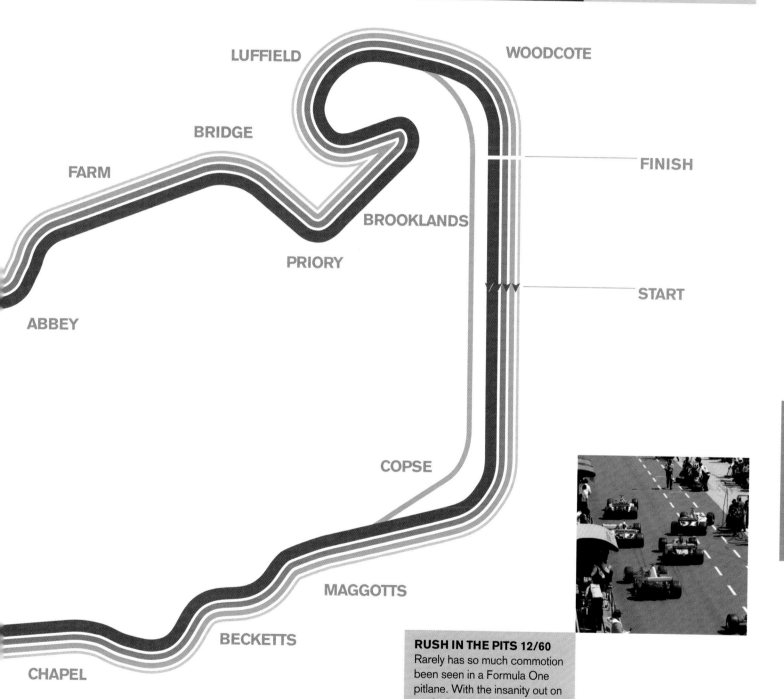

LUFFIELD

WOODCOTE

BRIDGE

FARM

FINISH

BROOKLANDS

PRIORY

START

ABBEY

COPSE

MAGGOTTS

BECKETTS

CHAPEL

RUSH IN THE PITS 12/60
Rarely has so much commotion been seen in a Formula One pitlane. With the insanity out on track, the pits filled up very quickly at the British Grand Prix, with many drivers having to sit behind their team-mates waiting for their turn to come - one such driver being Ferrari's Michael Schumacher.

Left: Kimi Raikkonen lines up for a pass on Jarno Trulli down the start-finish straight. Above right: The rush to the pits came when the safety car was deployed for the second time in the race. Below right: The Toyotas had a mixed day. Having led the race, only one finished in the points.

In a great season, the British Grand Prix at Silverstone stood out for the quality of the racing, a great victory by Rubens Barrichello - and the antics of protester Father Neil Horan, who ran in religious protest on to the fastest part of the track on the 12th lap.

Renault's Jarno Trulli led for the first five laps until the safety car was deployed for two laps on lap six while debris, the headrest from Coulthard's McLaren, was cleared away from Copse corner. Then came the Horan incident. Carrying a placard, he began running down Hangar Straight into the path of the cars exiting Chapel curve. The safety car was immediately redeployed as a marshal tackled Horan, and stayed out until lap 15.

On lap 12 Trulli, Barrichello (who had overtaken Raikkonen at Abbey curve on the 11th lap), Raikkonen, Ralf Schumacher, Michael Schumacher, Montoya, Alonso, Villeneuve, Webber, Heidfeld and Button, all dived for the pits to refuel. Some lost time as their team-mates were serviced. Alonso and M Schumacher suffered most, and though the Spaniard passed the German, both were leap-frogged by Montoya. Incredibly, Schumacher remained trapped in the midfield traffic for another 20 laps, frustrated by the never-say-die fight of Jacques Villeneuve.

When the safety car pitted on lap 16, the two Toyotas led. Cristiano da Matta and Olivier Panis had refuelled on lap six under the first safety car, and now led Coulthard, Trulli, Raikkonen, R Schumacher and Barrichello.

Raikkonen soon disposed of Panis, but had to wait until da Matta stopped to refuel on the 30th lap. Meanwhile, Barrichello had been busy making up ground after a slow stop, passing and moving ahead of Coulthard when the Scot made his second stop on lap 28. Schumacher Snr, however, was still trapped in 13th place.

Raikkonen's next stop on the 35th lap handed Barrichello the lead for the first time. They switched again when the Ferrari refuelled four laps later, but it was clear the Italian car was quicker. Under pressure from Barrichello on lap 42, Raikkonen slid wide at Bridge corner and Barrichello pounced. Six laps later, Raikkonen lost second to Montoya after a similar incident at Abbey.

Michael Schumacher worked up to fourth by lap 48, leaving Trulli to fend off Coulthard and da Matta. Closing in on them, Button, Alonso and Villeneuve waged a great battle which was resolved when Alonso's car lost its electrics, and Villeneuve spun trying to catch Button.

The victory boosted Ferrari's points lead and pushed Barrichello closer to the leading quartet, while Schumacher extended his lead over Raikkonen and Montoya jumped to third ahead of his team-mate.

The British Grand Prix will certainly be remembered for the errant spectator, and the rash of pit stops his appearance prompted. But the excellence of the racing was also memorable. There were more overtaking moves than in all other 2003 races put together; Barrichello v Raikkonen, Raikkonen v Trulli, Button v Fisichella, M Schumacher v Alonso, Barrichello v Trulli, Pizzonia v Webber, Button v M Schumacher, M Schumacher v Villeneuve, Webber v Firman, Montoya v Trulli, Button v Villeneuve, Barrichello v Raikkonen again, Montoya v Raikkonen, M Schumacher v Trulli, and finally, Coulthard v Trulli. And it all took place, not in the pits, but in full view of a highly appreciative crowd.

It was a superb win for the beleaguered Barrichello. Coincidentally, the last time anyone got on to a track during a race was at Hockenheim in 2000. The Brazilian won that one as well.

ROUND 12 AUGUST 03 GERMAN GRAND PRIX

HOCKENHEIM

Earlier in the season, BMW Williams had been criticised for its lack of pace. The German Grand Prix proved all the doubters wrong. Since winning the Monaco Grand Prix earlier in the season, Juan Pablo Montoya had been the man with the most consistent results in the sport - finishing on the podium at every race since. After his team-mate took out Barrichello and Raikkonen at Turn One, Montoya romped home to win his second race of the season, and put real pressure on Michael Schumacher's championship hopes, which were beginning to look as deflated as his left rear tyre.

TURN ONE CHAOS 1/67
A big accident at Turn One on the first lap took out two championship protagonists, and caused mayhem at the back of the grid as everyone tried to pick through the wreckage. Ralf Schumacher was blamed for the crash that saw the field decimated by the start of the second lap of the race.

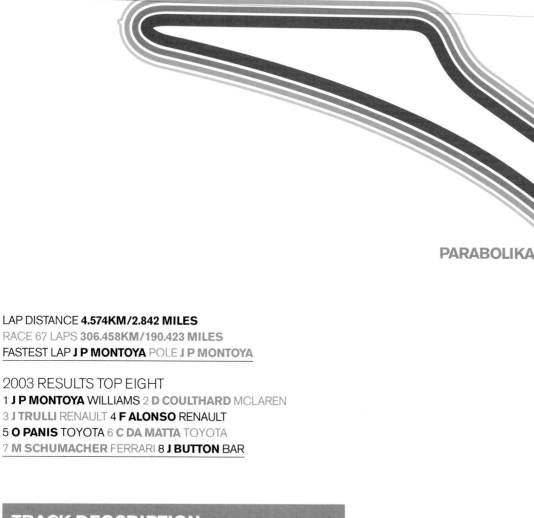

SPITZKEHRE

PARABOLIKA

EINFAHRT PARABOLIKA

LAP DISTANCE **4.574KM/2.842 MILES**
RACE 67 LAPS **306.458KM/190.423 MILES**
FASTEST LAP **J P MONTOYA** POLE **J P MONTOYA**

2003 RESULTS TOP EIGHT
1 **J P MONTOYA** WILLIAMS 2 **D COULTHARD** MCLAREN
3 **J TRULLI** RENAULT 4 **F ALONSO** RENAULT
5 **O PANIS** TOYOTA 6 **C DA MATTA** TOYOTA
7 **M SCHUMACHER** FERRARI 8 **J BUTTON** BAR

TRACK DESCRIPTION

Despite being drastically cut down in size and splendour from the original track, whose expanses roamed through the luscious forest that now forms the backdrop to the circuit, the home of the German GP has lost none of its verve. The sweeping section from turns two to six creates a fantastic opportunity to slipstream into the slow chicane, one of the best overtaking spots on the track. The track's stadium section remains as complicated as ever, and with 100,000 fans crammed into this amphitheatre, it's unsurprising that at times their cheers drown out the noise of the engines. The track was new in 2002, but in 2003 every team knew what to expect.

THE ASHES

Mark Webber and Jenson Button had a titanic battle in the 2003 German Grand Prix. Together for the majority of the race, they were scrapping over eighth position and the final world championship point. On the last lap Webber had a lunge but overshot and ended his race in the barriers.

BATTLE FOR SECOND

The battle for second place was a joy to watch. Jarno Trulli, David Coulthard and Michael Schumacher were all in contention, and all three fought hard for it, pulling off some fantastic overtaking manoeuvres, especially at the hairpin and on the wide run-off area it affords drivers.

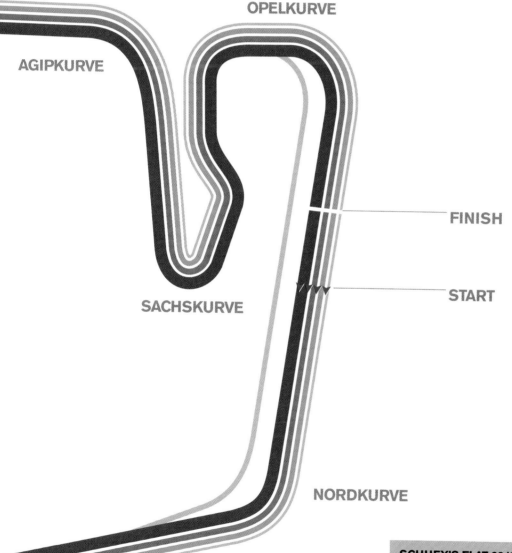

OPELKURVE

AGIPKURVE

FINISH

SACHSKURVE

START

NORDKURVE

SCHUEY'S FLAT 63/67

He had driven a sensational race, pulled off some brilliant moves and dragged himself up to second place. Then, with less than ten laps of the race remaining, Michael Schumacher's left rear tyre deflated and dropped him down the order. For once, his legendary luck was missing.

Left: Fifth and sixth places for Toyota who finally seemed to find some solid form in Germany. Above right: Trulli's popular podium finish came at a price. He was so exhausted that he missed the press conference. Below right: Schumacher finishes in seventh after his problems.

Juan Pablo Montoya's victory at Hockenheim, only the third of his career, was the most dominant of the season and moved him within six points of local hero Michael Schumacher who, by contrast, had a torrid weekend. Blown off in practice and qualifying, he had to play second fiddle to the Renaults of Jarno Trulli and Fernando Alonso for much of the race, and just when he had fought up to second place, his chances of a record sixth world crown took a serious dent with four laps to go when a punctured Bridgestone tyre dropped him to a seventh place finish.

Montoya's relationship with his team might have been strained with a switch to McLaren becoming ever more likely, but as he left the carnage at the start behind him, all he had to do was keep up the pace. And he did it with only 93 percent throttle movement which cost him 10 km/h off his top speed. Despite all that, it was, as he summarised, "A perfect finish to a perfect weekend."

An accident at the start accounted for Ralf Schumacher, Rubens Barrichello and Kimi Raikkonen. Schumacher Jnr's double blow proved that the bad luck at Hockenheim was not the exclusive preserve of his big brother. Slow away at the start, he moved to the left to defend his entry to the first corner against a challenge from British Grand Prix winner Barrichello, and ended up pinching the Brazilian into a collision with Raikkonen. Barrichello and Raikkonen retired immediately, while Schumacher only limped as far as the pits before retiring with heavy left-hand sidepod damage. The incident threatened to have a catastrophic effect on the championship aspirations of all three drivers. It also accounted for Jaguar debutant Justin Wilson, who hit Jacques Villeneuve's BAR Honda in the ensuing chain reaction. Heinz-Harald Frentzen and

Ralph Firman also took an early bath after the latter ran into the former.

Immediately after the race, a stewards' enquiry held Ralf to blame for the crash and he was awarded a 10 grid place penalty for the forthcoming Hungarian GP, but that would be replaced with a hefty fine following an FIA appeal hearing in Paris. Another stewards' enquiry, specially convened in Hungary, subsequently exonerated Barrichello and Raikkonen.

Once the safety car had pitted, Montoya initially eased away partially from the fast-starting Renaults and Schumacher's Ferrari, but soon his three-stop strategy paid dividends. He lost the lead to Alonso by refuelling on lap 18, but he was so crushingly dominant that he retained the lead when he stopped again on laps 33 and 50.

Schumacher and the Renaults were all on two-stop strategies and it took the champion until lap 31 to pass Alonso, as the Spaniard made a rare error and ran wide going into the stadium. But it took him until lap 59 to outfox Trulli by going round the outside at the hairpin. The Italian tried to hold him out wide, but Schumacher out-dragged him on the controversial new Tarmac run-off area. On-song David Coulthard, having moved up from an initial sixth place, pulled off a similar move on Trulli the following lap, even though the Italian held him wide for almost the entire length of the ensuing straight. Second place was a much-needed result for Coulthard after his troubled season, and he drove an attacking race. Both Renaults made places back when Schumacher's tyre failed on the 63rd lap.

The run of BMW Williams successes was ringing every alarm bell in Maranello, but the summer testing ban meant that Ferrari and Bridgestone had limited means of digging themselves out of trouble as the championships' climax loomed.

ROUND 13 AUGUST 24 HUNGARIAN GRAND PRIX

HUNGARORING

Fernando Alonso became the youngest ever winner of a Formula One Grand Prix when he completely obliterated his opposition from the second pole position of his career at the Hungaroring. If anyone needed further proof of this incredible young man's talents, all they needed to know was that in the course of the race he not only lapped Michael Schumacher's Ferrari, but he did the same to his own team-mate, Jarno Trulli. The eighth different winner of a race in 2003, Alonso's victory was yet another page in the incredible chapter of F1 history that the 2003 season was turning out to be.

MONTOYA'S MISSION
Montoya started the race on the dirty side of the track but despite this still came home in third place. He was angry he'd taken his final qualifying run cautiously and at the start of the race he fell back. Regardless, he ran a solid race and left Hungary just one point behind Michael Schumacher.

LAP DISTANCE **4.381KM/2.722 MILES**
RACE 70 LAPS **306.663KM/190.551 MILES**
FASTEST LAP **J P MONTOYA** POLE **F ALONSO**

2003 RESULTS TOP EIGHT
1 **F ALONSO** RENAULT 2 **K RAIKKONEN** MCLAREN
3 **J P MONTOYA** WILLIAMS 4 **R SCHUMACHER** WILLIAMS
5 **D COULTHARD** MCLAREN 6 **M WEBBER** JAGUAR
7 **J TRULLI** RENAULT 8 **M SCHUMACHER** FERRARI

TRACK DESCRIPTION

Hungary has always been a difficult circuit. It is thin, twisty and because it is rarely used, the track is coated in a layer of dust. For 2003 the Hungaroring had undergone some pretty major changes. The start-finish straight had been lengthened and the profile of the first corner tightened to promote overtaking. Similarly, the old Turn 12 had been replaced with a longer straight and tighter corner to again try and create the overtaking spots this circuit had once lacked. The track, despite these changes, still required a medium to high downforce setup to negotiate the many slippery and challenging corners.

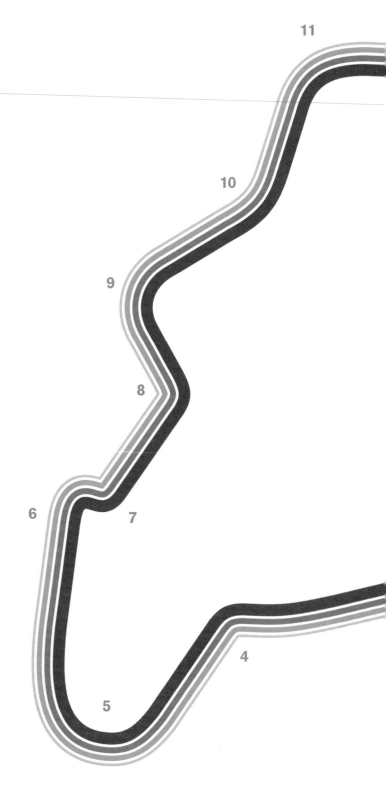

RALF IN A SPIN 1/70

Taking a fine, rather than a ten place grid demotion for his part in causing the first corner accident at the German Grand Prix, looked like a big mistake for Ralf Schumacher. At the start of the Hungarian race he was pushed onto the dirt at Turn Two and spun back to very last place on the track.

RUBENS' FRIGHT 20/70

On the run down to the new Turn 1, Rubens Barrichello was pushing hard in pursuit of Trulli and Raikkonen. As he stabbed on the brakes however, his left rear suspension literally exploded and the Brazilian was powerless to stop a big impact into the barriers from which he thankfully walked away unhurt.

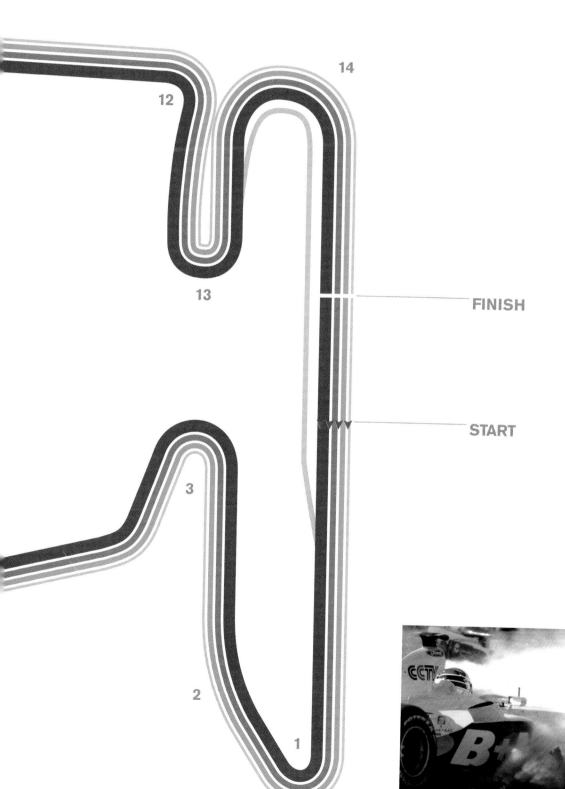

FINISH

START

12

14

13

3

2

1

LUCK OF THE IRISH

Ralph Firman was on a flying lap on Friday morning when the rear wing of his Jordan Ford fell off. With no rear end grip his car spun wildly out of control, launching the rookie sideways into the barriers at frightening speed. He was carried away from the wreckage and missed the next two races.

Left: Justin Wilson had a tough race for Jaguar. His engine blew and brought about an early end to his race. Above right: Fernando Alonso became the youngest winner of a grand prix. Below right: David Coulthard runs over the kerb in a great scrap with Ralf Schumacher.

For Fernando Alonso it was the greatest afternoon of his life, yet the 22 year-old celebrated with remarkable aplomb. It was his first victory in the big league, the first for a Spanish driver, the first for his Renault team in 20 years, and he deposed New Zealander Bruce McLaren as the youngest-ever winner after a 44-year reign. "It's too many things for one day!" he admitted. "The weekend was fantastic. With pole position and now victory it's a dream come true! I'm 22 years old and now I have my first victory in the pocket. It's too much like a dream, still. The car was perfect."

With eight laps left he'd also lapped Michael Schumacher.

The Hungarian GP, however, was not merely the story of an impressive young driver fulfilling his destiny with a performance that was just as dominant and impressive as Juan Pablo Montoya's had been three weeks earlier in Germany. It was symbolic that he lapped Schumacher, regardless of the embarrassingly clear discrepancy in the respective performance of their Michelin and Bridgestone tyres. Montoya and Raikkonen have won their first grands prix, and now the third young pretender had likewise confirmed his long-term potential. And he had done so in great style.

Cristiano da Matta stalled his Toyota on row eight, lending confusion to the start as yellow flags waved, but up front Alonso blasted straight into the lead. Behind him, Mark Webber's start for Jaguar was to play a crucial part in the eventual outcome. The Jaguar driver grabbed second place, having started third. Like Alonso, he was on the clean side of a dirty race track. On the dirty side, both BMW Williamses (Ralf Schumacher, second fastest, Juan Pablo Montoya, fourth) made poor getaways. Kimi Raikkonen and Rubens Barrichello sprinted ahead of them, and then to compound his gloom, Ralf spun in the second corner and condemned himself to an afternoon playing catch-up. Alonso checked out as Webber, who was driving superbly, was holding everyone back. "For the first two or three laps Mark was in the mirror, then on the eighth or ninth I asked the team on the radio where the others were and they told me they were 15 seconds away!" he laughed. "I started thinking of the victory when I was 20 seconds ahead. I started taking it easy with 50 laps to go."

Raikkonen passed Webber when the Jaguar driver made the first of three stops on lap 14, but Barrichello marred his chances when an early move to pass Webber saw him overshoot a chicane on lap three. Seventeen laps later, rear suspension failure sent him headlong into the wall in Turn 1. Montoya was thus promoted to third, but nearly threw it away with a spin on the 62nd lap. He just recovered before team-mate Schumacher came along. The latter had staged a remarkable recovery after his spin.

Behind them, David Coulthard's fortunes improved again with a solid fifth place, the Scot beating the valiant Webber and Jarno Trulli, who kept Michael Schumacher behind him to the flag. In short, the Hungarian Grand Prix was a disaster for Schumacher, Ferrari and Bridgestone. At one stage an attempt to make up ground with a light fuel load almost backfired when he ran short and only just sputtered into the pits to refuel.

The race dramatically changed the face of the title fight. Ferrari lost its Constructors' Championship lead to BMW Williams, and Schumacher barely clung to his drivers' points advantage.

It was the lowest point of the Scuderia's season, and left Schumacher looking like a spent force. As events would later prove, however, appearances can be deceptive.

ROUND 14 SEPTEMBER 14 **ITALIAN GRAND PRIX**

MONZA

Formula One arrived at Monza with the tyre controversy hanging over it. Bridgestone's rubber was fine, but Michelin's design was ruled just that little bit too wide. Modifications were made, arguments were had, and then 20 cars went about their business and ran the quickest race in the sport's history. Ferrari hadn't been within a sniff of victory for the previous three races, but at their home grand prix, Michael Schumacher put in a faultless drive to mark his return to the top step of the podium. The tifosi, as always, went absolutely mad, and this incredible season drew ever closer to its conclusion.

RETTIFILI·

PARABOLICA 4/53
Cristiano da Matta had qualified just twelfth for the Italian Grand Prix despite a good showing in Friday's session. His race was even more disappointing. In the high speed run down to the Parabolica, he suffered a left rear puncture, his car pitched onto the grass, launched over a kerb and into retirement.

CURVA PARABOLICA

VAF

LAP DISTANCE **5.793KM/3.599 MILES**
RACE 53 LAPS **306.720KM/190.586 MILES**
FASTEST LAP **M SCHUMACHER** POLE M SCHUMACHER

2003 RESULTS TOP EIGHT
1 **M SCHUMACHER** FERRARI 2 **J P MONTOYA** WILLIAMS
3 **R BARRICHELLO** FERRARI 4 **K RAIKKONEN** MCLAREN
5 **M GENE** WILLIAMS 6 **J VILLENEUVE** BAR
7 **M WEBBER** JAGUAR 8 **F ALONSO** RENAULT

FIRST LAP SPECIAL 1/53
Schumacher led, Montoya was all over him, and just in case either made a mistake Jarno Trulli was ready to pick up the pieces. The championship rivals almost collided at the second chicane, but after Trulli took a look at Montoya, his hydraulics died and the Italian was out of his home grand prix.

TRACK DESCRIPTION

After the shortening of Hockenheim, Monza is one of the few tracks left in Formula One that could really be termed "high speed." Flowing through mile-after-mile of woodland, Monza is also one of the most beautiful tracks on the calendar, and one with a fabled history. The seemingly endless straights have been dissected with quick chicanes, and as such overtaking is usually possible if a decent slingshot is gained out of the preceding corner. The track is home to some of the greatest corners in Formula One such as Curva Grande and the Parabolica. Low downforce settings are crucial here, as straight line speed is vital for a blistering lap.

SPEED DEMON
Michael Schumacher's Ferrari crossed the finish line at Monza just one hour, 14 minutes and 19.383 seconds after the lights had gone out at the start. It was the quickest grand prix in the history of the sport, beating Peter Gethin's record, set in 1971 at the same circuit. Yet another record for Schumacher.

LAUNCH CONTROL 1/53
Having spun at the first chicane on his final qualifying run, Fernando Alonso was forced to start the Italian Grand Prix from the back of the grid. The Renault's launch control system is renowned for its brilliance, but this time all it did was shoot him into the back of Verstappen and briefly into the sky.

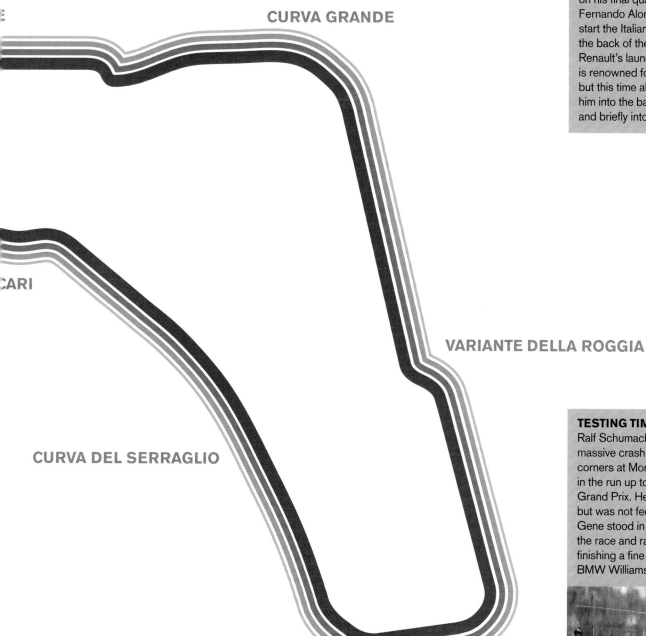

CURVA GRANDE

VARIANTE DELLA ROGGIA

CARI

CURVA DEL SERRAGLIO

CURVA DI LESMOS

TESTING TIMES
Ralf Schumacher had a massive crash at the Lesmo corners at Monza whilst testing in the run up to the Italian Grand Prix. He ran on Friday but was not feeling right. Marc Gene stood in for him during the race and ran brilliantly, finishing a fine fifth and helping BMW Williams in its title fight.

Left: Michael Schumacher silenced the Italian press with a brilliant win at Monza. Above right: The track commentators compared the first lap to one from the days of Gilles Villeneuve. Below right: The euphoric Ferrari mechanics celebrate a win that put both titles within reach.

Since Hungary, an acrimonious row broke out after Ferrari and Bridgestone protested to the FIA that, when worn, Michelin's front tyres exceeded the 270mm tread width limit by 5mm. Bad feelings abounded. But when it mattered, on a circuit where tyre and chassis performance were less important than engine power, low drag and braking efficiency, Michael Schumacher not only delivered pole position, but a perfect race performance.

His 50th victory since joining Ferrari back in 1996 finally unseated Englishman Peter Gethin as the victor of history's fastest-ever grand prix. In 1971 the jockey's son had ridden his BRM to a hair's breadth success at a speed of 242.615 km/h. Schumacher's winning average, on a circuit since raddled with chicanes, was 247.585 km/h.

"There were many things that came together here," said Schumacher. "It's quite a while ago since we last won in 2003. We've had some tough races behind us. Then we had the summer break and a big push in the team and at the factory. Everyone was very motivated, more than 100 percent. It's been an unbelievable thing to watch. Today was one of the greatest days of my career. I am so in love with all those guys in the team, from the designers and engineers and mechanics to the lady who sweeps the factory. To all of them, a big thank you!"

Schumacher had only one dangerous moment. It came after the first chicane, where he almost overshot. By the second, arch-rival Juan Pablo Montoya went sneaking down the outside and actually nosed ahead. Whoever emerged in the lead would almost certainly win the race. And since he was running a notch more rear wing than his team had recommended - and therefore would be slower on the straight than Schumacher - Montoya desperately needed the lead. But Schumacher

denied him, holding his nerve after some gripping side-by-side racing, and regained the initiative by the exit. The race was effectively over.

"It was very hard but fair," Schumacher said afterwards, "and a vital factor in winning the race."

Montoya got within a second of Schumacher late in the race, but was then blocked, first by rookie Zsolt Baumgartner, and then by veteran Heinz-Harald Frentzen. In the end Montoya settled for a damage-limiting second place. "I decided to pace myself to the end," he admitted. "It would have been very hard to pass Michael anyway."

Crucially, from a championship perspective, Barrichello fended off Raikkonen all the way, the duo finishing less than a second apart, six and half seconds behind Montoya. Coulthard should have been fifth but his McLaren lost fuel pressure on the 46th lap, handing the place to Spaniard Marc Gene, who substituted splendidly for Ralf Schumacher at BMW Williams after the German complained of dizziness on Friday in the wake of a testing accident at the track the previous week. Jacques Villeneuve had a reliable run to sixth, Mark Webber was seventh, and Fernando Alonso pipped Nick Heidfeld for eighth with a lap to run.

Suddenly, Ferrari was back on track and the Prancing Horse had broken into a full gallop again. But that only intensified the bad feelings. McLaren's Ron Dennis said of the disruption, "From my youth I remember seeing a film, Ben Hur, and there's one sequence where the slaves are flogged to row at what was called 'ramming speed,' the maximum speed for hitting rivals. And ramming speed is what a grand prix team achieves at the point at which a World Championship becomes as critical and finely balanced as it is now. This definitely had a negative influence and I think that was part of the strategy."

ROUND 15 SEPTEMBER 28 **US GRAND PRIX**

INDIANAPOLIS

Three drivers came to Indianapolis with a shot at the title, but as a despondent Juan Pablo Montoya left the track with his championship dreams in tatters, and with Kimi Raikkonen needing something just short of a miracle to close the gap to first place, Michael Schumacher stood on the brink of history. His masterful run in the changeable American conditions could easily be rated as one of his greatest ever drives. As his fellow title contenders battled through the field, Schumacher simply sat back, waited for them to wear themselves out, and then pounced to take the win. A record sixth title was now his to lose.

BUTTON LEADS THE RACE
As the track turned from damp
to wet, the Bridgestone tyres
came into their element. Jenson
Button subsequently found
himself leading a race for the
first time. He drove brilliantly,
and despite being passed by
Schumacher, looked certain for
his first podium finish until
engine failure stole it from him.

LAP DISTANCE **4.192KM/2.604 MILES**
RACE 73 LAPS **306.016KM/190.149 MILES**
FASTEST LAP **M SCHUMACHER** POLE **K RAIKKONEN**

2003 RESULTS TOP EIGHT
1 **M SCHUMACHER** FERRARI 2 **K RAIKKONEN** MCLAREN
3 **H H FRENTZEN** SAUBER 4 **J TRULLI** RENAULT
5 **N HEIDFELD** SAUBER 6 **J P MONTOYA** WILLIAMS
7 **G FISICHELLA** JORDAN 8 **J WILSON** JAGUAR

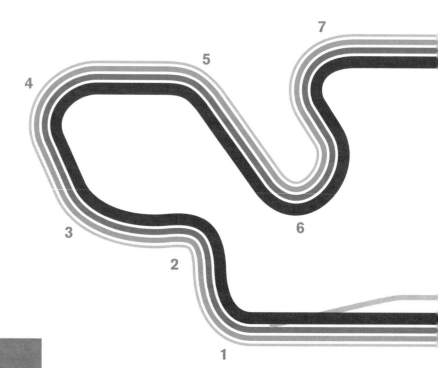

TRACK DESCRIPTION

Few F1 tracks have the racing pedigree of Indianapolis. The infield
section is remarkably tight and twisty, corners suddenly appearing
almost before the cars have fully completed the one before. What
makes the Brickyard so different, however, is the banked final
corner. The cars run clockwise around the oval, the wrong way as
far as the Americans are concerned, but the sight of a modern
Formula One car on full tilt, slipstreaming at full throttle, reminds you
of the days of the 10km Monza circuit, or even further back to the
days of Brooklands. Fast, challenging and very physical,
Indianapolis is a true test of the modern F1 driver.

SAUBER LUCKS IN
2003 had not been the sort of season that Sauber Petronas had been expecting. The competition in the midfield had been at its closest for a good few years, and even with the new points system Sauber was struggling. The team's great result at the US GP, however, turned their season around.

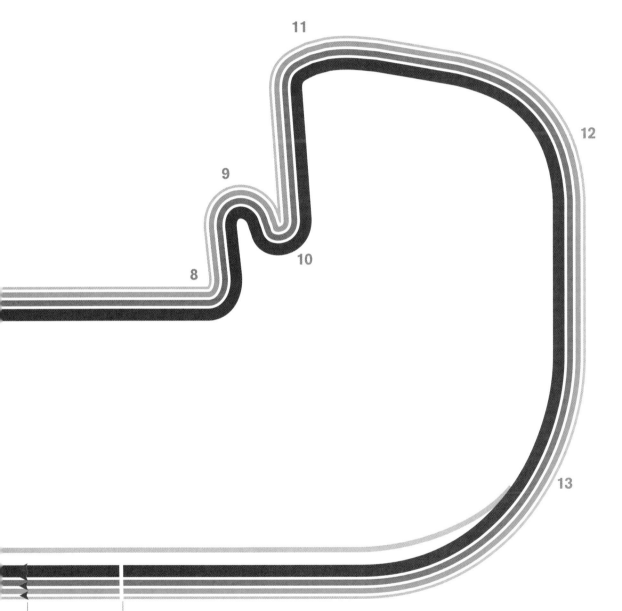

11

9

12

8

10

13

START   FINISH

MONTOYA'S FIGHT
Despite a problem with his pit stop, a drive-through penalty for his accident with Barrichello, and a spot of rain thrown in for good measure, Juan Pablo Montoya drove a gritty race and was unlucky to come home only sixth. At one point he overtook Schumacher, but the German was to have the last laugh.

Michael Schumacher was the 2003 World Champion for 17 laps of the US Grand Prix at Indianapolis Motor Speedway. As rivals Kimi Raikkonen and Juan Pablo Montoya met problems on a rainy day, and he deprived upstart Jenson Button of the lead on the 38th lap, Schumacher had amassed sufficient points to win a record sixth crown. But when Raikkonen moved up to second place on the 55th lap Schumacher no longer had the 10-point gap he needed. Raikkonen was only nine adrift, and so the title fight would go down to the wire in Japan a fortnight later. It was yet another cliffhanger, 2003 style. But on a day when the weather gods smiled on Schumacher, his only cloud was Olivier Panis's allegation that Schumacher had illegally passed him for third place under waved yellow flags on the fifth lap.

Bernie Ecclestone and Max Mosley could not have come up with a better scenario for this vital race. After qualifying, the third-placed driver in the championship fight (Raikkonen) had pole position, the second (Montoya) was fourth and the leader (Schumacher) was only seventh. And the weather was unsettled. After the second lap the race was a mish-mash of overtaking moves. Schumacher went from seventh to third at the start, but soon fell back as light rain favoured the Michelin runners. But Montoya was also in trouble. After colliding with Rubens Barrichello on the third lap he was awarded a drive-through penalty moments after a fuel rig problem delayed his first pit stop.

That left Raikkonen in an easy lead until he refuelled on lap 19. By now, however, light rain was dampening the track once more.

Schumacher stopped for fuel and gambled on new dry tyres on lap 20, but by lap 22 it was pouring, so he stopped again for wets. In the meantime, Mark Webber had a brief moment of glory leading for Jaguar, before crashing. On dry Michelins, new leader David Coulthard also lasted only a lap. Thus Button was promoted to the lead for the first time in his BAR Honda. Like Button, Heinz-Harald Frentzen had timed his stop right and was also on Bridgestone wets for Sauber Petronas, but Schumacher was catching them both. Frentzen succumbed on lap 33, Button on lap 38. While it lasted it had been an impressive and confident performance from the BAR Honda driver, whose engine then blew up after another four laps.

Now Schumacher was champion, because Raikkonen was only fourth behind the Saubers of Frentzen and Nick Heidfeld. Montoya had been lapped in ninth place, and was out of the points. But the race was far from over...

Raikkonen passed the Saubers as the track dried again, and eight points for second just kept him in the hunt for the championship. Further back Montoya eventually caught Giancarlo Fisichella's Jordan, but sixth place was one too low. The Colombian's title hopes were over.

"This was a very important outcome for my position for the championship," Schumacher said with great understatement. "I'm so pleased, it's such an emotional day today." Video evidence proved he had just beaten the yellow flags by a few feet.

After giving the 2002 race to Barrichello on the line Schumacher had been vilified. Now the Americans loved him again. But Raikkonen, though philosophical, was not daunted. "We lost the race because we were unlucky with the weather. What can you do?" he said. "Things are a lot more difficult, but at least we are still in the championship."

But only just. His chances were on life support, and it would take a miracle to revive them.

SUZUKA

It was Formula One showdown time once again, and as a thrilling season reached its conclusion, both championships were up for grabs. Michael Schumacher needed just one point to be assured his place in history as the sport's first six-time world champion, and Ferrari stood on the brink of a record-breaking fifth constructors' title in a row. The race itself was a fitting conclusion to what had been an unbelievable year of racing. Schumacher had a difficult day, but up front Barrichello recorded a brilliant victory, ensuring that both Schumacher and Ferrari won their world championships.

SHUT THAT DOOR 6/53
Takuma Sato was competing in the Japanese Grand Prix, but only after Jacques Villeneuve had quit BAR the day before running started. The Japanese driver acquitted himself well in the race and refused to buckle under pressure from Michael Schumacher, taking the German's front wing off.

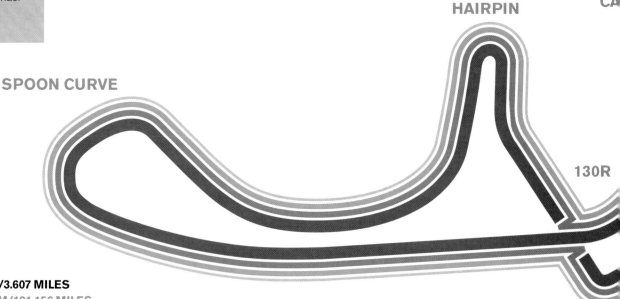

SPOON CURVE

HAIRPIN

CA

130R

LAP DISTANCE **5.807KM/3.607 MILES**
RACE 53 LAPS **307.771KM/191.156 MILES**
FASTEST LAP **R SCHUMACHER** POLE R BARRICHELLO

2003 RESULTS TOP EIGHT
1 **R BARRICHELLO** FERRARI 2 **K RAIKKONEN** MCLAREN
3 **D COULTHARD** MCLAREN 4 **J BUTTON** BAR
5 **J TRULLI** RENAULT 6 **T SATO** BAR
7 **C DA MATTA** TOYOTA 8 **M SCHUMACHER** FERRARI

TRACK DESCRIPTION

Built by Honda as a motorbike test track in 1962, Suzuka is the centrepiece of an enormous theme park. The first grand prix was held here in 1987 and since then the circuit has seen some nail-biting season finales. One of very few 'figure-of-eight' tracks in existence, Suzuka is a huge challenge. It is incredibly fast and highly technical, with almost relentless challenges facing both car and driver. Possibly the greatest challenge of all is the fabled 130 R corner which, after Eau Rouge at Spa Francorchamps, is one of the best corners F1 has ever known. If you listen carefully you can hear some drivers take this one flat out. It's an awesome track.

BROTHERS IN ARMS 41/53
Battling back through the field, after his collision with Sato, Schumacher Snr came up to da Matta's Toyota. On the run into the chicane he outbraked himself and his younger brother had to take evasive action. He missed taking his brother out, but broke his BMW Williams' front wing in the process.

GOOD DAY FOR BAR
Jenson Button led a Formula One grand prix for the second time in two races in Japan. He missed out on the podium again but came home a very respectable fourth. His new team-mate Takuma Sato also finished in the points and, with that, BAR wrapped up fifth place in the constructors' race.

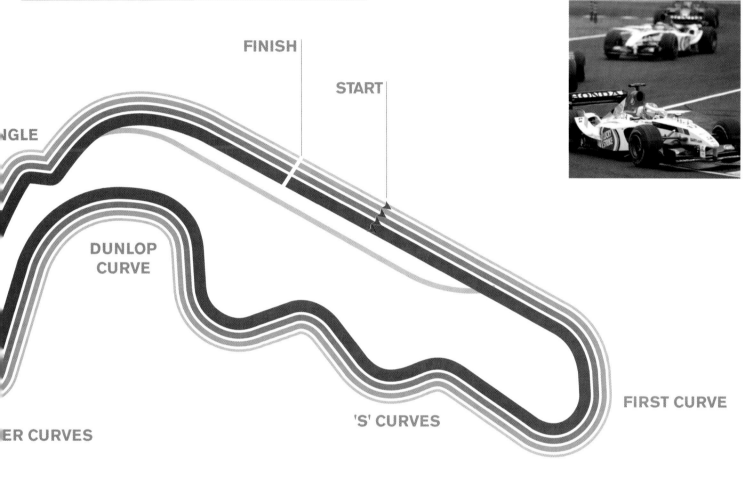

FINISH

START

NGLE

DUNLOP
CURVE

FIRST CURVE

'S' CURVES

ER CURVES

ALONSO RETIRES 18/53
Fernando Alonso finished his season off with another fine race in Japan. He reckoned he could have won the race, but his car retired on lap 18 when its engine blew. He parked up on the way to 130 R and looked genuinely depressed. It was a shame that such a brilliant year had finished with a DNF.

298

If Rubens Barrichello was somewhat overcome after the seventh victory of his career, it was understandable. As the hero of the hour, he had just helped team-mate Michael Schumacher to win a record sixth World Championship, and Ferrari its fifth constructors' title in succession. "I'm so proud to be part of this team. Most of the time it has been Michael doing the winning, but I am so proud to have been there so often and to have played a key role," the little Brazilian gasped.

The World Champion barely featured in a race made more notable for the errors he made. Chasing Takuma Sato for 12th place on the sixth lap he ruined his front wing crashing into the back of the Japanese driver's BAR Honda at the chicane, dropping to last place.

On lap 41 he got his braking wrong again at the chicane, locked his brakes to avoid hitting Cristiano da Matta's Toyota, and pulled into the path of battling brother Ralf, who couldn't avoid hitting his left rear tyre. Both Schumacher brothers slid down the escape road, and subsequently Michael admitted to worries about a puncture for the rest of his race to eighth place - the minimum he needed to win the crown even if rival Kimi Raikkonen won. Thanks to Barrichello, the Finn didn't even get close.

The Brazilian led off the line before being passed on the opening lap by Juan Pablo Montoya's BMW Williams. But the Colombian was soon out with hydraulic failure on the ninth lap. With Ralf Schumacher already spinning on lap two before attacking Frentzen at the chicane on lap nine, BMW Williams' hopes of the constructors' championship were quickly doomed.

Fernando Alonso challenged Barrichello, but retired with a blown engine on lap 18, promoting Kimi Raikkonen and David Coulthard, who had 'let' the Finn by early on. When Barrichello made the first of his three refuelling stops on lap 12, Raikkonen led the race. With Schumacher only 16th, the Finn had the title in his hands. But not for long. His two-stop strategy was inferior to that of Ferrari, and he never had the speed to challenge the dominant Barrichello.

Jenson Button drove brilliantly to bag fourth place for BAR Honda, leading for three laps during the early refuelling stops, and Jarno Trulli did an equally fine job to take fifth having started at the back of the grid after aborting his qualifying lap when it started to rain. Sato, who had suddenly replaced Jacques Villeneuve a race early, drove well for sixth. BAR's eight-point haul pushed it back in front of Sauber for fifth place in the constructors' championship,

It was an edgy race. At one point any slip from Barrichello could have gifted the title to Raikkonen, but in the end the result worked out the way most had predicted. Michael Schumacher won his record sixth World Championship crown, and Ferrari wrapped up the constructors' title.

Clearly affected by his success, which brought down the curtain on a fabulous season of Formula One, Schumacher said: "It's probably not appropriate to describe my emotions. It's been a tough year and this was a very tough race, probably one of my toughest. But much more to mention is the team. They did an incredible job. Rubens had a fantastic drive, so we won the constructors' title now five times in a row - the first time this has ever happened, and we did it in big style. You have seen what happened in Nurburgring, Hockenheim and Budapest, and how many people wrote us off. But here we are, back, because we never give up, we always fight. That's one of the strengths of a fantastic team."

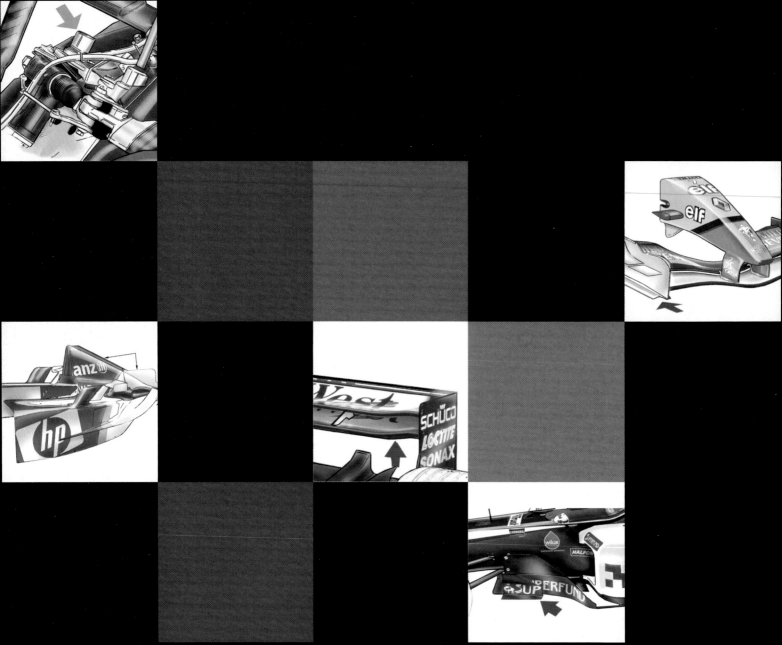

TECHNICAL REVIEW

BRIDGESTONE

Some people have criticised our performance this year but Ferrari have won the Constructors' Championship for an unprecedented fifth time in a row using our tyres, so I guess we can't be too bad! Throughout the year I never changed my opinion that the performance of our tyres is very good. People have to take into consideration that the tyres are just one part, albeit a very important part, of the total technical package.

You also have to take into consideration that last year we didn't have any rivals in our battle for the Championship, whereas this year it has been a good, long and hard battle to the end with our main competitor. Everyone has been talking about tyres and that can only be a good thing.

It is good for Bridgestone and good for the sport and also good for the road car user. At the Frankfurt motorshow this year a lot of the cars were using Bridgestone tyres, and awareness of our name within the motor trade is very strong and getting stronger all the time. This proves that Formula One is very important to our company.

Friday testing is a very good idea. This year we have had two teams, Jordan and Minardi participating in Friday testing and next year I hope we might have one more as the feedback we gather is very useful.

I am very proud of our success in 2003 and as usual we will be working hard in the winter to make important new developments for 2004.

MICHELIN

" **2003 was a very good year for Michelin. It was also a good year** for racing and that has to be positive for the sport. We had several top teams competing for the Championship which I think gave us a significant advantage which has been very important this year. For example if we had been completely dependant on BMW Williams at the beginning of the season then we would have been in trouble, but we worked together well and the team came up with a car that is well balanced in every condition. Conversely McLaren had a downpoint mid season and then came back at the end of the season. While Renault has been one of the big surprises of the year.

Friday testing is only useful if you have decent track conditions which are close to the race conditions. But usually the track is unused, and so it is cold, dirty or dusty and you really only get decent feedback in the last half an hour or so of the two hour session.

I was very disappointed by the vicious gossip against Michelin which occurred before the Italian Grand Prix and forced the FIA to reinterpret the rules. This is not the way to behave. I know the guys from Ferrari and I'm ashamed of them. This is not the spirit of Ferrari talking.

Formula One is very important to us as it provides a very strong pool of technology and research. I am proud to be part of a company like Michelin and I am looking forward to the challenges and triumphs of 2004. "

SCUDERIA FERRARI MARLBORO

" **Your references are always mixed. Last year we had a car which** won a lot of races and had a very dominant season and the F2003-GA car was better than last year's. However, clearly on certain occasions it was not good enough, because we were being beaten. I was pretty happy with the car, but I was not happy with all of the results. After the season we had in 2002, you automatically develop a sort of conservatism. You do not push things as aggressively as you might otherwise do after a less dominant season. Therefore you don't take any risks which might affect reliability. It holds you back a little bit. For sure this winter we will have to change that approach. That is not a criticism or a failure, it is normal to set priorities according to the situation you have.

There were a number of rule changes over the winter of 2002 that were designed to reduce Ferrari's competitiveness. I cannot think of a single regulation that helped us. One of them was to allow different tyres for different teams. When you have, like Michelin, three top teams, it is difficult to find the right compromise in supplying them with a tyre that suits all three of them. Now Michelin does not have that problem any more. Of course, there was a lot of talk about the tyre war. Tyres are a major factor, no doubt about that. You have to say that, in the majority of the races, perhaps the Michelins were stronger in 2003 than our Bridgestones. But when two serious competitors are fighting, that is the natural order of things. Fundamentally, a Michelin tyre ran cooler than a Bridgestone tyre, because of design philosophy, the car or whatever. So when it was very hot we were dealing with a higher temperature range than Michelin. We had this situation very often in the summer. Under normal conditions we still had a reasonable advantage in high-speed corners, whereas they were stronger in medium-speed corners. We have our plans to get that right for next year. We cannot just rely on Bridgestone to change the tyre. We have to look at the car as well and tune it to run lower tyre temperatures. We will work together to find a solution over the winter. "

The Ferrari engineers had to find a solution to a problem that seemed almost impossible to solve: How do you improve the best car in the field?

Three of the first four races demonstrated how good the Ferrari F2002 still was. Apart from Malaysia, where the Michelin factor dominated the excellence of the Ferrari-chassis, the old F2002 was the quickest car on the track. Due to mistakes by the team, Ferrari exploited the potential only at Imola, where Michael Schumacher celebrated an unchallenged victory.

Given the outstanding performance of the F2002, it was not a surprise to see at the presentation of the new car that the F2003-GA (the GA was a tribute to the late Fiat patriarch Gianni Agnelli) had a completely new face. In order to beat the F2002, it had to be different. The only similarities were the nose and the front wing, but even that had changed when you looked at it closely. In contrast to almost all other competitors (BAR being a notable exception), Ferrari lengthened the wheelbase. They did it for aerodynamic and weight reasons. The sidepods were lower than before and narrower than ever in the back to improve the airflow to the rear wing and the diffuser. This meant that both the tank and the gearbox/differential unit were reduced in width. Other new features were the asymmetric sidepods and the rear suspension. The rear wishbones were attached to the engine instead of the gearbox casing. That gave extra stiffness. Despite producing much better data than the F2002, the new car could not repeat the outstanding success of last year. The major factor was the weakness of the Bridgestone tyres in hot temperatures and on certain types of circuit. Slow corners, accelerating and braking favoured cars with Michelin-tyres.

F2003-GA TECHNICAL SPECIFICATIONS
ENGINE (052) **Ferrari V10 / 90 degree / 2997cc**
TRANSMISSION **Ferrari seven-speed semi-automatic gearbox**
CHASSIS **Carbon fibre**
SUSPENSION **Push-rod with torsion bar front and rear**
BRAKES **Brembo**
SHOCK ABSORBERS **Sachs**
WHEELS **BBS**
TYRES **Bridgestone Potenza**
ELECTRONICS **Magneti Marelli**

DIMENSIONS
WHEELBASE **3,100mm**
WEIGHT **600kg (including driver)**
TOTAL LENGTH **4,545mm**
FRONT TRACK **1,470mm**
REAR TRACK **1,405mm**

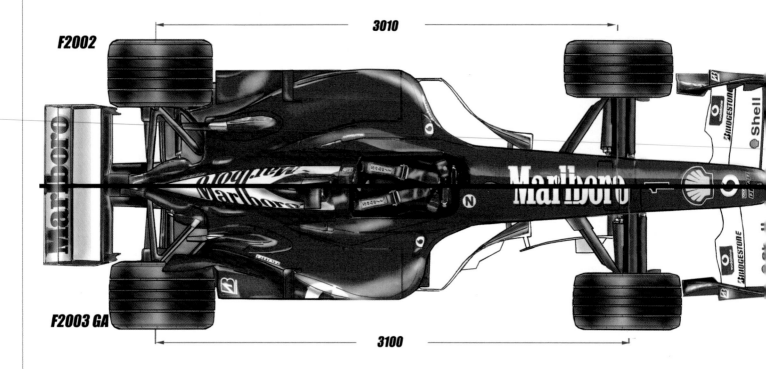

F2002

3010

F2003 GA

3100

THE WHEELBASE

The wheelbase was lengthened by five centimetres in comparison to the F2002. This moved the front wheels further forward to a section where the width of the chassis was no longer restricted by the rules. Although the chassis was only eight millimetres narrower than at the point where the old front suspension was, this meant a lot for Ferrari's aerodynamicist, Rory Byrne. He could get more air in between the front wheels and the chassis through to the undertray and the radiators. The cockpit moved a fraction backwards. That allowed the engineers to position the driver a bit lower in the car. The fuel tank's capacity was reduced by five percent, but the tank was no shorter. As Byrne wanted to have a narrow rear, he took away width from the tank. Logically the area between the front wheels and the sidepods increased. That gave more room to calm down the turbulent air coming off the front wheels. Inspired by McLaren, Ferrari later used double bargeboards to deal with the air coming from the front end of the car.

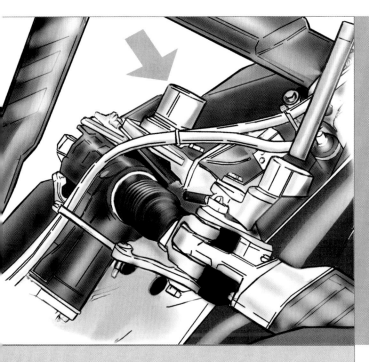

THE REAR SUSPENSION

The rear suspension was one of the best-kept secrets of the new Ferrari. In Monaco, the experts finally saw what Ferrari wanted to hide. In collaboration with Sachs, the team had developed a new rotational damper. The piston inside rotated instead of moving in a vertical axis. It brought a number of advantages: It took up less space, weighed less, and was more responsive. The rotational damper had many functions. It was used in the same location as the rocker for the push-rods and it included both the torsion bars and the third damper, which was mounted horizontally on top of the gearbox in between the two rotational dampers. The whole unit saved both space and 150 grams in weight. Due to reduced internal friction, the response was much quicker and the damping therefore more efficient. You could see that when the Ferrari went over kerbs and bumps, it swallowed them as if they were not there. And it used the rear tyres better, as they had improved contact with the road. The principle of a rotational damper was nothing new. Yamaha tried them on motorbikes, without success. The biggest problem was always avoiding leaks in the system. Costing five times more than a conventional component, this titamium cased technology did not come cheap.

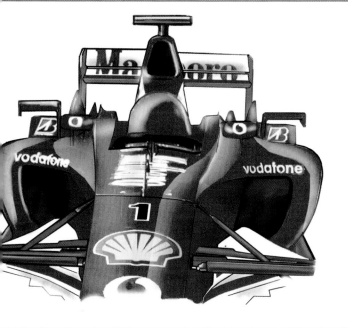

ASYMMETRIC SIDEPODS

It was hard to see, but the sidepods of the F2003-GA were not 100 percent identical. The right-hand pod was a bit lower than the one on the left, if you looked forwards from the rear of the car. The reason for that was because Ferrari strictly separated the water and oil radiator. It allowed two separate cooling circuits with better cooling results, and it saved weight due to fewer pipelines. Ferrari put the water radiators to the left. As they were taller than the oil radiators, that sidepod was a bit higher. On the oil side to the right, Ferrari's aerodynamicists demonstrated that Formula One technology is always taken to the extreme. The lower a sidepod, the better. Therefore they made it lower. The asymmetric design was no disadvantage.

In order to get the hot air out of the sidepods, the bodywork was fitted with different variations of gills. In Friday qualifying, when temperatures over one lap did not count, the sidepods were sometimes closed. For the races they opened both or, as in Barcelona, just one side. As oil temperatures were more critical on this type of circuit, the left-hand pod was fitted with the gills. In Monaco, where the water temperature was crucial, it was reversed.

BMW. WILLIAMSF1 TEAM

"**The early part of our year was worse than expected, and the** middle part better than we thought it would be. We had some problems with the FW25 in the beginning of the year, but I never lost confidence in the car. All the figures and the logic behind the new concept told us that it had to be a good car. It was just a matter of time to understand it. Another factor, which added to the improvements, was that we developed our abilities to test in the wind tunnel. Yaw, steer and different attitudes of the car were things we started to assess a long time ago, but they did not come on-stream until earlier this year. The standard of our model work has also become better, driven by John Davis. This has all has been beneficial to our aero department, now led by Antonia Terzi.

Obviously the Michelin tyres work much better than they did a year ago. I would not say they never suffer from graining any more, but they do not suffer in quite such a big way as they did in the past. We managed to produce a car which is no longer the heaviest on its tyres. We started our development work with the FW25 with a barge board concept, but we never got it to work well. Therefore we made the decision to go back to the FW24 guide-vanes. Another feature of the car is the much shorter wheelbase. It had consequences on the aerodynamics and the driving dynamics. Once we got over the teething problems, the shorter wheel base proved itself to be beneficial.

Since December 2002, we have been working towards an ongoing partnership with BMW. Both parties can say that they negotiated hard and came up with a mutually beneficial agreement. One of the principles we agreed on was how we operate together technically. In areas like electronics and transmission we have a close relationship. On the aerodynamic side there is room for improvement, but we have three guys from Munich working with us at the moment. As regards methodology, in many areas we have moved quite a long way towards using some of the methods that BMW apply. "

WILLIAMS TECHNICAL DEVELOPMENTS

The old rule, that a good racing car has to be quick out of the box, does not apply any more. If it has not already been proven wrong before, the Williams FW25 finally smashed this theory. BMW Williams Chief Operations Engineer Sam Michael thinks that modern technology has brought an end to that philosophy: "Nowadays a car is designed by a big group of people and there are a lot of calculations and wind tunnel work. You might not be quick from the first lap, but you have development programmes at hand, which deal with the problems." Williams had overturned all their design principles from the FW22, FW23, and FW24 family. The wheelbase has been shortened by approximately 15 centimetres, which is a lot in a modern Formula One car. Williams also reduced the tank capacity dramatically down to approximately 90 kilograms (120 litres). This came rather by accident than planning. Sam Michael admits: "At the time we had to decide about the tank, we did not know that the rules would change in favour of a smaller tank." Aerodynamically, Williams covered new ground. The FW25 had a slow start, but was developed more than any other car in the field. By Imola the engineers had understood the biggest mysteries, but the real breakthrough came in between Thursday and Saturday practice in Monaco. There the engineers found the settings that made a winning car out of what was perceived as a flop. Sam Michael translates that into laptimes: "If we compare the FW25 in Suzuka-spec with the version of the first test, we gained three seconds. And this is just in the car, without tyre development." Williams played the major role in Michelin's tyre programme. When Michelin presented a new family of tyres, at the Monaco GP, Williams were the only team to follow that up without compromise.

FW25 TECHNICAL SPECIFICATIONS
ENGINE (P83) **BMW V10 / 90 degree / 2998cc**
TRANSMISSION **Williams six-speed semi-automatic gearbox**
CHASSIS **Carbon fibre**
SUSPENSION **Push-rod with torsion bar front and rear**
BRAKES **Carbon Industrie / AP**
SHOCK ABSORBERS **WilliamsF1**
WHEELS **O.Z Racing**
TYRES **Michelin Pilot**
ELECTRONICS **BMW**

DIMENSIONS
WHEELBASE **Undisclosed**
WEIGHT **600kg (including driver)**
TOTAL LENGTH **Undisclosed**
FRONT TRACK **Maximum allowance**
REAR TRACK **Maximum allowance**

BARGEBOARDS

The Williams FW25 started with bargeboards mounted between the front wheels and the sidepods. After the initial test in Barcelona, they were replaced with an older concept - guide-vanes in the front suspension and a wing in front of the sidepods. The front wing and the bargeboards did not work in harmony. Patrick Head remembers: "When we tested the car first in that configuration, it was not unpleasant to drive, but it was just slow." From the second FW25 test in Jerez the Williams car drove with the guide-vanes and modified their shape a number of times during the season, including the final race at Suzuka. Generally the guide-vane concept gives more downforce at the front, whereas the other solution helps the diffusor to create more downforce. During the year McLaren and Ferrari combined both ideas. Sam Michael comments: "Our concept cannot be that bad if others copy parts of it." After staff changes in the aero-department and an updating of the windtunnel, Williams made big steps during the season. The improvement over the winter was about eight percent. During the season Antonia Terzis department, however, found around 15 percent in efficiency.

REAR BODYWORK DEVELOPMENT

The rear bodywork of the FW25 was one of the most frequently modified areas of the car throughout the season. The winglets placed on the top of the sidepods, the hot air vent chimneys, and of course the exhaust covers, were changed many times, providing at least five different configurations for the rear of the car. These were combined in various layouts according to the circuit's aerodynamics needs and (for the hot air vents) the heat conditions.

Another major change introduced in this area at the British Grand Prix, was a sort of shark dorsal fin placed on the top edge of the engine cover, extending for its entire length to the level of the rear wing support. In its rearmost section this fin featured an increased vertical extension, having the function of yaw control in corners with fast direction changes, such as the super-quick Becketts sequence at Silverstone.

This dorsal fin was kept for some of the following races, although at the German GP its rearmost extension was lower, to reduce the negative effects of a drag increase.

SHORTER WHEELBASE

The Williams FW22, FW23 and FW24 all had long wheelbases. With the FW25, Gavin Fisher's team went completely the opposite way. They shortened the wheelbase by well over 10 centimetres. It made the car more agile, it reduced the weight and, in turn, increased the amount of ballast available. More ballast means a lower centre of gravity. The shorter wheelbase had many side effects, and most of them were not easy to handle. Braking stability was more difficult to achieve. The car reacted differently at the apex of corners. The changed driving dynamics made it a tough job to learn the perfect set-ups for the FW25. The aerodynamics were affected as well, as all the dimensions relative to each other were different. Sam Michael explains: "You cannot just cut out a big piece of the chassis at the front and put the front wheels rearward. In this area you are restricted by the rules. You also do not want to have the front wheels too close to the sidepods. So you have to find a solution in the back where you can only play a little with the length of the engine and the gearbox." One area where Williams could cut something away was the fuel tank. The capacity decreased by an estimated 40 litres.

WEST McLAREN MERCEDES

"**Looking back over any race season is a time for reflection. 2003** has been a year of complex development work. We developed the MP4-17 into the MP4-17D, while at the same time building and developing the new car, the MP4-18. At McLaren we have a very strong technical team led by Adrian Newey with Mike Coughlan, Neil Oatley, Pat Fry, Paddy Lowe, Mark Williams and Tim Goss, so we had the resources to run two full programmes. But at the same time there has been an element of disappointment that the MP4-18 did not make its race debut.

The reality of the situation is that we over-estimated our performance deficit in relation to Ferrari, who obviously did a very competent job last year. In retrospect our desire to make big steps forward meant that we incorporated too many technical risks in the MP4-18 package. This ultimately caused us to take the decision to continue to develop the MP4-17.

When we conceived the MP4-18 we had no knowledge of the new racing format and the Parc Ferme conditions, or the new points scoring system and the unprecedented reliability of the principle Championship contenders this year, all of which slanted the car's requirements away from raw speed to serviceability and reliability. However, our future programme on the MP4-19 will benefit from the knowledge we have gained in working with the MP4-18.

Rules and regs? To be honest I'm not a big fan of this qualifying format. I think the drama of the final crescendo of the top drivers all going out in search of a last flying lap gave a sense of tension that is not present in this new format."

The technical review of McLaren-Mercedes is the story of two cars. On the one side there was the development of last year's MP4-17, on the other the somewhat unlucky career of the revolutionary MP4-18, which was destined to become one of the very few Formula One cars which never participated in a race.

Fortunately for McLaren, the updated MP4-17D was able to fight for the championship until the closing race of the season. In the first three races it was actually the dominant car. Development of the car to MP4-17D specification started at the end of the 2002 season, and a lot more work went into it over the winter. The new front suspension made its debut at the 2002 US Grand Prix. Before Christmas the car was running with a lighter and stiffer gearbox and a revised rear suspension. Very late before the start of the 2003 season, project leader Neil Oatley and his team introduced W-profile wings. Helped by a power gain of almost 50 bhp, the McLaren MP4-17D-soon became a winning car. Parallel to the tests with the MP4-18, McLaren developed the MP4-17D even further. For Monza the engineers merged the rear aerodynamics of the new car with the old one. Meanwhile, McLaren abandoned plans to race the MP4-18, mainly because of reliability problems and, it was rumoured, shortcomings with chassis strength. About 5100 test kilometres were completed, but the car failed a few crash tests and due to the very tight packaging of its bodywork it suffered from overheating. Kimi Raikkonen and Alexander Wurz had big shunts, which further delayed the development process. On pure lap times the MP4-18 showed significant progress compared to the old car, and will form the basis for 2004's MP4-19.

MP4-14D TECHNICAL SPECIFICATIONS
ENGINE (F0110M) **Mercedes-Benz V10 / 90 degree / Approx: 3000 cc**
TRANSMISSION **McLaren seven-speed semi-automatic gearbox**
CHASSIS **Carbon fibre**
SUSPENSION **Push-rod with torsion bar front and rear**
BRAKES **Penske / McLaren**
SHOCK ABSORBERS **Enkei**
WHEELS **BBS**
TYRES **Michelin Pilot**
ELECTRONICS **TAG Electronic Systems**

DIMENSIONS
WHEELBASE **Undisclosed**
WEIGHT **600 kg (including driver)**
TOTAL LENGTH **Undisclosed**
FRONT TRACK **Undisclosed**
REAR TRACK **Undisclosed**

W-PROFILE WINGS

In the final pre-season test the McLaren MP4-17D ran with a wing profile never seen before, reminiscent of a W shape. The middle part of the wing was the lowest, then the plane rose slightly before going downwards close to the endplates. From a front view the wing shape followed the lines of the car. McLaren introduced this type of wing both front and rear. The latter used a double plane for high-downforce circuits. It was not long before other teams started to copy the principle; Williams at the front, Sauber, Renault and BAR at the rear. The W-wings were originally part of the MP4-18 concept, and McLaren Technical Director Adrian Newey used the MP4-17 D as a test-bed for them. "We developed the idea towards the end of the 2002 season," he explained, "but we decided not to run it during the winter tests, so it wasn't in the public eye. This type of wing improves the efficiency. As you could see from 2003's top speeds, our car was always among the fastest." One characteristic of the W-wing was to minimise the traditional losses of downforce at the edges between the main plane and the endplates. This is a critical area because of the different airflows.

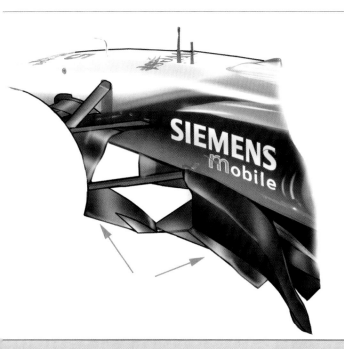

DOUBLE BARGEBOARDS

McLaren were the first team to use bargeboards. In 1993 the MP4-8 had Bargeboards between the front wheels and the sidepods. The bargeboard is not a device that creates downforce, but one that cleans up the air which flows underneath the car. The diffuser gets the benefit of it, which results in more downforce. Over the years, engineers have become divided over two philosophies. Some developed the classic bargeboards in all kinds of shapes. Others moved these deflectors forward into the front suspension and called them guide-vanes. This puts more emphasis on front-end downforce.

McLaren were the first team to combine both ideas. They mounted little guide-vanes at the bottom of the twin chassis keels and kept the bargeboards. Newey said: "We chose the tandem version mainly to improve the cooling." The problem of having the two devices in a row is that the second one gets the air disturbed by the first and therefore partly loses its efficiency. Just like one car following the other in a slipstream 'tow'. McLaren obviously found a good solution to minimise that effect. Newey: "As long as you do your research and optimise it, it is not too much of a problem. After all, any aircraft has two wings running in tandem." As do these race cars.

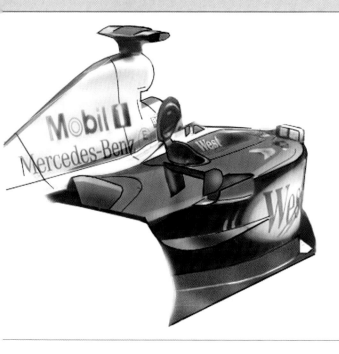

MERGING THE REAR BODYWORK OF MP4-18 WITH MP4-17D

For the Italian Grand Prix, McLaren introduced their biggest development step of the year. New rear bodywork borrowed many details from the MP4-18. The sidepods were lower and had the same cut-in ahead of the rear wheels. The exit for the hot air was just in front of the little winglet, which had a twisted plate. The flip-up had the same shape as the MP4-18, and the same diffuser was used.

Ilmor Engine boss Mario Illien revised both the injection and the exhaust system of his FO110M-engine. The new spec version had 16 further bhp with decreased fuel consumption. Apart from the changes to the engine, the other mechanical components underneath the bodywork - the gearbox and rear suspension - were unchanged. Adrian Newey reported a significant step forward: "In Monza we lost 0.3 seconds a lap to Ferrari and Williams. Without these modifications we would not have been able to be so close on that type of circuit." The potential of this update was shown in Indianapolis, where the McLaren MP4-17D was clearly the best compromise between top speed on the oval section and downforce in the infield.

MILD SEVEN RENAULT F1 TEAM

We got our new chassis out earlier than we had ever done before, actually running it for the first time on November 26 2002. There were two reasons behind this: First, to get enough test mileage on the engine, the transmission and the chassis before the start of the season, and second to give ourselves more time to develop the aerodynamic package, which we only put on the car as late as February. We already had a reasonably good aero package in 2002, but the R23 represented a big step forward. The only limitation over the winter was a lack of engines due to some serious reliability problems. When we went to Australia, we were not confident of finishing the race, but the weak spots were sorted out at the very last minute. The first long run on the dyno was only completed on the Thursday before the Australian Grand Prix.

As we progressed through the season, we introduced detailed aerodynamic changes at almost every race. A B-version of the car, with a new aerodynamic package, was introduced at Silverstone. Furthermore, the engine guys got on top of the problems during the first part of the season so that, by Suzuka, we ran our eighth major variation of engine spec. All the different parts of the team have stepped up and produced a solid level of development over the year. We maintained our level of competitiveness throughout the season and were only overtaken by Williams, who began the year at a very low point. In this, we have certainly been helped by Michelin, who had the dominant tyre in the dry. The rule allowing each team to run individual tyres also benefited us, as on several occasions we were able to run softer compounds and different constructions to our rivals, which suited our car a little bit better.

The decision to opt for two hours extra practice on Friday morning also paid off and gave us a good advantage at many of the circuits. We studied it very carefully and for our team, with the resources we had available, it was the right thing to do. We have not got the money to do 100 days of testing a year like some other teams. Looking back on the year, I have to say that finishing fourth is not where our ambitions lie. It was not a bad and not a great season, but it was a solid fourth place and we had the satisfaction of being able to compete for race wins. The next step we have to take is difficult, but I believe it is within our reach.

The Renault R23 is one of those racing cars that doesn't overtly display its potential by being a spectacular design. You always tended to ask yourself: Why is this car so quick? The secret was in its detail. The R23 was probably the best car in terms of aerodynamic efficiency. It had the lowest centre of gravity due to the wide angle engine concept and it provided the drivers with excellent mechanical grip. Without doubt, Renault's launch control system was the class of the field. The weak point was the lack of power from the Renault engine. Maybe it was not as much as 100 bhp, as some speculated, but it was definitely between 50 and 70 bhp. You just have to look at the revs. The maximum at the shifting points were 17,500 rpm. The BMW V10 reached as much as 19,100 rpm. The lack of power was offset by advantages such as lower fuel consumption. On most of the circuits the Renault could go a lap longer with the same fuel load as others.

The car had very good traction, because its control systems worked very well. On top of that, the car was very kind to its tyres. Symonds: "Partly because we hadn't the strongest engine in the field, that sometimes allowed us to use softer compounds than our competitors." The careful treatment of the tyres was helpful for the race but sometimes a handicap in qualifying. Especially in the Friday practice sessions with a low fuel load, Renault struggled to generate the right tyre temperatures as quickly as their rivals. Renault opted for the restriction to 20 test days in exchange for two hours of testing on Friday morning. In particular on circuits where testing was not possible, that turned out to be a big advantage. One of them was Hungary, where Renault celebrated pole position and its first victory as a car maker for 20 years.

R23B TECHNICAL SPECIFICATIONS
ENGINE (RS23) **Renault V10 / 110 degree / 2998cc**
TRANSMISSION **Renault six-speed semi-automatic gearbox**
CHASSIS **Carbon fibre**
SUSPENSION **Push-rod with torsion bar front and rear**
BRAKES **HITCO / AP**
SHOCK ABSORBERS **Penske**
WHEELS **O.Z Racing**
TYRES **Michelin Pilot**
ELECTRONICS **Magneti Marelli**

DIMENSIONS
WHEELBASE **3,100mm**
WEIGHT **600kg (including driver)**
TOTAL LENGTH **4,600mm**
FRONT TRACK **1,450mm**
REAR TRACK **1,400mm**

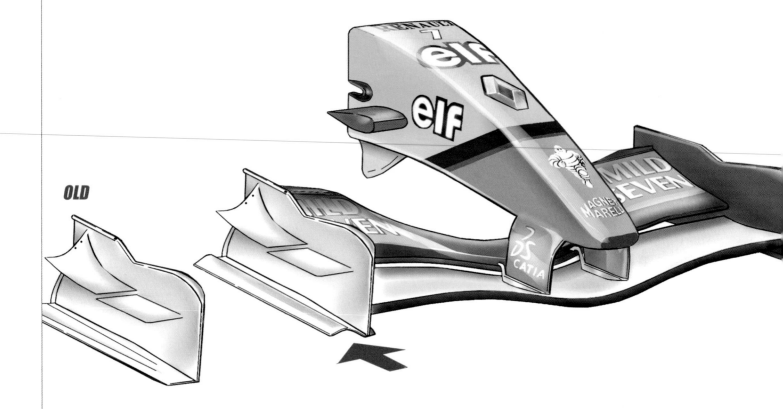

OLD

FRONT WING

The front wing was the part of the Renault R23 that was most emulated by the competition. In particular the endplates with their curved foot plates. Both McLaren and Ferrari tried similar solutions. These endplates helped to make the aerodynamics more efficient and less sensitive towards changes in the car's ride height. Counting all the flap and endplate configurations, Renault tried nine different front wing variations in 2003.

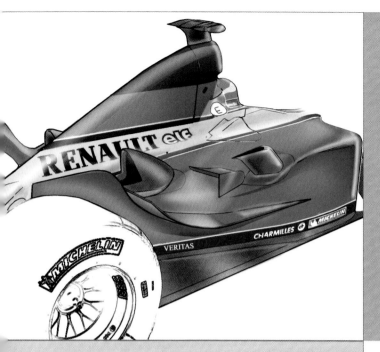

SILVERSTONE B-VERSION

The work towards the aero-update in Silverstone started in February. The last bits left the wind tunnel by the beginning of June. Renault had modified the top bodywork, the undertray including the diffuser, and the front wing. There were also changes to the rear wing, which could not be used, as Silverstone required a different downforce level. All the changes increased the aerodynamic efficiency. Pat Symonds explained the qualities of the car: "The R23 was aerodynamically extremely efficient. It liked fast and medium fast corners and quick changes of direction." The brilliance of the car's aerodynamics were demonstrated at the low downforce circuit in Montreal. Against all forecasts, Alonso could not only follow the leaders, but even managed to set the fastest lap time. Symonds: "Due to the lack of fast corners, it was possible to run less downforce without any negative consequences." In Budapest the engineers applied a different approach. They set-up Alonso's car to provide more downforce than the competition. The idea was to give up further top speed for speed in the corners. As Alonso was so fast in the last corner, he could defend himself easily on the main straight. Although the Renault was among the slowest in all four speed traps, it was producing consistently the fastest lap times.

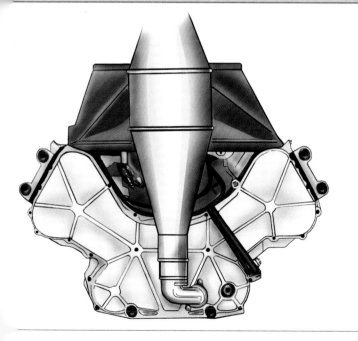

LOW CENTRE OF GRAVITY ENGINE CONCEPT

A racing car is always a compromise. Renault's engine, with a suspected cylinder angle of 110 degrees, offered advantages and disadvantages. It certainly helped to have a car with a low centre of gravity and low rear bodywork. On the other hand the unit produced a lot of vibrations. Components around it had to be made a bit stronger and this added weight. The engine lacked not only top-end power but also mid-range torque. And it needed good ideas to install the low V10 in the car from a structural point of view. The wide angle demanded solutions in order to guarantee vertical stiffness. As the 2004 rules require engines to last for a whole Grand Prix weekend, Renault had to give up the experiment with their wide-angle V10. Due to shortness of time, Renault will start the season with an engine whose basic architecture will closely resemble the Supertec V10, which means an angle of 71 degrees. This V10 will be updated with technologies from the current engine. After the three overseas grand prix, Renault will debut an all-new narrow-angle engine.

LUCKY STRIKE BAR HONDA

In terms of design, structural integrity and engineering quality the BAR Honda 005 was a much better racing car than its predecessor. The chassis was significantly lighter and passed all its crash tests without problems. The car was simpler, had fewer parts, a much lower centre of gravity and was easier to work on. Aerodynamically we made, over the winter, a step of at least one and a half years' worth of development and almost as much again throughout the season.

The Honda engine was smaller, lighter and produced more power than the previous one right from the start of the season. It was continuously updated from the initial step one engine to step eight at Suzuka. The whole package, therefore, resulted in a much better racing car. On the negative side we had too many realiability issues. This is possibly because we did not complete enough testing mileage over the winter. Before the season started we completed 7000 to 8000 kilometres of testing, whereas the top teams had done over 25,000 kilometres. Most of the problems we faced were small, such as faulty sensors or the leak from a brake crossover pipe, but we also had gearbox problems and problems with the engine and control-systems. Had we had more running over the winter, we would have seen most of these problems earlier, in testing, rather than in the race events.

As Bridgestone runners, our benchmark has always been Ferrari. The tyre situation has changed from last year. In 2002 Michelin had a very strong tyre in qualifying whereas Bridgestone clearly had the better race tyre. It was obvious to us from pre-season testing that Michelin had caught up a lot in that area and, maybe, Bridgestone reacted a little bit late. As a result we were struggling in mid-season, particularly on low grip-circuits. Would we go for a wider front tyre? We definitely would. In some ways we have worked better with Bridgestone than Ferrari and we have already started a programme with different constructions and compounds, which will be one of the major tasks over the winter.

If we had known the new rules when we designed the car, we would have probably built a smaller fuel tank. Considering the effect on strategy, it took us a few races to adapt fully to the fact, that you have to qualify in race trim. Two-stop strategies became a norm with three stops on limited occasions. I think we got it right in most cases this year.

During the first four years, BAR produced a quite bulky and big car. The new technical director Geoff Willis put an end to it. It was not a surprise that the 005 shared similarities with recent Williams designs. Former Williams aerodynamicist Willis adopted the long wheelbase, the guide-vane concept and the split of water and oil radiators over the two sidepods. Although the BAR is the longest car in the pitlane, Willis was able to reduce the overall weight by 10 percent, mainly in the chassis area. The aero department improved the efficiency by a big margin, but even more so the stability. Stiffness has been increased and the centre of gravity lowered. This made the BAR a car which was kind to its tyres. At the beginning of the year BAR were using stiffer construction techniques than Ferrari. Later, Bridgestone convinced BAR that it was better for them if all their clients followed the same route. Quite often the Japanese tyre manufacturer seemed to lose direction by bringing up to eight different types of tyres for their five teams. In order to judge the true potential, BAR was looking at Ferrari. Taking the fastest lap in the race as a comparison, in 2003 BAR gained 0.9 seconds per lap over the 2002 spec car, the 004. A major contribution towards this was thanks to a 60 bhp gain from Honda during the season. The Honda V10 is still quite big and heavy, but in power it was not far off the top engines. The 900 bhp barrier was cracked.

BAR005 TECHNICAL SPECIFICATIONS
ENGINE (RA003E) **Honda V10 / 90 degree /Approx: 3000cc.**
TRANSMISSION **BAR seven-speed semi-automatic gearbox**
CHASSIS **Carbon fibre**
SUSPENSION **Push-rod with torsion bar front and rear**
BRAKES **AP**
SHOCK ABSORBERS **Koni**
WHEELS **BBS**
TYRES **Bridgestone Potenza**
ELECTRONICS **Pi / Athena**

DIMENSIONS
WHEEL BASE **3,140mm**
WEIGHT **600 / 605kg (including driver)**
TOTAL LENGTH **4,465mm**
FRONT TRACK **1,460mm**
REAR TRACK **1,420mm**

GUIDE VANES

Geoff Willis kept his concept of the guide-vanes. The aero-team did some tests with classic bargeboards, but they could not find a promising solution. Willis explains: "We faced problems with the aerodynamic stability, which was one of the major problems of last year's car the BAR 004." In fact BAR was introducing guide-vanes already in Canada 2002. On the old car they used two little vanes, mounted at the bottom of the chassis. The support went downwards, the endplates upwards. The BAR 005 solution was the other way around with a much neater finish. Again, the support was attached to the lower edge of the chassis, but in a 90 degree angle. The endplates were hanging down.

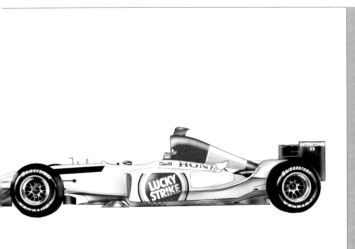

LONG WHEELBASE CONCEPT

BAR shortened the wheelbase in comparison to last years car, but still had a longer one than any other car in the pitlane. The main reason to stick to that, whereas most of the competitors were favouring shorter cars, was the aero-stability. Willis: "Although I was pretty sure what the problems of the old car were, I wasn't 100 percent certain. Therefore I wanted to be on the safe side, rather than risk anything with a much shorter wheelbase." In fact the BAR005 turned out to be a car which was easy to drive - and predictable for the men in the cockpit. Both Jenson Button and Jacques Villeneuve had, compared with most of the other drivers, fewer spins and accidents when in race trim. For Willis, the downsides of the long wheelbase were less important than the benefits. "A longer car adds a little bit of weight, but in our case it was no more than two kilograms. We probably had more trouble with understeer than other teams on some circuits, but all in all it cost us not more than one or two tenths. However, if you go too short with it, you can easily lose three quarters of a second." The long wheelbase allowed them to put the driver lower in the cockpit as well as to lower the tank. Both helped to bring down the centre of gravity dramatically.

NEW BODYWORK

At Silverstone BAR presented half of a new car. It was the result of three months of work. In lap-time it was worth three tenths. Jacques Villeneuve immediately said: "The car is balanced much more neutrally after these changes." The whole rear bodywork changed. The engine cover was lower, which improved the airflow to the lower rear wing element. The sidepods came in sharper, which allowed more air to go through inside the rear wheels and the bodywork. The winglet in front of the rear tyres had a different shape. Instead of having just one support, it formed a tunnel with the upper of the two flip-ups. This gave extra stiffness and directed the air more efficiently into the area where the exhaust pipes were exiting in relatively low chimneys. In summary, it accelerated the airflow. The roll structure was modified for three reasons. There was a gain in weight of 700 grams at the highest point of the car, an aerodynamic advantage and the modified shape of the airbox helped Honda to find a bit more power. The modification made it necessary to pass the structural test of the roll-hoop again. With the rear wing, the team positioned the endplate with both upper wings in line, in order to minimise the losses due to turbulences at the edge of the endplate and the main plate.

SAUBER PETRONAS

We started this season with a not very satisfactory performance level. On one side we faced a few reliability problems with our engine which on occasion cost us valuable track time in practice. On the other hand the car was not quick enough. We managed to maintain the gap between ourselves and the top teams, but our closest rivals had caught up over the winter. Therefore we fell back in the ranking.

We therefore initiated an ambitious development programme on the aerodynamic side, starting with the front wing. This caused most of the problems in the early part of the season, as we struggled to find a good balance and turn-in with the car. As a result the C22 was difficult to drive. Once we got over those problems, we modified the undertray and the rear part of the car with promising results. The new rear bodywork brought the biggest performance step. Since Silverstone, we were able to improve the car continuously with many detailed changes. In addition, we tried new front suspension geometries and new settings of dampers and springs, which we worked out on our seven-post-rig. The target was to use the tyres better over a long distance. Until then we had acceptable results in qualifying, but could not repeat that performance in the races. We got over this weakness mainly by finding better set-ups.

The positive aspect for me was that we solved most of the problems with restricted resources. With hindsight it would probably have been better to join the Heathrow-testing teams. There were a few occasions where the teams who tested two extra hours on Friday mornings benefited from that. The new rules did not affect us too much. We adapted very quickly to new race strategies. In fact Sauber was one of the first teams to do short first stints. The grid position is more important than the ability to run longer in the first stint.

The technical story of Sauber in 2003 was very much a story of
their wind tunnel. The tunnel at Emmen was built in 1948. Until 2001 it
delivered quite good results. But in the last two years there were no
more huge gains to find by any single modification. Instead it was a
matter of the addition of small improvements on the detail. In Formula
One today, a tunnel needs to be good enough to measure steps even
as small as half a point. This was the area where the old Sauber tunnel
reached its limit. Another problem was that in the tunnel at Emmen you
can only turn the front wheels on the running belt to a maximum of three
degrees. When Sauber booked two weeks in the Lola wind tunnel, they
were able to turn the front wheels to seven degrees. It was as late as
July that they found the true reason why their front wing was producing
good data in the ideal configuration, but lost massive downforce when
the car was cornering.

A series of changes helped Sauber to make significant steps forward
in the second half of the season. They started with a new rear wing at the
Nürburgring, followed by double barge-boards in Hockenheim and a
tighter engine cover for Monza. As a compensation for the hard work,
Sauber earned 10 points at Indianapolis, the biggest ever payday in the
Swiss team's Formula One history. Although rain and the superiority of
the Bridgestone tyres in these conditions helped, it became apparent
that the Sauber C22 had also made progress in the dry. "Our guideline",
Peter Sauber said, "was always BAR. By the end of the season we got
pretty close. Sometimes we were even able to beat them."

C22 TECHNICAL SPECIFICATIONS
ENGINE (03A) **Petronas (Ferrari) V10 / 90 degree / 2997cc**
TRANSMISSION **Sauber seven-speed semi-automatic gearbox**
CHASSIS **Carbon fibre**
SUSPENSION **Push-rod with torsion bar front and rear**
BRAKES **Brembo**
SHOCK ABSORBERS **Sachs**
WHEELS **O.Z Racing**
TYRES **Bridgestone Potenza**
ELECTRONICS **Magneti Marelli**

DIMENSIONS
WHEEL BASE **3,100mm**
WEIGHT **600kg (including driver)**
TOTAL LENGTH **4,470mm**
FRONT TRACK **1,470mm**
REAR TRACK **1,410mm**

NEW BODYWORK AT MONZA

Just before the Italian Grand Prix, Sauber introduced rear bodywork which borrowed inspiration from Ferrari. The bodywork was lower in the back and in the wind tunnel showed a significant step forward in efficiency. It improved the airflow to the lower main plane of the rear wing. The winglets produced downforce and guided the air away from the rear tyres. A tighter package resulted in less space for the radiators underneath the bodywork, so there was a danger of overheating. In order to avoid that, Sauber cut Ferrari-style gills into the sidepods to draw out the hot air.

The next obstacle to overcome was finding the right aerodynamic balance. After Heidfeld had a testing shunt at Monza, the new version was not deemed to have been tested sufficiently. When Sauber tried it again in Friday practice they discovered far too much rear downforce, which they could not balance out with the front wing. Therefore they were forced to go back temporarily to the old solution. Willy Rampf anticipated that the balance problem would only occur in low downforce trim. At Indianapolis, where higher downforce levels are needed, the cars were well balanced.

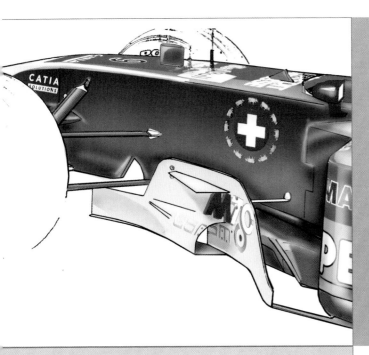

BARGEBOARD-DEVELOPMENT

In Hockenheim Sauber had new bargeboards which extended forwards. The front section built a kind of tunnel with the main bargeboard, which had a little horizontal fin at the top. With this solution it was possible to catch the turbulent air at an earlier point in order to improve the airflow underneath the car. These guide-vanes did not create any downforce directly. The front wing dictates what quantity of air hits the back of the car. Sauber produced more than 10 front wing variations during the year. They experimented with the ride height and the width of the main plane. Willy Rampf said: "The trend is to have a smaller main plane and endplates just inboard of the tyres."

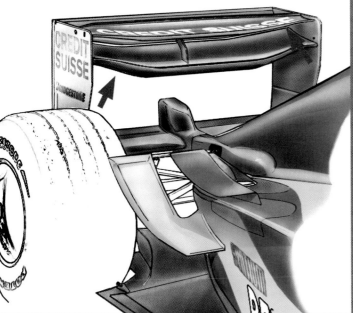

REAR WING DEVELOPMENT

At the Nürburgring Sauber changed the rear wing profile. It had the shape of a W, just like McLaren's and Renault's. Due to a lack of time and the non-availability of their own wind tunnel for a few more months, Sauber relied completely on results from the CFD. So the wing was fitted to the car before it was tested in the wind tunnel. And it worked. The purpose of the twisted profile was to increase the aero-stability at the rear. It put more emphasis on the downforce, which is created in the middle part of the wing rather than the sides near to the endplates. These areas are critical when the car is not going straight or if there is a sidewind. The middle part of the wing always gets an unspoiled airflow, no matter what the car's yaw angle might be.

DR MARK GILLAN HEAD OF VEHICLE PERFORMANCE

JAGUAR RACING

In 2003 we completely revamped our trackside operations, which has stabilised the engineering side of Jaguar Racing. There are no superstars, just people who get on with the job. There are four engineering groups; Vehicle Performance; Vehicle Design; Aerodynamics and Vehicle Science. Above these groups we have Malcolm Oastler who is our Chief Engineer, and Ian Pocock who is Director of Engineering.

This year's car, the R4, is significantly better than the R3 and we finally have a sound basis from which to develop next year's car, the R5. Our main disappointment was Silverstone. We struggled with trying to get the best from the chassis and tyres, but then we found the answer and started to make progress, which has been apparent in the last few races. Mark Webber has done a great job this year and Justin Wilson has also fitted in very well, earning his first well deserved point at Indianapolis.

Our participation in the Heathrow Agreement has been a great success. We have two hours on the track on Friday mornings to prepare the car and sort out any problems. Renault have run a third car for long runs doing tyre development and race preparation, and I think that is something we need to look at for 2004.

Surprises? Michelin's continual improvement throughout the season. They have been fantastic. I was surprised by how much Williams improved during the year, and also surprised that McLaren did not run the MP4-18. Development of a car that hasn't made it is a very expensive business.

Jaguar started pretty late with the design of the R4. The reason for this was that first of all they had to trace the problems of the R3. That took until September 2002. Mainly the R3 was weak in torsional stiffness and aerodynamic efficiency. The structural weaknesses never permitted a clear judgement of how good or bad the R3 really was. Therefore the design team chose to wait until the final results from a rig test in Cologne confirmed that the old car was too weak torsionally both in the front and the rear.

Taking into account that the design office was upgraded with engineers from McLaren, Renault, Arrows and BAR, and therefore had only worked a few months as a unit, they delivered a remarkable result. It was no surprise that radical solutions were missing. Any adventurous solution would have been a big risk. "Back to the basics", as Mark Gillan would say. So the engineers took over the good points of the R3 by eliminating the bad ones. Compared with the R3 in early 2002 guise they found 16 percent more downforce. One of the targets was to get more out of the Michelin tyres. The designers also got a present from the engine department. Cosworth changed the new CR-5's cylinder angle from 72 to 90 degrees, which as a consequence helped to lower the centre of gravity. Due to reliability problems the maximum revs were restricted to 18,200 rpm, which was substantially less then the targeted 19,000 rpm.

The season started with quite a few technical problems such as a mysterious fuel pick-up problem. This obliged Jaguar in the first three races to use 15 to 20 kilos more fuel than they would have liked. Gillan blamed these initial problems on the team's limited test mileage over the winter. Because of a tight budget, Jaguar opted for the so-called 'Heathrow' testing solution, allowing them to test for two hours on Friday morning on each of the circuits.

R4 TECHNICAL SPECIFICATIONS
ENGINE (CR-5) **Cosworth V10 / 90 degree / 2998cc**
TRANSMISSION **Jaguar seven-speed semi-automatic gearbox**
CHASSIS **Carbon fibre**
SUSPENSION **Push rod with torsion bar front and rear**
BRAKES **Brembo / AP**
SHOCK ABSORBERS **Jaguar / Penske**
WHEELS **O.Z Racing**
TYRES **Michelin Pilot**
ELECTRONICS **Pi**

DIMENSIONS
WHEELBASE **Undisclosed**
WEIGHT **600kg (including driver)**
TOTAL LENGTH **Undisclosed**
FRONT TRACK **Undisclosed**
REAR TRACK **Undisclosed**

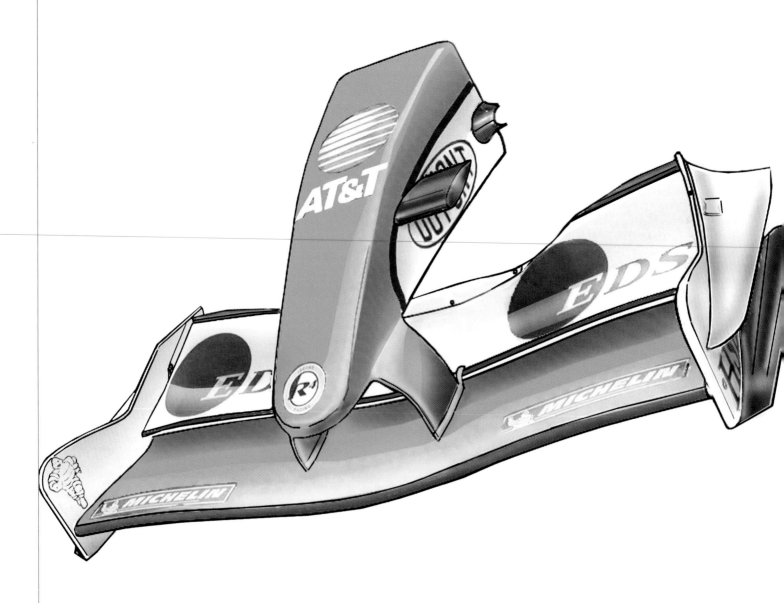

FRONT SUSPENSION

One month of rig testing in Cologne in the late summer of 2002 proved that the Jaguar R3 lacked torsional stiffness. The front of the car was 55 percent less stiff than it should have been. This was partly due to the carbon fibre material that Jaguar sourced from Japan, and partly due to bad design. So the design team decided to build a much simpler package that was stiffer, easy to set up and easy to work on. This had priority over the aerodynamic advantage of the twin-keel solution. The new front suspension on the R4 followed the classic single-keel philosophy. By Barcelona, Jaguar introduced a modified version of the front suspension that gave further improved stiffness and helped to use the tyres better. The anti-dive characteristics were also changed to help Antonio Pizzonia.

The Brazilian struggled with the nervous back end of the car. Pizzonia explained that his driving style was different to Mark Webber's. He liked to carry the speed into the corner and needed a car that was really stable under braking. After the changes to the suspension the handling definitely improved.

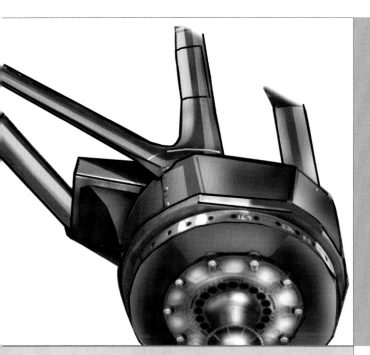

REAR SUSPENSION

The Jaguar R3 also had a problem with torsional stiffness at the back end of the car. This was less a problem within the rear suspension and more to do with the connecting points between chassis and engine and the engine and gearbox. The rear uprights were still flexing too much even after an initial redesign. In order to sort that out, Jaguar focussed on these weak points. The programme started in 2002. By Silverstone that year they changed from a multi-link suspension to a conventional system with double wishbones. At Spa 2002 they introduced titanium cast uprights to improve stiffness. The R4's rear suspension was only a slightly modified version and was still rather old-fashioned, with three shock absorbers and the third element mounted longitudinally instead of transversely. On some occasions, notably in Brazil, the R4 was working its rear tyres too hard. Mark Gillan explained: "We invested a lot of work in order to find out the reason for that. Due to the limited testing it was not easy, but by the British Grand Prix we had found an answer." In Monza, for example, the engineers corrected it with a lot of downforce, but this cost 32 kph on the straight. Nevertheless, Mark Webber managed to score two points.

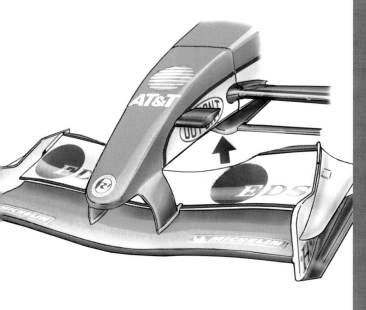

FRONT WING

Chief aerodynamicist Ben Agathangelou worked previously for Renault and details in the front wing design betrayed that fact, such as the twist in the main plane and the flap as well as the shape of the endplates. Also the wing hung on relatively short supports as the logical consequence of having a low-nose concept. According to Mark Gillan, the starting point of the design was very similar, but from then on went in a different direction. "We adapted it to the R4 design package quite a lot."

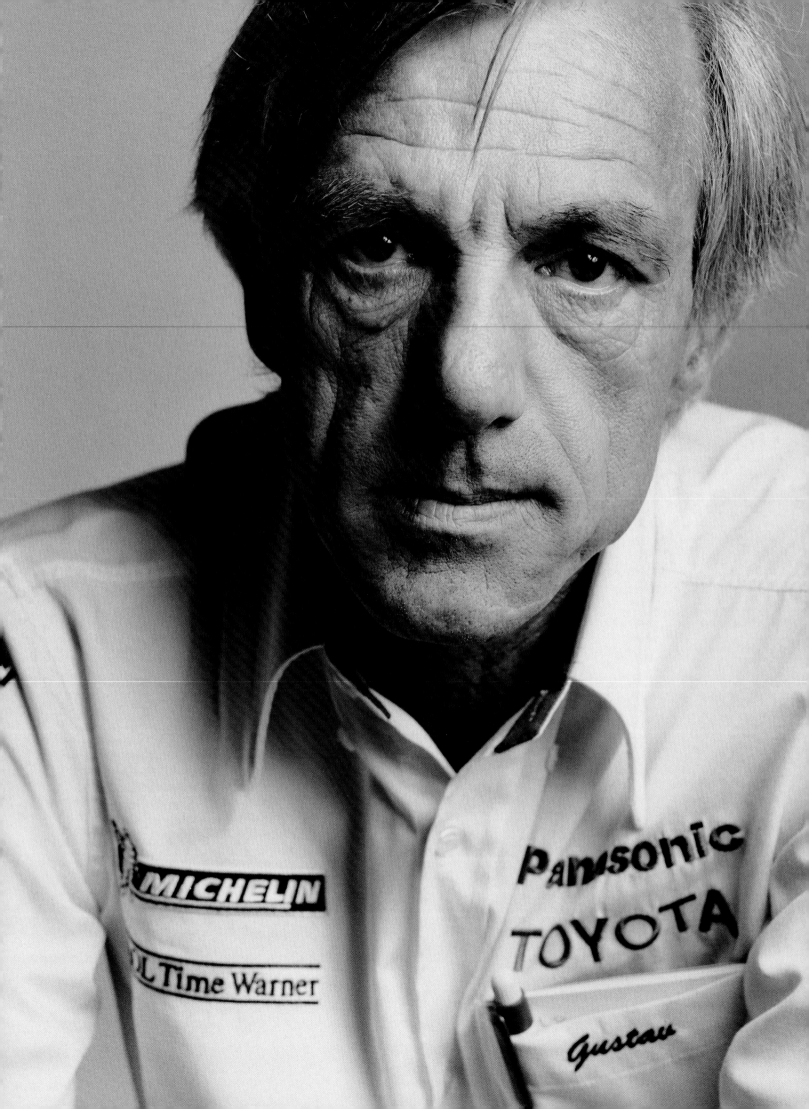

PANASONIC TOYOTA RACING

"**From Toyota's point of view we did not quite reach our target of** 20 points, but we were pretty happy though. In comparison to last year we managed to make good improvements both on the engine and the car, mainly in the aerodynamics department. In 2002 we dropped back after a good start to the season. This time we had a consistent development programme which resulted in a promising performance at the end of the year. In particular, the qualifying results both in Indianapolis and Suzuka demonstrated our progress. Many people thought that Olivier's third place on the grid at Indy was a 'show-time' with little fuel on board, but I can tell you that we had 60 kilos in the tank.

We also improved the car significantly in terms of stiffness, weight, engineering quality and the understanding of the set-up. Mechanically the Toyota TF103 was a very solid car. We constantly modified the suspension, the uprights and the brakes. Toyota is a young team. Our wind tunnel only became operational in June 2002 and was updated during this season to fulfill our latest requirements. Despite this handicap we delivered encouraging aerodynamic progress, which makes us confident for 2004 where we need to make another big step forward. We are also quite satisfied with the fact that we had no structural problems. For a car manufacturer like Toyota, who are so proud of the reliability of their road cars, it wouldn't have been acceptable to see their cars breaking down in every race. We finished fifth in the ranking of the completed race laps. Most of the reliability issues were stupid ones such as a fuel pick-up problem, which cost us the first two races.

Unfortunately, we always tested over the winter in cold conditions and were caught out in the first two hot events. Another problem we had to address was that very often in free practice sessions we were able to do quick lap times, which we could not repeat in qualifying. This was more a human issue. Toyota are a big team with a lot of expectations. Sometimes the drivers struggled to stand up to this pressure. By mid-season we were fighting with high wear of the rear tyres. This had to do with too much aero-balance at the front. So during the race the rear tyres slid, overheated and lost grip, which made the car oversteer. That was corrected quickly. We trimmed the cars more to understeer and made some changes to the traction control system."

When Toyota launched their new TF103, many people saw it as a red and white Ferrari. In fact there were many similarities to last year's F2002. Chief designer Gustav Brunner does not see any problem with that. "Obviously you are influenced more by the best car in the field than by the slowest. To say that it is a 100 percent copy, however, is unfair. That would not work as we are running on Michelin tyres and the Ferrari on Bridgestones. That means that we could never use a 1:1 copy of their aerodynamics, given the fact that the shape of the Michelin tyres was different."

After promising test results over the winter, the start of the season was something of a disappointment. Problems with the fuel pick-up and the gearbox cost points in the first few races. In Imola the car showed its weaknesses. Chief engineer Norbert Kreyer explained the early troubles: "We had a problem riding over bumps and kerbs. Circuits where you had to brake hard and turn into tight chicanes were like poison for our car." One of the reasons for that was a lack of aerodynamic stability. Toyota got it right with constant updates through the season, the biggest ones in Barcelona, Silverstone and Monza. On tracks with long corners such as Barcelona and Silverstone, the TF103 showed good speed. "Maybe we tested over the winter a bit too much in Barcelona and got misled by the results," Kreyer mused. In the second half of the season Toyota were almost constantly running in the top 10, though it did not always translate that speed into points. The engine, which gained three percent over the season from four development steps, gave no problems. With maximum revs of 18,800 rpm the Toyota V10 reached a similar level to Ferrari. Despite all the improvements there is still a lot to do. Kreyer commented "Under normal circumstances we lost 0.6 to 0.8 seconds compared to the fastest cars. That meant that we relied on them having problems in order to score points. It is our task for 2004 to build a car capable of ending up in the points on its own merit."

TF103 TECHNICAL SPECIFICATIONS
ENGINE (RVX-03) **Toyota V10 / 90 degree / 2998cc**
TRANSMISSION **Toyota seven-speed semi-automatic gearbox**
CHASSIS **Carbon fibre**
SUSPENSION **Push-rod with torsion bar front and rear**
BRAKES **Brembo**
SHOCK ABSORBERS **Sachs**
WHEELS **BBS**
TYRES **Michelin Pilot**
ELECTRONICS **Magneti Marelli**

DIMENSIONS
WHEEL BASE **3,090mm**
WEIGHT **600kg (including driver)**
TOTAL LENGTH **4,547mm**
FRONT TRACK **1,424mm**
REAR TRACK **1,411mm**

SILVERSTONE AERO UPDATE

The biggest modification during the year on the Toyota TF103 was presented at Silverstone. In three months the aerodynamics team under René Hilhorst changed the front wing, the engine cover, the sidepods, the bargeboards, the undertray and the exhaust chimneys. The arrangement on the sidepods, with the one-legged winglets, the chimneys and gills, looked similar to the Ferrari F2003-GA. Hilhorst protested: "The gills for example were our idea, the car had them already in 2002, but lower. Now we moved them upwards to improve the cooling. Our flip-up has two elements, whereas the Ferrari solution is out of one piece." The bargeboard development was done in two steps. Finally, they became smaller in order to get more air into the radiators. According to Brunner, two percent in aerodynamic efficiency was found. The modification gained Toyota 0.3 seconds in lap time. Only the rear wing development was not ready in time for Silverstone and was tried a race later in Hockenheim. As it produced too much downforce for this kind of circuit, its race debut was postponed until Budapest.

WINGLET, FLIP-UP, EXHAUST CHIMNEY

The three elements – winglet, flip-up and exhaust chimney – are aerodynamically one unit. When you move one of the items just a little bit, it can have a detrimental effect on the airflow. Or a positive one. Norbert Kreyer was not so happy with the solutions that his aero-department tested over the season. In particular the flip-ups, which try to guide the air around the rear wheels. "Our flip-ups create too much drag. In our case the double element works better, but Ferrari showed that they get it right with a flip-up in one piece. So we obviously still have to learn in that area."

Chimneys nowadays are almost a must. Lacking the space on the bottom of the car the exhaust has to exit at the top. "You build a chimney in order to support extraction of the hot air. During the year these chimneys got bigger and bigger. They use the exhaust gas to accelerate the airflow to the rear wing. The winglets, however, are just a device to create downforce. It is in the area of one to two percent."

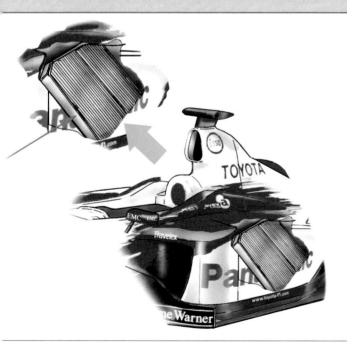

RADIATOR CONCEPT

Toyota mounted the radiators at a forward-leaning angle like Ferrari, rather than upright inside the sidepods. The main reason for that configuration was to bring more weight forward. In order to help the rear tyres, the intention was to change the weight distribution. This solution was already tested in the hybrid TF102B over the winter and then carried over to the TF103. In the beginning Toyota had split water/oil radiators in each sidepod, but before Barcelona they separated the two cooling circuits completely, just as Ferrari did. From then on the water was on the left side and the oil on the right. This reduced the number of parts and therefore the weight. Norbert Kreyer explained: "Obviously we had that step in mind right from the beginning. The engine and all the water and oil lines were designed in a way to switch without complications from one race to the other." The only question remained whether the two cooling systems worked independently without any disadvantages. They did. Aluminium radiators with Toyota's distinctive shape are pretty difficult to fabricate, but Denso finally managed to find a good solution to the problem.

GARY ANDERSON DIRECTOR OF RACE AND TEST ENGINEERING

JORDAN FORD

" **We started the 2003 season with a new engine partner, going from** Honda to a Ford Cosworth engine. This engine was basically the 2002 Jaguar V10, updated. This in itself sounds simple, but for us it was a new package with a new set of problems. It was smaller and lighter, but had a lot more vibration. It also entailed setting up a working relationship with a completely new group of people.

That vibration problem caused a few initial reliability problems and reduced our pre-season testing. We also had seven engine failures during the season. This was something neither Cosworth nor ourselves expected as the engine design was in effect a year old. The planned updates never really came. But we had a small one for the last three races, but nothing particularly special. We started the season in reasonable shape, got a 10-point bonus from our win in Brazil, but that was really the highlight. We were working on a limited budget, but still should have been able to hold onto that fifth place in the championship. If we had reacted at that time and put a comprehensive development programme in place we could have ended the season with 25 to 30 points easily. We suffered throughout the year with a lack of overall grip and this basically meant we didn't really have the performance to be in the good scoring positions, which is where we needed to be and should have been. We did develop a new specification that we would have introduced in Silverstone, but decided that it did not have the potential we needed. So after that it was a case of seeing the season out, doing whatever we could with the existing package and hoping for some luck.

Other problems we faced throughout the year consisted of suspension failures in Brazil and Malaysia, and a rear wing failure in Hungary for Firman. Fisichella had a couple of gearbox problems. In the middle of the season there was a lull when our tyre rivals responded to Bridgestone's strength and in the end I think we lost the advantage. We're all working hard to make sure we get the most from the entire package in 2004.

To sum it up, it has been a disappointing year for everyone at Jordan. However, a lot of lessons have been learnt and structures put in place whereby the 2004 car will be a substantial improvement upon the aptly named EJ13, both initially and in its development package. We need to believe in ourselves and get on with it. That way we can hope for a better chance next year. "

355

JORDAN TECHNICAL DEVELOPMENTS

Jordan had quite a heavy task over the winter. An engine change always means that a lot of things have to alter on the car as well. That is due to the different dimensions and the different weight between a Honda V10 and a Cosworth V10. The Honda had an angle of 90 degrees, whereas Cosworth used a 72 degree concept. The weight difference was about 20 kg in Cosworth's favour, which was significant. Therefore, Director of Design and Development, Henri Durand, and Director of Race and Test Engineering, Gary Anderson, decided to start with a completely new car.

It followed the usual principles: small, simple, efficient. According to the numbers, the EJ13 should have been 1.2 seconds per lap faster than its predecessor, but in reality the performance gain turned out to be just 0.5 seconds. The car was reasonably balanced, but did not produce enough downforce. As Jordan had to live on a smaller budget than in previous years, they did less testing than most of the other teams. Their 20 year-old wind tunnel was supplying valuable data, but was restricted in terms of what precisely could be measured. During the year there was only minor development on the car, such as front wing endplates, diffuser modifications, new Gurney flaps and slight suspension alterations. The rule changes did not help either. Had the engineers known it, they would have gone for a smaller fuel tank and a shorter wheelbase. But Gary Anderson saw a good side to that. "The big fuel tank was for sure a major factor in our win in Brazil. We called Fisichella in quite early and filled it up. By adopting that strategy we were able to keep him out until the race was stopped, without any further refuelling."

EJ13 TECHNICAL SPECIFICATIONS
ENGINE (RS1) **Cosworth V10 / 72 degree / 2998cc**
TRANSMISSION **Jordan GP seven-speed semi-automatic gearbox**
CHASSIS **Carbon fibre**
SUSPENSION **Push-rod with torsion bar front and rear**
BRAKES **AP**
SHOCK ABSORBERS **Jordan / Penske**
WHEELS **BBS**
TYRES **Bridgestone Potenza**
ELECTRONICS **Pi**

DIMENSIONS
WHEEL BASE **3,000mm**
WEIGHT **600kg (including driver)**
TOTAL LENGTH **4,600mm**
FRONT TRACK **1,500mm**
REAR TRACK **1,418mm**

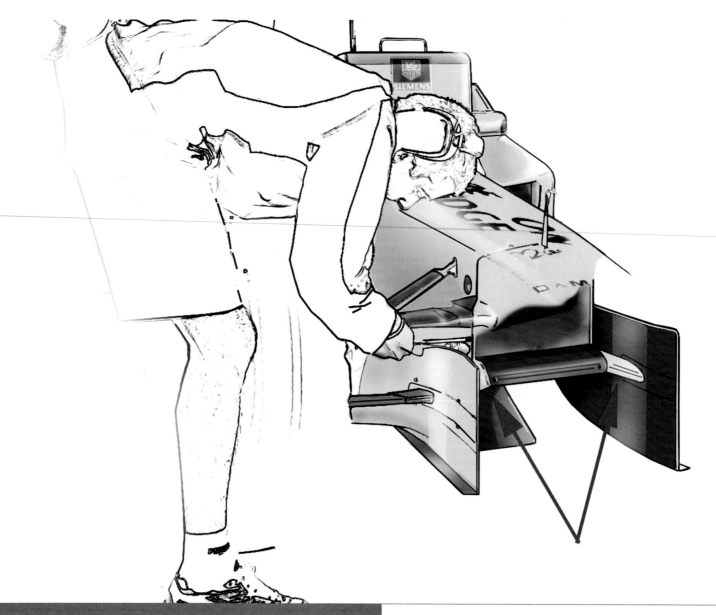

TWIN-KEEL CONCEPT

Despite problems with the twin-keel on the 2002 EJ12, Jordan stuck to that design philosophy. But this time the two keels were not vertical, they were given an angle of 45 degrees. That improved the stiffness and decreased the weight. The angled keels allowed Durand to mount the front wishbones higher, so the brake callipers could be mounted below the brake discs to lower the centre of gravity. Jordan also stiffened the front uprights, which had given some problems in 2002 with flexing.

Gary Anderson was not sure whether the twin-keel concept was the right way to go. "You have to weigh up the advantages and disadvantages. You definitely gain aerodynamically, as you have no suspension parts in the airflow underneath the chassis. On the other hand you have to accept disadvantages in both stiffness and weight. It is more difficult to create a competitive package with it. Three of the four top cars use the single keel still, so that solution cannot be too bad. In the end it is quite simple. Basically there are very few things that make your car go quicker. They are; a lower centre of gravity, more downforce, more horsepower and less weight."

REAR WING

The Jordan's rear wing looked different to all the others. In particular the underwing had a complicated shape. It was difficult to build it as a light package. Anderson did not like the design too much. "It was too complicated and too heavy at a spot where you do not want to have extra weight. It hangs out at the back of the car, so the polar moment of inertia is high because of it. You have to add weight to make it stiff. You want to move weight forward instead. And the whole effort was only for half a kilo of downforce, maybe." The quite significant vibrations from the engine did not help either. However, this was not the reason for Ralph Firman's practice shunt in Hungary when the rear wing fell off. Analysis showed that bad manufacturing was responsible for that. "The wing was designed for much higher loads than we experienced at this spot on the circuit in Budapest. Other wings did 4000 to 5000 kilometres without any problem", Anderson said. But not those they brought to Hungary. All of the wings on the three EJ13s showed cracks in the aluminium plates which strengthened the connection between the underwing and the endplates. After the crash, the team repaired the parts in question.

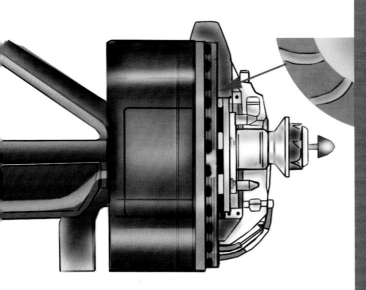

BRAKE DEVELOPMENT

The brake system of the Jordan EJ13 used underslung callipers front and rear. The 2002 EJ12 had problems with brake knock-off. Anderson: "After a fast corner when you hit the next brake pedal it would have a long movement where the pads had been knocked back." The pad wear was too high as well. Therefore, Jordan modified the brakes completely in order to eliminate that. The callipers went from the side to the bottom of the disc. A lower position of the weight was another positive effect, and the old cooling system was replaced by a more efficient design. Anderson however thought: "We definitely improved in this area, but to use the potential of the brakes to the optimum, we needed more downforce."

EUROPEAN MINARDI COSWORTH

"**The 2003 season was a difficult one because of a very limited** budget at our disposal. To start with, we had to use the 2002 chassis which obliged us to make at least a couple of crucial changes: first of all we had to fit Justin Wilson in to the 2002 cockpit, and we are talking about the tallest man in the 2003 F1 drivers' line up. In the end we managed to settle Justin in a pretty comfortable position at the wheel and secure him in the cockpit. The second major change came from the necessity to fit a new engine in the existing chassis which meant that a remarkable amount of components were affected, starting with the engine plugs and the snorkel, including the water plant and the gearbox, the oil and fuel systems, the exhaust pipes and the hydraulic system. Moreover, the car layout required quite a few modifications as well in order to accommodate the new engine, and last but not least we operated on the electronics, especially the engine management and software. We dealt with a massive amount of work using minimal budget and we're aware that we could not add any particular innovation to the car that could improve its performance apart from the engine.

That said, European Minardi's technical staff concentrated all their efforts to achieve a reliable, simple car, despite all the changes involved to fit the engine. In addition to that, we also focused on putting in as much ballast as possible as this was a great opportunity to obtain a little advantage to help improve the car's performance.

In the end, our technical staff did a good job as we managed to have a car which proved reliable, handled well and was driveable throughout the season.

One further obstacle we had to tackle this year was a total lack of windtunnel testing. We only managed to do seven days of testing over the whole 2003 season because right at the end of January our development programme, which was planned for the PS03 chassis, had to be interrupted."

Before the season even started, Minardi had a handicap from a technical point of view. The PS03 was designed for Michelin tyres.

As the French manufacturer refused to supply more then five teams, Minardi had to switch to Bridgestone rubber. The difference in the philosophy of the two manufacturers explained the problem for Gabriele Tredozi's design team: He had a car designed for a different tyre.

With its limited budget, Minardi was not a team that could adapt their car via endless windtunnel sessions or thousands of test kilometres. Here's a comparison that demonstrates the gulf between Formula One's biggest and smallest teams: Between January 7th and the end of the season in Suzuka in October, Ferrari ran 49,615 test kilometres over 126 days, Minardi only 6822, and that included the 16 Friday private test sessions during the grand prix weekends plus 10 private sessions. Taking that into account, on the reliability side Minardi did an amazing job. With 1548 completed race laps out of a possible 2036, they made a better job than most of the wealthier teams. Sauber, BAR, Jaguar and Jordan had a worse finishing record.

On the performance side Minardi suffered from a lack of downforce, a lack of horsepower and the late change of the tyre manufacturer. Due to the restrictions there was only little development on the car. During the season, however, Minardi introduced a new front wing, new barge-boards and modifications to the undertray.

PS03 TECHNICAL SPECIFICATIONS
ENGINE (CR-3) **Cosworth V10 / 72 degree / 2998cc**
TRANSMISSION **Minardi six-speed semi-automatic gearbox**
CHASSIS **Carbon fibre**
SUSPENSION **Push-rod with torsion bar front and rear**
BRAKES **Brembo**
SHOCK ABSORBERS **Sachs**
WHEELS **O.Z Racing**
TYRES **Bridgestone Potenza**
ELECTRONICS **Pi**

DIMENSIONS
WHEEL BASE **3,097mm**
WEIGHT **600kg (including driver)**
TOTAL LENGTH **4,548mm**
FRONT TRACK **1,480mm**
REAR TRACK **1,410mm**

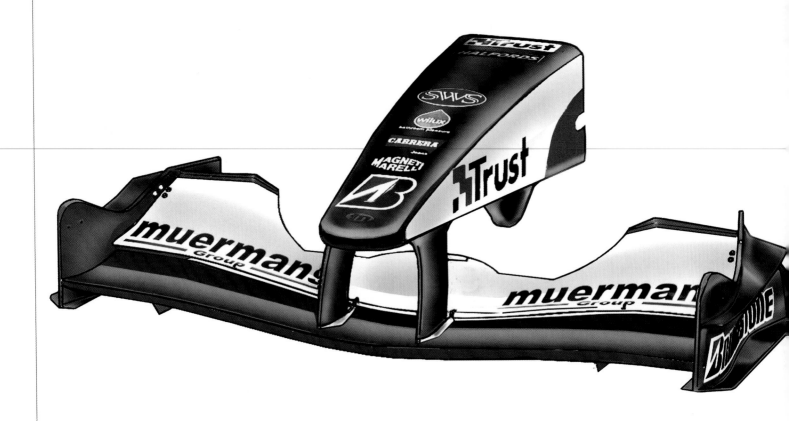

CAR DEVELOPMENT

The development work on a number of car components such as front wing, bargeboards, floor, diffuser and clearly some bodywork, was never completed thus affecting the whole optimisation of the car performance during the season.

Gabriele Tredozi explains: "The only chance for us to obtain some improvement in terms of car performance was to try and carry out our development programme straight on track. We built a number of full scale pieces which we tested at the circuit, despite not being completely delveloped in the wind tunnel, during the hours at our disposal on Friday's private tests. We were therefore able to calculate the potential of those parts directly on board the car, but clearly we had to make quite a few modifications before obtaining the final optimisation of a piece compared to the original one."

"This was the case with our front wing which we modified in its spoon profile, now smoother and less sharp in comparison to the previous version. This helped us to achieve some improvement in the pitch sensitivity and furthermore, it worked well coupled to the developed versions of the barge boards we introduced."

BARGEBOARDS

The first evolution of bargeboards, were introduced at the European GP, adding a smaller deflector to the original ones. Then we developed this solution so to maximise the air flow passing through the sidepods and underneath, by increasing the area of the deflector at Silverstone.
A further and last development of barge boards took place in Germany at Hockenheim where we placed the deflector forward at the level of the front axle, improving front end stability.

DIFFUSER

A small development of the diffuser was also put in place, modifying its side channels and in particular their angle so to increase the downforce provided by the undertray.

Tredozi states: "These changes were minimal ones, based on the previous version of the diffuser, as we didn't test for a long period in the windtunnel. Therefore it was only possible to add small bits and pieces to these elements as configuring a major change to the diffuser requires long windtunnel testing sessions, and due to our limited resources we tried to maximise the efficiency of what we already had.

In the end a good 80% of those car parts and components, which had been optimized in this way, were fitted in the car at the final Japanese GP. Therefore, we believe we got an overall positive result considering the team's potential and the economical difficulties we had to face this year.

FAMOUS FANS

> "To wear a diamond of this magnitude is unique. I'm absolutely thrilled."
>
> HELENA CHRISTENSEN
> MONACO 2003

The season's most glamorous weekend was at Monaco, when the stars of fashion, film and racing gathered to celebrate the launch of one of the world's rarest diamonds. The Diamond Trading Company, Jaguar and Formula One Publishing, on behalf of Moussaieff and Steinmetz, collaborated to unveil the Monaco Rose, a 59.6-carat flawless pink diamond.

From left to right: Antonio Pizzonia, Helena Christensen and Mark Webber at the Hotel de Paris on Thursday 29th May.

> " Party, party, party...
> Fun, fun, fun! "
>
> WESLEY SNIPES
> MONACO 2003

Clockwise from far left: Helena Christensen, Hollywood actor Wesley Snipes, and Naomi Campbell wearing diamonds from the Moussaieff Flawless collection; BAR F1 driver Jenson Button and his girlfriend Louise Griffiths at the gala dinner; BMW Williams Technical Director, Patrick Head; Beny Steinmetz, chairman of the Steinmetz Diamond Group; BMW Williams driver and Monaco winner, Juan Pablo Montoya and Prince Rainier of Monaco; Nir Livnat, CEO of the Steinmetz Diamond Group, and Beny Steinmetz with Helena Christensen.

> " I was delighted to attend the British Grand Prix as a guest of Jaguar Racing, which, like the film itself, was about pure action! What a thrilling race! "
>
> ARNOLD SCHWARZENEGGER
> SILVERSTONE 2003

Clockwise from far left: Terminator 3: Rise of the Machines star co-star, Kristanna Loken, Mark Webber, Antonio Pizzonia and Arnold Schwarzenegger; Sex Pistols front man, Johnny Rotten at Indianapolis; Heidi Klum and Flavio Briatore at Monaco; Patrick Head and Dennis Hopper at Monza.

Clockwise from far left: Brazilian football superstar, Ronaldo and rock
front man, Bono at Monaco; Wild man of rock Ozzy Osbourne and Juan
Pablo Montoya at Montreal; Leon star Jean Reno at Monaco; Matrix star
Lawrence Fishburne at Monza.

BAHRAIN

The 4th of April 2004 marks the arrival of the Middle East as a member of the Formula One family. This is the day of the inaugural Bahrain Grand Prix, a race that brings the mystique of the desert into the high-tech modern world of Formula One racing.

The circuit is under construction at Sakhir, a short drive from the Bahraini capital of Manama, where the desert has natural rock strewn escarpments, rather than the traditional sea of sand. For thousands of years, this land has endured the slow and sleepy pace of fishermen, farmers, merchants and camel traders. In keeping with the pace of Bahrain as an international centre of commerce and finance, it will now echo to the roar of twenty V10 engines.

His Excellency Shaikh Fawaz bin Mohammed Al Khalifa, Chairman of the Bahrain International Circuit says, "The inaugural Grand Prix in the Middle East is a dream come true. 04.04.04 will be a very special day for the people of Bahrain, and indeed for everyone in the Gulf Region. The vision of His Highness the Crown Prince to stage a round of the FIA Formula One World Championship in Bahrain has received universal support from all corners of the globe."

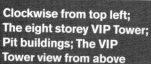
**Clockwise from top left;
The eight storey VIP Tower;
Pit buildings; The VIP
Tower view from above**

A combination of superb, modern facilities set against the
evocative and beautiful backdrop of Bahrain will make this one of the most
popular grands prix in years to come. The striking feature of this venue is
the unusual track character. Spectators will have the experience of seeing
the cars heading into the external desert area, before coming back to the
oasis-styled infield. This modern track is set to offer the driver a unique,
experience in the way the track's width varies at the end of the different
straights. It also enables diverse racing lines, therefore offering
opportunities for overtaking manoeuvres.

As circuit architects Hermann Tilke and Peter Wahl say, "Beautiful
landscape design leads the visitor into the oasis of the circuit, which is
formed by the unique double serving paddock areas. These allow two
circuits to operate independently. The connection of both circuits creates
a maximum loop-length of 5.475m for the Formula One track.

Besides the character of a desert track, the circuit gains its particular
charm from the attractive mixture of traditional Bahraini and modern
architecture combined with the high-tech look of a Formula One race circuit.

TRACK DESCRIPTION

Circuit length **5.475 Km / 12 corners**
Estimated lap time **1min 33.63 secs**
Estimated Top speed **317 Km/h**
Special features **The circuit is a stunning oasis set in the
midst of the desert. It combines the most modern
technology with a clever use of traditional features. For
example, the control tower resembles an old fort, while on
top of the grandstands, wind towers grace the skyline.**

FINISH | START

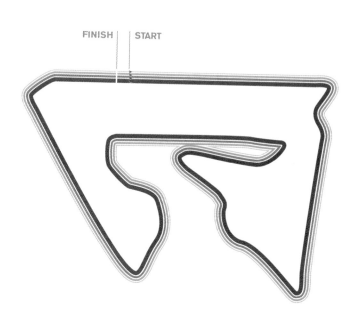

CHINA

In 2004, China joins the Formula One fraternity, bringing the magic and mystery of a country rich in history and ancient culture still largely unexplored by the outside world. This welcome entrant to Formula One racing will offer the international community an opportunity to explore its cultural, economic and sporting traditions.

Shanghai is a rapidly developing commercial centre, and hosting a grand prix will allow the world to see more of this fascinating place, with its past traditions and modern approach to life.

Mr. Mao Xiaohan, President of the Shanghai International Circuit says, "Our objective is not only to deliver an exciting circuit and hold a successful Chinese Grand Prix, but also to create a facility that will fulfill social, cultural and business objectives, creating sports, recreational and cultural opportunities

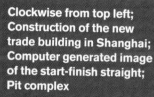

Clockwise from top left; Construction of the new trade building in Shanghai; Computer generated image of the start-finish straight; Pit complex

The Shanghai International Circuit is a race circuit for the new millennium. The modern racetrack and stunning architecture is set to provide China's gateway to the world of racing.

Circuit architects HermannTilke and Peter Wahl say, "The 5.4 kilometre racing track is shaped like the Chinese character 'shang', which stands for 'high' or 'above.' Other symbols represented in the architecture originate from Chinese history, such as the team buildings arranged like pavilions in a lake to resemble the ancient Yuyan-Garden in Shanghai. Here, nature and technology are carefully used to create harmony between the elements."

Not only will the course be remarkable for its change of acceleration and deceleration in different winding turns, but also for its high-speed straights making high demands on the driver as well as the car. This will offer many opportunities for overtaking and give an intense and exciting motorsport experience to the spectators. The Main Grandstand with 29,500 seats presents a spectacular view of almost 80 percent of the track-one of the new features in race track design realised in Shanghai.

TRACK DESCRIPTION

Circuit length **5.451 km**
Estimated lap time **1min 34.64 secs**
Estimated top speed **327 km/h**

Special Features **In keeping with Chinese tradition, there will be a "Yang" corner which will be slow in, fast out, while the "Ying" corner will be fast in, and slow out.**

START
FINISH

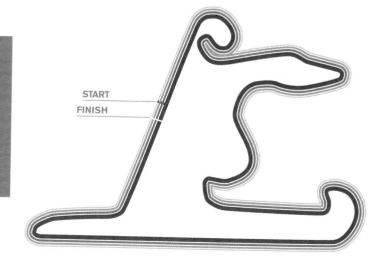

2003 SEASON STATISTICS

MELBOURNE AUSTRALIAN GRAND PRIX ROUND 01

QUALIFYING 1: FRIDAY MARCH 07

DRIVER	TIME	GAP	ORDER
1 R BARRICHELLO	1M26.372		2
2 K RAIKKONEN	1M26.551	+0.179	6
3 J VILLENEUVE	1M26.832	+0.460	11
4 M SCHUMACHER	1M27.103	+0.731	1
5 J BUTTON	1M27.159	+0.787	7
6 D COULTHARD	1M27.242	+0.870	5
7 F ALONSO	1M27.255	+0.883	15
8 O PANIS	1M27.352	+0.980	12
9 J TRULLI	1M27.411	+1.039	8
10 JP MONTOYA	1M27.450	+1.078	3
11 C DA MATTA	1M27.478	+1.106	20
12 N HEIDFELD	1M27.510	+1.138	9
13 HH FRENTZEN	1M27.563	+1.191	14
14 G FISICHELLA	1M27.633	+1.261	10
15 M WEBBER	1M27.675	+1.303	13
16 R SCHUMACHER	1M28.266	+1.894	4
17 R FIRMAN	1M29.977	+3.605	16
18 J VERSTAPPEN	1M30.053	+3.681	19
19 A PIZZONIA	1M30.092	+3.720	17
20 J WILSON	1M30.479	+4.107	18

QUALIFYING 2: SATURDAY MARCH 08

DRIVER	TIME	GAP	ORDER
1 M SCHUMACHER	1M27.173		17
2 R BARRICHELLO	1M27.418	+0.245	20
3 JP MONTOYA	1M28.101	+0.928	11
4 HH FRENTZEN	1M28.274	+1.101	8
5 O PANIS	1M28.288	+1.115	13
6 J VILLENEUVE	1M28.420	+1.247	18
7 N HEIDFELD	1M28.464	+1.291	9
8 J BUTTON	1M28.682	+1.509	16
9 R SCHUMACHER	1M28.830	+1.657	5
10 F ALONSO	1M28.928	+1.755	14
11 D COULTHARD	1M29.105	+1.932	15
12 J TRULLI	1M29.136	+1.963	12
13 G FISICHELLA	1M29.344	+2.171	7
14 M WEBBER	1M29.367	+2.194	6
15 K RAIKKONEN	1M29.470	+2.297	19
16 C DA MATTA	1M29.538	+2.365	10
17 R FIRMAN	1M31.242	+4.069	4
18 A PIZZONIA	1M31.723	+4.550	2
19 J VERSTAPPEN	NO TIME		3
20 J WILSON	NO TIME		1

RACE: SUNDAY MARCH 09

DRIVER	TEAM	TIM/RET	LAPS
1 D COULTHARD	MCLAREN MERCEDES	1HR34M42.124	58
2 JP MONTOYA	WILLIAMS BMW	+08.675	58
3 K RAIKKONEN	MCLAREN MERCEDES	+09.192	58
4 M SCHUMACHER	FERRARI	+09.942	58
5 J TRULLI	RENAULT	+38.801	58
6 HH FRENTZEN	SAUBER PETRONAS	+43.928	58
7 F ALONSO	RENAULT	+45.074	58
8 R SCHUMACHER	WILLIAMS BMW	+45.745	58
9 J VILLENEUVE	BAR HONDA	+65.536	58
10 J BUTTON	BAR HONDA	+65.974	58
11 J VERSTAPPEN	MINARDI COSWORTH	+1 LAP	57
12 G FISICHELLA	JORDAN FORD	GEARBOX	52
13 A PIZZONIA	JAGUAR COSWORTH	SUSPENSION	52
RET O PANIS	TOYOTA	FUEL PRESSURE	32
RET N HEIDFELD	SAUBER PETRONAS	SUSPENSION	21
RET J WILSON	MINARDI COSWORTH	RADIATOR	16
RET M WEBBER	JAGUAR COSWORTH	SUSPENSION	15
RET C DA MATTA	TOYOTA	SPIN	7
RET R FIRMAN	JORDAN FORD	ACCIDENT	6
RET R BARRICHELLO	FERRARI	ACCIDENT	5

FASTEST LAP: K RAIKKONEN MCLAREN MERCEDES 1M27.724

SEPANG MALAYSIAN GRAND PRIX ROUND 02

QUALIFYING 1: FRIDAY MARCH 21

DRIVER	TIME	GAP	ORDER
1 M SCHUMACHER	1M34.980		4
2 R BARRICHELLO	1M35.681	+0.701	20
3 JP MONTOYA	1M35.939	+0.959	2
4 K RAIKKONEN	1M36.038	+1.058	3
5 D COULTHARD	1M36.297	+1.317	1
6 J TRULLI	1M36.301	+1.321	5
7 N HEIDFELD	1M36.407	+1.427	15
8 HH FRENTZEN	1M36.615	+1.635	6
9 J BUTTON	1M36.632	+1.652	10
10 F ALONSO	1M36.693	+1.713	7
11 C DA MATTA	1M36.706	+1.726	18
12 G FISICHELLA	1M36.759	+1.779	12
13 R SCHUMACHER	1M36.805	+1.825	8
14 O PANIS	1M36.995	+2.015	14
15 J VILLENEUVE	1M37.585	+2.605	9
16 M WEBBER	1M37.669	+2.689	17
17 R FIRMAN	1M38.240	+3.260	19
18 J VERSTAPPEN	1M38.904	+3.924	11
19 J WILSON	1M39.354	+4.374	16
20 A PIZZONIA	NO TIME		13

QUALIFYING 2: SATURDAY MARCH 22

DRIVER	TIME	GAP	ORDER
1 F ALONSO	1M37.044		11
2 J TRULLI	1M37.217	+0.173	15
3 M SCHUMACHER	1M37.393	+0.349	20
4 D COULTHARD	1M37.454	+0.410	16
5 R BARRICHELLO	1M37.579	+0.535	19
6 N HEIDFELD	1M37.766	+0.722	14
7 K RAIKKONEN	1M37.858	+0.814	17
8 JP MONTOYA	1M37.974	+0.930	18
9 J BUTTON	1M38.073	+1.029	12
10 O PANIS	1M38.094	+1.050	7
11 C DA MATTA	1M38.097	+1.053	10
12 J VILLENEUVE	1M38.289	+1.245	6
13 HH FRENTZEN	1M38.291	+1.247	13
14 G FISICHELLA	1M38.416	+1.372	9
15 A PIZZONIA	1M38.516	+1.472	1
16 M WEBBER	1M38.624	+1.580	5
17 R SCHUMACHER	1M38.789	+1.745	8
18 J VERSTAPPEN	1M40.417	+3.373	3
19 J WILSON	1M40.599	+3.555	2
20 R FIRMAN	1M40.910	+3.866	4

RACE: SUNDAY MARCH 23

DRIVER	TEAM	TIM/RET	LAPS
1 K RAIKKONEN	MCLAREN MERCEDES	1HR32M22.195	56
2 R BARRICHELLO	FERRARI	+39.286	56
3 F ALONSO	RENAULT	+1MIN 4.007	56
4 R SCHUMACHER	WILLIAMS BMW	+1MIN 28.026	56
5 J TRULLI	RENAULT	+1 LAP	55
6 M SCHUMACHER	FERRARI	+1 LAP	55
7 J BUTTON	BAR HONDA	+1 LAP	55
8 N HEIDFELD	SAUBER PETRONAS	+1 LAP	55
9 HH FRENTZEN	SAUBER PETRONAS	+1 LAP	55
10 R FIRMAN	JORDAN FORD	+1 LAP	55
11 C DA MATTA	TOYOTA	+1 LAP	55
12 JP MONTOYA	WILLIAMS BMW	+3 LAPS	53
13 J VERSTAPPEN	MINARDI COSWORTH	+4 LAPS	52
RET A PIZZONIA	JAGUAR COSWORTH	SPIN	42
RET J WILSON	MINARDI COSWORTH	RETIRED	42
RET M WEBBER	JAGUAR COSWORTH	ENGINE	41
RET O PANIS	TOYOTA	FUEL PRESSURE	35
RET D COULTHARD	MCLAREN MERCEDES	ELECTRICAL	2
RET G FISICHELLA	JORDAN FORD	ELECTRICAL	0
RET J VILLENEUVE	BAR HONDA	ELECTRICAL	0

FASTEST LAP: M SCHUMACHER FERRARI 1M36.412

INTERLAGOS BRAZILIAN GRAND PRIX ROUND 03

QUALIFYING 1: FRIDAY APRIL 04

DRIVER	TIME	GAP	ORDER
1 M WEBBER	1M23.111		19
2 R BARRICHELLO	1M23.249	+0.138	4
3 K RAIKKONEN	1M24.607	+1.496	1
4 D COULTHARD	1M24.655	+1.544	2
5 M SCHUMACHER	1M25.585	+2.474	6
6 O PANIS	1M25.614	+2.503	20
7 J VILLENEUVE	1M25.672	+2.561	12
8 A PIZZONIA	1M25.764	+2.653	17
9 F ALONSO	1M26.203	+3.092	5
10 HH FRENTZEN	1M26.375	+3.264	9
11 C DA MATTA	1M26.554	+3.443	15
12 J TRULLI	1M26.557	+3.446	7
13 R SCHUMACHER	1M26.709	+3.598	8
14 G FISICHELLA	1M26.726	+3.615	16
15 J VERSTAPPEN	1M26.886	+3.775	14
16 N HEIDFELD	1M27.111	+4.000	11
17 JP MONTOYA	1M27.961	+4.850	3
18 R FIRMAN	1M28.083	+4.972	13
19 J WILSON	1M28.317	+5.206	18
20 J BUTTON	NO TIME		10

QUALIFYING 2: SATURDAY APRIL 05

DRIVER	TIME	GAP	ORDER
1 R BARRICHELLO	1M13.807		19
2 D COULTHARD	1M13.818	+0.011	17
3 M WEBBER	1M13.851	+0.044	20
4 K RAIKKONEN	1M13.866	+0.059	18
5 J TRULLI	1M13.953	+0.146	9
6 R SCHUMACHER	1M14.124	+0.317	8
7 M SCHUMACHER	1M14.130	+0.323	16
8 G FISICHELLA	1M14.191	+0.384	7
9 JP MONTOYA	1M14.223	+0.416	4
10 F ALONSO	1M14.384	+0.577	12
11 J BUTTON	1M14.504	+0.697	1
12 N HEIDFELD	1M14.631	+0.824	5
13 J VILLENEUVE	1M14.668	+0.861	14
14 HH FRENTZEN	1M14.839	+1.032	11
15 O PANIS	1M14.839	+1.032	15
16 R FIRMAN	1M15.240	+1.433	3
17 A PIZZONIA	1M15.317	+1.510	13
18 C DA MATTA	1M15.641	+1.834	9
19 J VERSTAPPEN	1M16.542	+2.735	6
20 J WILSON	1M16.586	+2.779	2

RACE: SUNDAY APRIL 06

DRIVER	TEAM	TIM/RET	LAPS
1 G FISICHELLA	JORDAN FORD	1HR31M17.748	54
2 K RAIKKONEN	MCLAREN MERCEDES	+0.945	54
3 F ALONSO	RENAULT	+6.348	54
4 D COULTHARD	MCLAREN MERCEDES	+8.096	54
5 HH FRENTZEN	SAUBER PETRONAS	+8.642	54
6 J VILLENEUVE	BAR HONDA	+16.054	54
7 R SCHUMACHER	WILLIAMS BMW	+38.526	54
8 J TRULLI	RENAULT	+45.927	54
9 M WEBBER	JAGUAR COSWORTH	ACCIDENT	53
10 C DA MATTA	TOYOTA	+1 LAP	53
RET R BARRICHELLO	FERRARI	FUEL FEED	46
RET J BUTTON	BAR HONDA	ACCIDENT	32
RET J VERSTAPPEN	MINARDI COSWORTH	SPIN	30
RET M SCHUMACHER	FERRARI	ACCIDENT	26
RET JP MONTOYA	WILLIAMS BMW	ACCIDENT	24
RET A PIZZONIA	JAGUAR	ACCIDENT	24
RET O PANIS	TOYOTA	ACCIDENT	17
RET R FIRMAN	JORDAN FORD	SUSPENSION	17
RET J WILSON	MINARDI COSWORTH	SPIN	15
RET N HEIDFELD	SAUBER PETRONAS	ENGINE	8

FASTEST LAP: R BARRICHELLO FERRARI 1M22.032

IMOLA SAN MARINO GRAND PRIX ROUND 04

QUALIFYING 1: FRIDAY APRIL 18

DRIVER	TIME	GAP	ORDER
1 M SCHUMACHER	1M20.628		8
2 R BARRICHELLO	1M21.082	+0.454	7
3 R SCHUMACHER	1M21.193	+0.565	9
4 JP MONTOYA	1M21.490	+0.862	6
5 M WEBBER	1M21.669	+1.041	14
6 J BUTTON	1M21.891	+1.263	12
7 J VILLENEUVE	1M21.926	+1.298	11
8 K RAIKKONEN	1M22.147	+1.519	1
9 D COULTHARD	1M22.326	+1.698	2
10 HH FRENTZEN	1M22.531	+1.903	10
11 G FISICHELLA	1M22.734	+2.096	4
12 O PANIS	1M22.765	+2.137	20
13 F ALONSO	1M22.809	+2.181	3
14 N HEIDFELD	1M22.911	+2.283	13
15 A PIZZONIA	1M22.919	+2.291	18
16 J TRULLI	1M23.100	+2.472	5
17 R FIRMAN	1M24.360	+3.732	16
18 C DA MATTA	1M24.854	+4.226	15
19 J VERSTAPPEN	1M24.990	+4.362	17
20 J WILSON	1M25.195	+4.567	19

QUALIFYING 2: SATURDAY APRIL 19

DRIVER	TIME	GAP	ORDER
1 M SCHUMACHER	1M22.327		20
2 R SCHUMACHER	1M22.341	+0.014	18
3 R BARRICHELLO	1M22.557	+0.230	19
4 JP MONTOYA	1M22.789	+0.462	17
5 M WEBBER	1M23.015	+0.688	16
6 K RAIKKONEN	1M23.148	+0.821	13
7 J VILLENEUVE	1M23.160	+0.833	14
8 F ALONSO	1M23.169	+0.842	8
9 J BUTTON	1M23.381	+1.054	15
10 O PANIS	1M23.460	+1.133	9
11 N HEIDFELD	1M23.700	+1.373	7
12 D COULTHARD	1M23.818	+1.491	12
13 C DA MATTA	1M23.838	+1.511	3
14 HH FRENTZEN	1M23.932	+1.605	11
15 A PIZZONIA	1M24.147	+1.820	6
16 J TRULLI	1M24.190	+1.863	5
17 G FISICHELLA	1M24.317	+1.990	10
18 J WILSON	1M25.826	+3.499	1
19 R FIRMAN	1M26.357	+4.030	4
20 J VERSTAPPEN	NO TIME		2

RACE: SUNDAY APRIL 20

DRIVER	TEAM	TIM/RET	LAPS
1 M SCHUMACHER	FERRARI	1HR28M12.058	62
2 K RAIKKONEN	MCLAREN MERCEDES	+1.882	62
3 R BARRICHELLO	FERRARI	+2.291	62
4 R SCHUMACHER	WILLIAMS BMW	+8.803	62
5 D COULTHARD	MCLAREN MERCEDES	+9.411	62
6 F ALONSO	RENAULT	+43.689	62
7 JP MONTOYA	WILLIAMS BMW	+45.271	62
8 J BUTTON	BAR HONDA	+1 LAP	61
9 O PANIS	TOYOTA	+1 LAP	61
10 N HEIDFELD	SAUBER PETRONAS	+1 LAP	61
11 HH FRENTZEN	SAUBER PETRONAS	+1 LAP	61
12 C DA MATTA	TOYOTA	+1 LAP	61
13 J TRULLI	RENAULT	+1 LAP	61
14 A PIZZONIA	JAGUAR COSWORTH	+2 LAPS	60
15 G FISICHELLA	JORDAN FORD	+5 LAPS	57
RET M WEBBER	JAGUAR COSWORTH	DRIVESHAFT	54
RET R FIRMAN	JORDAN FORD	ENGINE	51
RET J VERSTAPPEN	MINARDI COSWORTH	ELECTRICAL	38
RET J WILSON	MINARDI COSWORTH	FUEL FLAP	23
RET J VILLENEUVE	BAR HONDA	ENGINE	19

FASTEST LAP: M SCHUMACHER FERRARI 1M22.491

CATALUNYA SPANISH GRAND PRIX ROUND 05

QUALIFYING 1: FRIDAY MAY 02

DRIVER	TIME	GAP	ORDER
1 M SCHUMACHER	1M17.130		3
2 J TRULLI	1M17.149	+0.019	9
3 R BARRICHELLO	1M17.218	+0.088	5
4 C DA MATTA	1M17.443	+0.313	16
5 J BUTTON	1M17.613	+0.483	12
6 O PANIS	1M17.746	+0.616	15
7 M WEBBER	1M17.793	+0.663	14
8 K RAIKKONEN	1M17.862	+0.732	1
9 D COULTHARD	1M18.060	+0.930	2
10 F ALONSO	1M18.100	+0.970	4
11 R SCHUMACHER	1M18.409	+1.279	6
12 J VILLENEUVE	1M18.461	+1.331	11
13 A PIZZONIA	1M18.528	+1.398	19
14 JP MONTOYA	1M18.607	+1.477	8
15 G FISICHELLA	1M18.879	+1.749	7
16 HH FRENTZEN	1M18.909	+1.779	10
17 N HEIDFELD	1M19.050	+1.920	13
18 R FIRMAN	1M19.195	+2.065	17
19 J VERSTAPPEN	1M20.822	+3.692	18
20 J WILSON	1M21.100	+3.970	20

QUALIFYING 2: SATURDAY MAY 03

DRIVER	TIME	GAP	ORDER
1 M SCHUMACHER	1M17.762		20
2 R BARRICHELLO	1M18.020	+0.258	18
3 F ALONSO	1M18.223	+0.471	11
4 J TRULLI	1M18.615	+0.853	19
5 J BUTTON	1M18.704	+0.942	12
6 O PANIS	1M18.811	+1.049	15
7 R SCHUMACHER	1M19.006	+1.244	10
8 D COULTHARD	1M19.128	+1.366	12
9 JP MONTOYA	1M19.377	+1.615	7
10 HH FRENTZEN	1M19.427	+1.665	5
11 J VILLENEUVE	1M19.563	+1.801	9
12 M WEBBER	1M19.615	+1.853	14
13 C DA MATTA	1M19.623	+1.861	17
14 N HEIDFELD	1M19.646	+1.884	4
15 R FIRMAN	1M20.215	+2.453	3
16 A PIZZONIA	1M20.308	+2.546	8
17 G FISICHELLA	1M20.976	+3.214	6
18 J WILSON	1M22.104	+4.342	1
19 J VERSTAPPEN	1M22.237	+4.475	2
20 K RAIKKONEN	NO TIME		13

RACE: SUNDAY MAY 04

DRIVER	TEAM	TIM/RET	LAPS
1 M SCHUMACHER	FERRARI	1HR33M46.933	65
2 F ALONSO	RENAULT	+5.716	65
3 R BARRICHELLO	FERRARI	+18.001	65
4 JP MONTOYA	WILLIAMS BMW	+1M02.022	65
5 R SCHUMACHER	WILLIAMS BMW	+1 LAP	64
6 C DA MATTA	TOYOTA	+1 LAP	64
7 M WEBBER	JAGUAR COSWORTH	+1 LAP	64
8 R FIRMAN	JORDAN FORD	+2 LAPS	63
9 J BUTTON	BAR HONDA	+2 LAPS	63
10 N HEIDFELD	SAUBER PETRONAS	+2 LAPS	63
11 J WILSON	MINARDI COSWORTH	+2 LAPS	63
12 J VERSTAPPEN	MINARDI COSWORTH	+3 LAPS	62
RET G FISICHELLA	JORDAN FORD	ENGINE	43
RET O PANIS	TOYOTA	GEARBOX	41
RET HH FRENTZEN	SAUBER PETRONAS	SUSPENSION	38
RET D COULTHARD	MCLAREN MERCEDES	ACCIDENT	17
RET J VILLENEUVE	BAR HONDA	ELECTRICAL	12
RET J TRULLI	RENAULT	ACCIDENT	0
RET A PIZZONIA	JAGUAR COSWORTH	ACCIDENT	0
RET K RAIKKONEN	MCLAREN MERCEDES	ACCIDENT	0

FASTEST LAP: R BARRICHELLO FERRARI 1M20.143

ZELTWEG AUSTRIAN GRAND PRIX ROUND 06

QUALIFYING 1: FRIDAY MAY 16

DRIVER	TIME	GAP	ORDER
1 M SCHUMACHER	1M07.908		2
2 R BARRICHELLO	1M08.187	+0.279	4
3 M WEBBER	1M08.512	+0.604	14
4 J VILLENEUVE	1M08.680	+0.772	11
5 J BUTTON	1M08.831	+0.923	13
6 JP MONTOYA	1M08.839	+0.931	7
7 D COULTHARD	1M08.947	+1.039	5
8 K RAIKKONEN	1M08.978	+1.070	1
9 A PIZZONIA	1M09.024	+1.116	20
10 G FISICHELLA	1M09.281	+1.373	8
11 J TRULLI	1M09.450	+1.542	9
12 N HEIDFELD	1M09.479	+1.571	15
13 F ALONSO	1M09.680	+1.772	3
14 O PANIS	1M09.764	+1.856	17
15 HH FRENTZEN	1M10.055	+2.147	10
16 C DA MATTA	1M10.370	+2.462	12
17 J VERSTAPPEN	1M10.894	+2.986	18
18 J WILSON	1M11.056	+3.148	19
19 R FIRMAN	1M11.171	+3.263	16
20 R SCHUMACHER	NO TIME		6

QUALIFYING 2: SATURDAY MAY 17

DRIVER	TIME	GAP	ORDER
1 M SCHUMACHER	1M09.150		20
2 K RAIKKONEN	1M09.189	+0.039	13
3 JP MONTOYA	1M09.391	+0.241	15
4 N HEIDFELD	1M09.725	+0.575	9
5 R BARRICHELLO	1M09.784	+0.634	19
6 J TRULLI	1M09.890	+0.740	10
7 J BUTTON	1M09.935	+0.785	16
8 A PIZZONIA	1M10.045	+0.895	12
9 G FISICHELLA	1M10.105	+0.955	11
10 R SCHUMACHER	1M10.279	+1.129	1
11 O PANIS	1M10.402	+1.252	7
12 J VILLENEUVE	1M10.618	+1.468	17
13 C DA MATTA	1M10.834	+1.684	5
14 D COULTHARD	1M10.893	+1.743	14
15 HH FRENTZEN	1M11.307	+2.157	6
16 R FIRMAN	1M11.505	+2.355	2
17 M WEBBER	1M11.662	+2.512	18
18 J WILSON	1M14.508	+5.358	3
19 F ALONSO	1M20.113	+10.963	8
20 J VERSTAPPEN	NO TIME		4

RACE: SUNDAY MAY 18

DRIVER	TEAM	TIM/RET	LAPS
1 M SCHUMACHER	FERRARI	1HR24M04.888	69
2 K RAIKKONEN	MCLAREN MERCEDES	+3.362	69
3 R BARRICHELLO	FERRARI	+3.951	69
4 J BUTTON	BAR HONDA	+42.243	69
5 D COULTHARD	MCLAREN MERCEDES	+59.740	69
6 R SCHUMACHER	WILLIAMS BMW	+1 LAP	68
7 M WEBBER	JAGUAR COSWORTH	+1 LAP	68
8 J TRULLI	RENAULT	+1 LAP	68
9 A PIZZONIA	JAGUAR COSWORTH	+1 LAP	68
10 C DA MATTA	TOYOTA	+1 LAP	68
11 R FIRMAN	JORDAN FORD	+1 LAP	68
12 J VILLENEUVE	BAR HONDA	+1 LAP	68
13 J WILSON	MINARDI COSWORTH	+2 LAPS	67
RET G FISICHELLA	JORDAN FORD	FUEL	60
RET N HEIDFELD	SAUBER PETRONAS	ENGINE	46
RET F ALONSO	RENAULT	ENGINE/SPIN	44
RET JP MONTOYA	WILLIAMS BMW	ENGINE	32
RET O PANIS	TOYOTA	DAMAGE	6
RET J VERSTAPPEN	MINARDI COSWORTH	ELECTRONICS	0
RET HH FRENTZEN	SAUBER PETRONAS	CLUTCH	0

FASTEST LAP: M SCHUMACHER FERRARI 1M08.337

MONTE CARLO MONACO GRAND PRIX ROUND 07

QUALIFYING 1: FRIDAY MAY 30

DRIVER	TIME	GAP	ORDER
1 M SCHUMACHER	1M16.305		2
2 R BARRICHELLO	1M16.636	+0.331	3
3 J BUTTON	1M16.895	+0.590	10
4 J TRULLI	1M16.905	+0.600	9
5 D COULTHARD	1M17.059	+0.754	5
6 R SCHUMACHER	1M17.063	+0.758	6
7 G FISICHELLA	1M17.080	+0.775	8
8 JP MONTOYA	1M17.108	+0.803	7
9 M WEBBER	1M17.637	+1.332	12
10 N HEIDFELD	1M17.912	+1.607	15
11 K RAIKKONEN	1M17.926	+1.621	1
12 J VILLENEUVE	1M18.109	+1.804	13
13 R FIRMAN	1M18.286	+1.981	16
14 F ALONSO	1M18.370	+2.065	4
15 A PIZZONIA	1M18.967	+2.662	17
16 J VERSTAPPEN	1M19.421	+3.116	19
17 J WILSON	1M19.680	+3.375	20
18 O PANIS	1M19.903	+3.598	18
19 C DA MATTA	1M20.374	+4.069	14
20 HH FRENTZEN	NO TIME		11

QUALIFYING 2: SATURDAY MAY 31

DRIVER	TIME	GAP	ORDER
1 R SCHUMACHER	1M15.259		15
2 K RAIKKONEN	1M15.295	+0.036	10
3 JP MONTOYA	1M15.415	+0.156	13
4 J TRULLI	1M15.500	+0.241	17
5 M SCHUMACHER	1M15.644	+0.385	20
6 D COULTHARD	1M15.700	+0.441	16
7 R BARRICHELLO	1M15.820	+0.561	19
8 F ALONSO	1M15.884	+0.625	7
9 M WEBBER	1M16.237	+0.978	12
10 C DA MATTA	1M16.744	+1.485	2
11 J VILLENEUVE	1M16.755	+1.496	9
12 G FISICHELLA	1M16.967	+1.708	14
13 A PIZZONIA	1M17.103	+1.844	6
14 N HEIDFELD	1M17.176	+1.917	11
15 HH FRENTZEN	1M17.402	+2.143	1
16 R FIRMAN	1M17.452	+2.193	8
17 O PANIS	1M17.464	+2.205	3
18 J VERSTAPPEN	1M18.706	+3.447	5
19 J WILSON	1M20.063	+4.804	4
20 J BUTTON	DNS		18

RACE: SUNDAY JUNE 01

DRIVER	TEAM	TIM/RET	LAPS
1 JP MONTOYA	WILLIAMS BMW	1HR42M19.010	78
2 K RAIKKONEN	MCLAREN MERCEDES	+0.602	78
3 M SCHUMACHER	FERRARI	+1.720	78
4 R SCHUMACHER	WILLIAMS BMW	+28.518	78
5 F ALONSO	RENAULT	+36.251	78
6 J TRULLI	RENAULT	+40.972	78
7 D COULTHARD	MCLAREN MERCEDES	+41.227	78
8 R BARRICHELLO	FERRARI	+53.266	78
9 C DA MATTA	TOYOTA	+1 LAP	77
10 G FISICHELLA	JORDAN FORD	+1 LAP	77
11 N HEIDFELD	SAUBER PETRONAS	+2 LAPS	76
12 R FIRMAN	JORDAN FORD	+2 LAPS	76
13 O PANIS	TOYOTA	+4 LAPS	74
RET J VILLENEUVE	BAR HONDA	ENGINE	63
RET J WILSON	MINARDI COSWORTH	FUEL	29
RET J VERSTAPPEN	MINARDI COSWORTH	FUEL	28
RET M WEBBER	JAGUAR COSWORTH	ENGINE	16
RET A PIZZONIA	JAGUAR COSWORTH	ELECTRICAL	10
RET HH FRENTZEN	SAUBER PETRONAS	ACCIDENT	0
DNS J BUTTON	BAR HONDA	WITHDRAWN	-

FASTEST LAP: K RAIKKONEN MCLAREN MERCEDES 1M14.545

MONTREAL CANADIAN GRAND PRIX ROUND 08

QUALIFYING 1: FRIDAY JUNE 13

DRIVER	TIME	GAP	ORDER
1 R BARRICHELLO	1M30.925		4
2 M SCHUMACHER	1M31.969	+1.044	2
3 N HEIDFELD	1M32.778	+1.853	15
4 R FIRMAN	1M34.759	+3.834	16
5 F ALONSO	1M35.173	+4.248	3
6 K RAIKKONEN	1M35.373	+4.448	1
7 HH FRENTZEN	1M35.776	+4.851	11
8 D COULTHARD	1M36.463	+5.538	6
9 M WEBBER	1M36.699	+5.774	12
10 O PANIS	1M37.313	+6.388	18
11 J VERSTAPPEN	1M37.426	+6.501	19
12 JP MONTOYA	1M37.479	+6.554	5
13 J WILSON	1M38.088	+7.163	20
14 J BUTTON	1M38.109	+7.184	10
15 R SCHUMACHER	1M38.210	+7.285	7
16 C DA MATTA	1M38.244	+7.319	13
17 A PIZZONIA	1M38.255	+7.330	17
18 G FISICHELLA	1M38.617	+7.692	9
19 J TRULLI	1M41.413	+10.488	8
20 J VILLENEUVE	1M44.702	+13.777	14

QUALIFYING 2: SATURDAY JUNE 14

DRIVER	TIME	GAP	ORDER
1 R SCHUMACHER	1M15.529		6
2 JP MONTOYA	1M15.923	+0.394	9
3 M SCHUMACHER	1M16.047	+0.518	19
4 F ALONSO	1M16.048	+0.519	16
5 R BARRICHELLO	1M16.143	+0.614	20
6 M WEBBER	1M16.182	+0.653	12
7 O PANIS	1M16.598	+1.069	11
8 J TRULLI	1M16.718	+1.189	2
9 C DA MATTA	1M16.826	+1.297	5
10 HH FRENTZEN	1M16.939	+1.410	14
11 D COULTHARD	1M17.024	+1.495	13
12 N HEIDFELD	1M17.086	+1.557	18
13 A PIZZONIA	1M17.337	+1.808	4
14 J VILLENEUVE	1M17.347	+1.818	1
15 J VERSTAPPEN	1M18.014	+2.485	10
16 G FISICHELLA	1M18.036	+2.507	3
17 J BUTTON	1M18.205	+2.676	7
18 J WILSON	1M18.560	+3.031	8
19 R FIRMAN	1M18.692	+3.163	17
20 K RAIKKONEN	NO TIME		15

RACE: SUNDAY JUNE 15

DRIVER	TEAM	TIM/RET	LAPS
1 M SCHUMACHER	FERRARI	1HR31M13.591	70
2 R SCHUMACHER	WILLIAMS BMW	+0.784	70
3 JP MONTOYA	WILLIAMS BMW	+1.355	70
4 F ALONSO	RENAULT	+4.481	70
5 R BARRICHELLO	FERRARI	+1M04.261	70
6 K RAIKKONEN	MCLAREN MERCEDES	+1M10.502	70
7 M WEBBER	JAGUAR COSWORTH	+1 LAP	69
8 O PANIS	TOYOTA	+1 LAP	69
9 J VERSTAPPEN	MINARDI COSWORTH	+2 LAPS	68
10 A PIZZONIA	JAGUAR COSWORTH	+4 LAPS	66
11 C DA MATTA	TOYOTA	+6 LAPS	64
RET J WILSON	MINARDI COSWORTH	GEARBOX	60
RET J BUTTON	BAR HONDA	GEARBOX	51
RET D COULTHARD	MCLAREN MERCEDES	GEARBOX	47
RET N HEIDFELD	SAUBER PETRONAS	ENGINE	47
RET J TRULLI	RENAULT	DAMAGE	22
RET G FISICHELLA	JORDAN FORD	GEARBOX	20
RET R FIRMAN	JORDAN FORD	ENGINE	20
RET J VILLENEUVE	BAR HONDA	BRAKES	14
RET HH FRENTZEN	SAUBER PETRONAS	ELECTRONICS	6

FASTEST LAP: F ALONSO RENAULT 1M16.040

2003 SEASON STATISTICS

NURBURGRING EUROPEAN GRAND PRIX ROUND 09

QUALIFYING 1: FRIDAY JUNE 27

DRIVER	TIME	GAP	ORDER
1 K RAIKKONEN	1M29.989		2
2 M SCHUMACHER	1M30.353	+0.364	1
3 JP MONTOYA	1M30.378	+0.389	5
4 R SCHUMACHER	1M30.522	+0.533	4
5 R BARRICHELLO	1M30.842	+0.853	6
6 D COULTHARD	1M30.903	+0.914	7
7 J TRULLI	1M31.143	+1.154	8
8 F ALONSO	1M31.533	+1.544	3
9 G FISICHELLA	1M32.196	+2.207	9
10 HH FRENTZEN	1M32.201	+2.212	11
11 J BUTTON	1M32.479	+2.490	10
12 M WEBBERA	1M35.972	+5.983	12
13 N HEIDFELD	1M52.300	+22.311	16
14 R FIRMAN	1M53.893	+23.904	17
15 J WILSON	1M54.546	+24.557	20
16 J VERSTAPPEN	1M55.921	+25.932	19
17 O PANIS	1M57.327	+27.338	15
18 A PIZZONIA	1M57.435	+27.446	18
19 C DA MATTA	NO TIME		13
20 J VILLENEUVE	NO TIME		14

QUALIFYING 2: SATURDAY JUNE 28

DRIVER	TIME	GAP	ORDER
1 K RAIKKONEN	1M31.523		20
2 M SCHUMACHER	1M31.555	+0.032	19
3 R SCHUMACHER	1M31.619	+0.096	17
4 JP MONTOYA	1M31.765	+0.242	18
5 R BARRICHELLO	1M31.780	+0.257	16
6 J TRULLI	1M31.976	+0.453	14
7 O PANIS	1M32.350	+0.827	4
8 F ALONSO	1M32.424	+0.901	13
9 D COULTHARD	1M32.742	+1.219	15
10 C DA MATTA	1M32.949	+1.426	2
11 M WEBBER	1M33.066	+1.543	9
12 J BUTTON	1M33.395	+1.872	10
13 G FISICHELLA	1M33.553	+2.030	12
14 R FIRMAN	1M33.827	+2.304	7
15 HH FRENTZEN	1M34.000	+2.477	11
16 A PIZZONIA	1M34.159	+2.636	3
17 J VILLENEUVE	1M34.596	+3.073	1
18 J VERSTAPPEN	1M36.318	+4.795	5
19 J WILSON	1M36.485	+4.962	6
20 N HEIDFELD	NO TIME		8

RACE: SUNDAY JUNE 29

DRIVER	TEAM	TIM/RET	LAPS
1 R SCHUMACHER	WILLIAMS BMW	1HR34M43.622	60
2 JP MONTOYA	WILLIAMS BMW	+16.821	60
3 R BARRICHELLO	FERRARI	+39.673	60
4 F ALONSO	RENAULT	+1M05.731	60
5 M SCHUMACHER	FERRARI	+1M06.162	60
6 M WEBBER	JAGUAR COSWORTH	+1 LAP	59
7 J BUTTON	BAR HONDA	+1 LAP	59
8 N HEIDFELD	SAUBER PETRONAS	+1 LAP	59
9 HH FRENTZEN	SAUBER PETRONAS	+1 LAP	59
10 A PIZZONIA	JAGUAR COSWORTH	+1 LAP	59
11 R FIRMAN	JORDAN FORD	+2 LAPS	58
12 G FISICHELLA	JORDAN FORD	+2 LAPS	58
13 J WILSON	MINARDI COSWORTH	+2 LAPS	58
14 J VERSTAPPEN	MINARDI COSWORTH	+3 LAPS	57
15 D COULTHARD	MCLAREN MERCEDES	+4 LAPS	56
RET C DA MATTA	TOYOTA	ENGINE	53
RET J VILLENEUVE	BAR HONDA	GEARBOX	51
RET J TRULLI	RENAULT	FUEL PRESSURE	37
RET O PANIS	TOYOTA	SPIN	37
RET K RAIKKONEN	MCLAREN MERCEDES	ENGINE	25

FASTEST LAP: K RAIKKONEN MCLAREN MERCEDES 1M32.621

MAGNY COURS FRENCH GRAND PRIX ROUND 10

QUALIFYING 1: FRIDAY JULY 4

DRIVER	TIME	GAP	ORDER
1 J VERSTAPPEN	1M20.817		19
2 R FIRMAN	1M23.496	+2.679	17
3 N HEIDFELD	1M24.042	+3.225	15
4 O PANIS	1M24.175	+3.358	16
5 A PIZZONIA	1M24.642	+3.825	18
6 J VILLENEUVE	1M24.651	+3.834	14
7 M WEBBER	1M25.178	+4.361	11
8 HH FRENTZEN	1M26.151	+5.334	12
9 C DA MATTA	1M26.975	+6.158	13
10 R BARRICHELLO	1M27.095	+6.278	6
11 M SCHUMACHER	1M27.929	+7.112	1
12 G FISICHELLA	1M28.502	+7.685	9
13 D COULTHARD	1M28.937	+8.120	7
14 JP MONTOYA	1M28.988	+8.171	4
15 J TRULLI	1M29.024	+8.207	8
16 K RAIKKONEN	1M29.120	+8.303	2
17 R SCHUMACHER	1M29.327	+8.510	3
18 F ALONSO	1M29.455	+8.638	5
19 J BUTTON	1M30.731	+9.914	10
20 J WILSON	TIME DELETED		20

QUALIFYING 2: SATURDAY JULY 5

DRIVER	TIME	GAP	ORDER
1 R SCHUMACHER	1M 15.019		4
2 JP MONTOYA	1M15.136	+0.117	7
3 M SCHUMACHER	1M15.480	+0.461	10
4 K RAIKKONEN	1M15.533	+0.514	5
5 D COULTHARD	1M15.628	+0.609	8
6 J TRULLI	1M15.967	+0.948	6
7 F ALONSO	1M16.087	+1.068	3
8 R BARRICHELLO	1M16.166	+1.147	11
9 M WEBBER	1M16.308	+1.289	14
10 O PANIS	1M16.345	+1.326	17
11 A PIZZONIA	1M16.965	+1.946	16
12 J VILLENEUVE	1M16.990	+1.971	15
13 C DA MATTA	1M17.068	+2.049	12
14 J BUTTON	1M17.077	+2.058	2
15 N HEIDFELD	1M17.445	+2.426	18
16 HH FRENTZEN	1M17.562	+2.543	13
17 G FISICHELLA	1M18.431	+3.412	9
18 R FIRMAN	1M18.514	+3.495	19
19 J VERSTAPPEN	1M18.709	+3.690	20
20 J WILSON	1M19.619	+4.600	1

RACE: SUNDAY JULY 6

DRIVER	TEAM	TIM/RET	LAPS
1 R SCHUMACHER	WILLIAMS BMW	1HR30M49.213	70
2 JP MONTOYA	WILLIAMS BMW	+13.813	70
3 M SCHUMACHER	FERRARI	+19.568	70
4 K RAIKKONEN	MCLAREN MERCEDES	+38.047	70
5 D COULTHARD	MCLAREN MERCEDES	+40.289	70
6 M WEBBER	JAGUAR COSWORTH	+1M06.380	70
7 R BARRICHELLO	FERRARI	+1 LAP	69
8 O PANIS	TOYOTA	+1 LAP	69
9 J VILLENEUVE	BAR HONDA	+1 LAP	69
10 A PIZZONIA	JAGUAR COSWORTH	+1 LAP	69
11 C DA MATTA	TOYOTA	+1 LAP	69
12 HH FRENTZEN	SAUBER PETRONAS	+2 LAPS	68
13 N HEIDFELD	SAUBER PETRONAS	+2 LAPS	68
14 J WILSON	MINARDI COSWORTH	+3 LAPS	67
15 R FIRMAN	JORDAN FORD	+3 LAPS	67
16 J VERSTAPPEN	MINARDI COSWORTH	+4 LAPS	66
RET J TRULLI	RENAULT	ENGINE	45
RET F ALONSO	RENAULT	ENGINE	43
RET G FISICHELLA	JORDAN FORD	ENGINE	42
RET J BUTTON	BAR HONDA	FUEL	21

FASTEST LAP: JP MONTOYA WILLIAMS BMW 1M15.512

SILVERSTONE BRITISH GRAND PRIX ROUND 11

QUALIFYING 1: FRIDAY JULY 18

DRIVER	TIME	GAP	ORDER
1 M SCHUMACHER	1M19.474		1
2 JP MONTOYA	1M19.749	+0.275	4
3 R SCHUMACHER	1M19.788	+0.314	3
4 F ALONSO	1M19.907	+0.433	6
5 O PANIS	1M19.959	+0.485	15
6 J TRULLI	1M19.963	+0.489	8
7 D COULTHARD	1M19.968	+0.494	7
8 M WEBBER	1M20.171	+0.697	9
9 J BUTTON	1M20.569	+1.095	11
10 C DA MATTA	1M20.765	+1.291	14
11 A PIZZONIA	1M20.877	+1.403	18
12 K RAIKKONEN	1M21.065	+1.591	2
13 J VILLENEUVE	1M21.084	+1.610	13
14 N HEIDFELD	1M21.211	+1.737	16
15 HH FRENTZEN	1M21.363	+1.889	12
16 G FISICHELLA	1M21.500	+2.026	10
17 R FIRMAN	1M22.335	+2.881	17
18 J VERSTAPPEN	1M23.418	+3.944	19
19 R BARRICHELLO	NO TIME		5
20 J WILSON	NO TIME		20

QUALIFYING 2: SATURDAY JULY 19

DRIVER	TIME	GAP	ORDER
1 R BARRICHELLO	1M21.209		2
2 J TRULLI	1M21.381	+0.172	15
3 K RAIKKONEN	1M21.695	+0.486	9
4 R SCHUMACHER	1M21.727	+0.518	18
5 M SCHUMACHER	1M21.867	+0.658	20
6 C DA MATTA	1M22.081	+0.872	11
7 JP MONTOYA	1M22.214	+1.005	19
8 F ALONSO	1M22.404	+1.195	17
9 J VILLENEUVE	1M22.591	+1.382	8
10 A PIZZONIA	1M22.634	+1.425	10
11 M WEBBER	1M22.647	+1.438	13
12 D COULTHARD	1M22.811	+1.602	14
13 O PANIS	1M23.042	+1.833	16
14 HH FRENTZEN	1M23.187	+1.978	6
15 G FISICHELLA	1M23.574	+2.365	5
16 N HEIDFELD	1M23.844	+2.635	7
17 R FIRMAN	1M24.385	+3.175	4
18 J WILSON	1M25.468	+4.259	1
19 J VERSTAPPEN	1M25.759	+4.550	3
20 J BUTTON	NO TIME		12

RACE: SUNDAY JULY 20

DRIVER	TEAM	TIM/RET	LAPS
1 R BARRICHELLO	FERRARI	1HR28M37.554	60
2 JP MONTOYA	WILLIAMS BMW	+5.462	60
3 K RAIKKONEN	MCLAREN MERCEDES	+10.656	60
4 M SCHUMACHER	FERRARI	+25.648	60
5 D COULTHARD	MCLAREN MERCEDES	+36.827	60
6 J TRULLI	RENAULT	+43.067	60
7 C DA MATTA	TOYOTA	+45.085	60
8 J BUTTON	BAR HONDA	+45.478	60
9 R SCHUMACHER	WILLIAMS BMW	+58.032	60
10 J VILLENEUVE	BAR HONDA	+1:03.569	60
11 O PANIS	TOYOTA	+1:05.207	60
12 HH FRENTZEN	SAUBER PETRONAS	+1:05.564	60
13 R FIRMAN	JORDAN FORD	+1 LAP	59
14 M WEBBER	JAGUAR COSWORTH	+1 LAP	59
15 J VERSTAPPEN	MINARDI COSWORTH	+2 LAPS	58
16 J WILSON	MINARDI COSWORTH	+2 LAPS	58
17 N HEIDFELD	SAUBER PETRONAS	+2 LAPS	58
RET F ALONSO	RENAULT	ENGINE	52
RET G FISICHELLA	JORDAN FORD	ENGINE	44
RET A PIZZONIA	JAGUAR COSWORTH	FUEL	32

FASTEST LAP: R BARRICHELLO FERRARI 1M22.236

HOCKENHEIM GERMAN GRAND PRIX ROUND 12

QUALIFYING 1: FRIDAY AUGUST 01

DRIVER	TIME	GAP	ORDER
1 R SCHUMACHER	1M14.427		4
2 JP MONTOYA	1M14.673	+ 0.246	3
3 J TRULLI	1M15.004	+ 0.577	8
4 M WEBBER	1M15.030	+ 0.603	9
5 F ALONSO	1M15.214	+ 0.787	6
6 K RAIKKONEN	1M15.276	+ 0.849	2
7 J WILSON	1M15.373	+ 0.946	19
8 R BARRICHELLO	1M15.399	+ 0.972	5
9 M SCHUMACHER	1M15.456	+ 1.029	1
10 O PANIS	1M15.471	+ 1.044	15
11 D COULTHARD	1M15.557	+ 1.130	7
12 J BUTTON	1M15.754	+ 1.327	10
13 HH FRENTZEN	1M15.968	+ 1.541	12
14 N HEIDFELD	1M15.985	+ 1.558	16
15 C DA MATTA	1M16.450	+ 2.023	13
16 R FIRMAN	1M17.044	+ 2.617	17
17 G FISICHELLA	1M17.111	+ 2.684	11
18 J VERSTAPPEN	1M17.702	+ 3.275	18
19 J VILLENEUVE	NO TIME		14
20 N KIESA	NO TIME		20

QUALIFYING 2: SATURDAY AUGUST 02

DRIVER	TIME	GAP	ORDER
1 JP MONTOYA	1M15.167		19
2 R SCHUMACHER	1M15.185	+ 0.018	20
3 R BARRICHELLO	1M15.488	+ 0.321	13
4 J TRULLI	1M15.679	+ 0.512	18
5 K RAIKKONEN	1M15.874	+ 0.707	15
6 M SCHUMACHER	1M15.898	+ 0.731	12
7 O PANIS	1M16.034	+ 0.867	11
8 F ALONSO	1M16.483	+ 1.316	16
9 C DA MATTA	1M16.550	+ 1.383	6
10 D COULTHARD	1M16.666	+ 1.499	10
11 M WEBBER	1M16.775	+ 1.608	17
12 G FISICHELLA	1M16.831	+ 1.664	4
13 J VILLENEUVE	1M17.090	+ 1.923	2
14 HH FRENTZEN	1M17.169	+ 2.002	8
15 N HEIDFELD	1M17.557	+ 2.390	7
16 J WILSON	1M18.021	+ 2.854	14
17 J BUTTON	1M18.085	+ 2.918	9
18 R FIRMAN	1M18.341	+ 3.174	5
19 J VERSTAPPEN	1M19.023	+ 3.856	3
20 N KIESA	1M19.174	+ 4.007	1

RACE: SUNDAY AUGUST 03

DRIVER	TEAM	TIM/RET	LAPS
1 JP MONTOYA	WILLIAMS BMW	1HR28M48.769	67
2 D COULTHARD	MCLAREN MERCEDES	+1M05.459	67
3 J TRULLI	RENAULT	+1M09.060	67
4 F ALONSO	RENAULT	+1M09.344	67
5 O PANIS	TOYOTA	+1 LAP	66
6 C DA MATTA	TOYOTA	+1 LAP	66
7 M SCHUMACHER	FERRARI	+1 LAP	66
8 J BUTTON	BAR HONDA	+1 LAP	66
9 J VILLENEUVE	BAR HONDA	+2 LAPS	65
10 N HEIDFELD	SAUBER PETRONAS	+2 LAPS	65
11 M WEBBER	JAGUAR COSWORTH	+3 LAPS	64
12 N KIESA	MINARDI COSWORTH	+5 LAPS	62
13 G FISICHELLA	JORDAN FORD	+7 LAPS	60
RET J VERSTAPPEN	MINARDI COSWORTH	HYDRAULICS	23
RET J WILSON	JAGUAR COSWORTH	TRANSMISSION	6
RET R SCHUMACHER	WILLIAMS BMW	DAMAGE	1
RET HH FRENTZEN	SAUBER PETRONAS	DAMAGE	1
RET R BARRICHELLO	FERRARI	ACCIDENT	0
RET K RÄIKKONEN	MCLAREN MERCEDES	ACCIDENT	0
RET R FIRMAN	JORDAN FORD	ACCIDENT	0

FASTEST LAP: JP MONTOYA WILLIAMS BMW 1M14.917

HUNGARORING HUNGARIAN GRAND PRIX ROUND 13

QUALIFYING 1: FRIDAY AUGUST 22

DRIVER	TIME	GAP	ORDER
1 J TRULLI	1M22.358		8
2 R SCHUMACHER	1M22.413	+0.055	4
3 M WEBBER	1M22.625	+0.267	10
4 D COULTHARD	1M22.786	+0.428	7
5 R BARRICHELLO	1M22.892	+0.534	5
6 F ALONSO	1M22.953	+0.595	6
7 O PANIS	1M22.986	+0.628	14
8 JP MONTOYA	1M23.305	+0.947	2
9 M SCHUMACHER	1M23.430	+1.072	1
10 N HEIDFELD	1M23.482	+1.124	16
11 HH FRENTZEN	1M23.660	+1.302	13
12 K RAIKKONEN	1M23.695	+1.337	3
13 J BUTTON	1M24.313	+1.955	9
14 J VILLENEUVE	1M24.333	+1.975	15
15 J WILSON	1M24.343	+1.985	19
16 G FISICHELLA	1M24.725	+2.367	11
17 R FIRMAN	1M25.223	+2.617	17
18 J VERSTAPPEN	1M26.052	+3.694	18
19 N KIESA	1M27.023	+4.665	20
20 C DA MATTA	1M55.138	+32.780	12

QUALIFYING 2: SATURDAY AUGUST 23

DRIVER	TIME	GAP	ORDER
1 F ALONSO	1M21.688		15
2 R SCHUMACHER	1M21.944	+0.256	19
3 M WEBBER	1M22.027	+0.339	18
4 JP MONTOYA	1M22.180	+0.492	13
5 R BARRICHELLO	1M22.180	+0.492	16
6 J TRULLI	1M22.610	+0.922	20
7 K RAIKKONEN	1M22.742	+1.054	9
8 M SCHUMACHER	1M22.755	+1.067	12
9 D COULTHARD	1M23.060	+1.372	17
10 O PANIS	1M23.369	+1.681	14
11 N HEIDFELD	1M23.621	+1.933	11
12 J WILSON	1M23.660	+1.972	6
13 G FISICHELLA	1M23.726	+2.038	5
14 J BUTTON	1M23.847	+2.159	8
15 C DA MATTA	1M23.982	+2.294	2
16 J VILLENEUVE	1M24.100	+2.412	7
17 HH FRENTZEN	1M24.569	+2.881	10
18 J VERSTAPPEN	1M26.423	+4.735	4
19 Z BAUMGARTNER	1M26.678	+4.990	1
20 N KIESA	1M28.907	+7.219	3

RACE: SUNDAY AUGUST 24

DRIVER	TEAM	TIM/RET	LAPS
1 F ALONSO	RENAULT	1HR39M01.460	70
2 K RAIKKONEN	MCLAREN MERCEDES	+16.768	70
3 JP MONTOYA	WILLIAMS BMW	+34.537	70
4 R SCHUMACHER	WILLIAMS BMW	+35.620	70
5 D COULTHARD	MCLAREN MERCEDES	+56.535	70
6 M WEBBER	JAGUAR COSWORTH	+1M12.643	70
7 J TRULLI	RENAULT	+1 LAP	69
8 M SCHUMACHER	FERRARI	+1 LAP	69
9 N HEIDFELD	SAUBER PETRONAS	+1 LAP	69
10 J BUTTON	BAR HONDA	+1 LAP	69
11 C DA MATTA	TOYOTA	+2 LAPS	68
12 J VERSTAPPEN	MINARDI COSWORTH	+3 LAPS	67
13 N KIESA	MINARDI COSWORTH	+4 LAPS	66
RET HH FRENTZEN	SAUBER PETRONAS	FUEL	47
RET J WILSON	JAGUAR COSWORTH	ENGINE	42
RET Z BAUMGARTNER	JORDAN FORD	ENGINE	34
RET O PANIS	TOYOTA	GEARBOX	33
RET G FISICHELLA	JORDAN FORD	ENGINE	28
RET R BARRICHELLO	FERRARI	SUSPENSION	19
RET J VILLENEUVE	BAR HONDA	HYDRAULICS	14

FASTEST LAP: JP MONTOYA WILLIAMS BMW 1M22.095

MONZA ITALIAN GRAND PRIX ROUND 14

QUALIFYING 1: FRIDAY SEPTEMBER 12

DRIVER	TIME	GAP	ORDER
1 JP MONTOYA	1M20.656		2
2 R BARRICHELLO	1M20.784	+0.128	6
3 M SCHUMACHER	1M21.268	+0.612	1
4 C DA MATTA	1M21.829	+1.173	12
5 K RAIKKONEN	1M21.966	+1.310	3
6 M WEBBER	1M21.966	+1.310	10
7 J TRULLI	1M22.034	+1.378	8
8 F ALONSO	1M22.103	+1.447	6
9 HH FRENTZEN	1M22.203	+1.547	13
10 O PANIS	1M22.372	+1.716	14
11 J BUTTON	1M22.495	+1.839	9
12 N HEIDFELD	1M22.547	+1.891	16
13 J VILLENEUVE	1M22.858	+2.202	15
14 D COULTHARD	1M23.154	+2.498	7
15 J WILSON	1M23.609	+2.953	19
16 G FISICHELLA	1M24.179	+3.523	11
17 Z BAUMGARTNER	1M24.872	+4.216	17
18 N KIESA	1M26.299	+5.643	20
19 R SCHUMACHER	DISQUALIFIED		4
20 J VERSTAPPEN	NO TIME		18

QUALIFYING 2: SATURDAY SEPTEMBER 13

DRIVER	TIME	GAP	ORDER
1 M SCHUMACHER	1M20.963		18
2 JP MONTOYA	1M21.014	+0.051	20
3 R BARRICHELLO	1M21.242	+0.279	19
4 K RAIKKONEN	1M21.466	+0.503	16
5 M GENE	1M21.834	+0.871	1
6 J TRULLI	1M21.944	+0.981	14
7 J BUTTON	1M22.301	+1.338	10
8 D COULTHARD	1M22.471	+1.508	7
9 O PANIS	1M22.488	+1.525	11
10 J VILLENEUVE	1M22.717	+1.754	8
11 M WEBBER	1M22.754	+1.791	15
12 C DA MATTA	1M22.914	+1.951	17
13 G FISICHELLA	1M22.992	+2.029	5
14 HH FRENTZEN	1M23.216	+2.253	12
15 J WILSON	1M23.484	+2.521	6
16 N HEIDFELD	1M23.803	+2.840	9
17 J VERSTAPPEN	1M25.078	+4.115	2
18 Z BAUMGARTNER	1M25.881	+4.918	4
19 N KIESA	1M26.778	+5.815	3
20 F ALONSO	1M40.405	+19.442	13

RACE: SUNDAY SEPTEMBER 14

DRIVER	TEAM	TIM/RET	LAPS
1 M SCHUMACHER	FERRARI	1H14M19.838	53
2 JP MONTOYA	WILLIAMS BMW	+5.294	53
3 R BARRICHELLO	FERRARI	+11.835	53
4 K RAIKKONEN	MCLAREN MERCEDES	+12.834	53
5 M GENE	WILLIAMS BMW	+27.891	53
6 J VILLENEUVE	BAR HONDA	+1 LAP	52
7 M WEBBER	JAGUAR COSWORTH	+1 LAP	52
8 F ALONSO	RENAULT	+1 LAP	52
9 N HEIDFELD	SAUBER PETRONAS	+1 LAP	52
10 G FISICHELLA	JORDAN FORD	+1 LAP	52
11 Z BAUMGARTNER	JORDAN FORD	+2 LAPS	51
12 N KIESA	MINARDI COSWORTH	+2 LAPS	51
13 HH FRENTZEN	SAUBER PETRONAS	+3 LAPS	50
RET D COULTHARD	MCLAREN MERCEDES	FUEL PRESSURE	45
RET O PANIS	TOYOTA	BRAKES	35
RET J VERSTAPPEN	MINARDI COSWORTH	RADIATOR	27
RET J BUTTON	BAR HONDA	GEARBOX	24
RET C DA MATTA	TOYOTA	PUNCTURE	3
RET J WILSON	JAGUAR COSWORTH	TRANSMISSION	2
RET J TRULLI	RENAULT	HYDRAULICS	0

FASTEST LAP: M SCHUMACHER FERRARI 1M21.832

INDIANAPOLIS UNITED STATES GRAND PRIX ROUND 15

QUALIFYING 1: FRIDAY SEPTEMBER 26

DRIVER	TIME	GAP	ORDER
1 J TRULLI	1M09.566		8
2 R BARRICHELLO	1M09.835	+0.269	5
3 M WEBBER	1M10.081	+0.515	9
4 R SCHUMACHER	1M10.222	+0.656	4
5 JP MONTOYA	1M10.372	+0.806	2
6 D COULTHARD	1M10.450	+0.884	7
7 F ALONSO	1M10.556	+0.990	6
8 M SCHUMACHER	1M10.736	+1.170	1
9 K RAIKKONEN	1M10.756	+1.190	3
10 J BUTTON	1M11.847	+2.281	10
11 C DA MATTA	1M11.949	+2.383	12
12 G FISICHELLA	1M12.227	+2.661	11
13 HH FRENTZEN	1M13.541	+3.975	13
14 O PANIS	1M17.666	+8.100	14
15 N HEIDFELD	1M17.768	+8.202	16
16 J VILLENEUVE	1M18.547	+8.981	15
17 R FIRMAN	1M19.383	+9.817	17
18 J WILSON	1M19.491	+9.925	19
19 N KIESA	1M21.973	+12.407	20
20 J VERSTAPPEN	NO TIME		18

QUALIFYING 2: SATURDAY SEPTEMBER 27

DRIVER	TIME	GAP	ORDER
1 K RAIKKONEN	1M11.670		12
2 R BARRICHELLO	1M11.794	+0.124	19
3 O PANIS	1M11.920	+0.250	7
4 JP MONTOYA	1M11.948	+0.278	16
5 R SCHUMACHER	1M12.078	+0.408	17
6 F ALONSO	1M12.087	+0.417	14
7 M SCHUMACHER	1M12.194	+0.524	13
8 D COULTHARD	1M12.297	+0.627	15
9 C DA MATTA	1M12.326	+0.656	10
10 J TRULLI	1M12.566	+0.896	20
11 J BUTTON	1M12.695	+1.025	11
12 J VILLENEUVE	1M13.050	+1.380	5
13 N HEIDFELD	1M13.083	+1.413	6
14 M WEBBER	1M13.269	+1.599	18
15 HH FRENTZEN	1M13.447	+1.777	8
16 J WILSON	1M13.585	+1.915	3
17 G FISICHELLA	1M13.798	+2.128	9
18 R FIRMAN	1M14.027	+2.357	4
19 J VERSTAPPEN	1M15.360	+3.690	1
20 N KIESA	1M15.644	+3.974	2

RACE: SUNDAY SEPTEMBER 28

DRIVER	TEAM	TIM/RET	LAPS
1 M SCHUMACHER	FERRARI	1HR33M35.997	73
2 K RAIKKONEN	MCLAREN MERCEDES	+18.258	73
3 HH FRENTZEN	SAUBER PETRONAS	+37.964	73
4 J TRULLI	RENAULT	+48.329	73
5 N HEIDFELD	SAUBER PETRONAS	+56.403	73
6 JP MONTOYA	WILLIAMS BMW	+1 LAP	72
7 G FISICHELLA	JORDAN FORD	+1 LAP	72
8 J WILSON	JAGUAR COSWORTH	+2 LAPS	71
9 C DA MATTA	TOYOTA	+2 LAPS	71
10 J VERSTAPPEN	MINARDI COSWORTH	+4 LAPS	69
11 N KIESA	MINARDI COSWORTH	+4 LAPS	69
RET J VILLENEUVE	BAR HONDA	ENGINE	63
RET R FIRMAN	JORDAN FORD	SPIN	48
RET D COULTHARD	MCLAREN MERCEDES	GEARBOX	45
RET F ALONSO	RENAULT	ENGINE	44
RET J BUTTON	BAR HONDA	ENGINE	41
RET O PANIS	TOYOTA	SPIN	27
RET M WEBBER	JAGUAR COSWORTH	ACCIDENT	21
RET R SCHUMACHER	WILLIAMS BMW	ACCIDENT	21
RET R BARRICHELLO	FERRARI	ACCIDENT	2

FASTEST LAP: M SCHUMACHER FERRARI 1M11.473

SUZUKA JAPANESE GRAND PRIX ROUND 16

QUALIFYING 1: FRIDAY OCTOBER 10

DRIVER	TIME	GAP	ORDER
1 J TRULLI	1M30.281		8
2 R SCHUMACHER	1M30.343	+0.062	4
3 M SCHUMACHER	1M30.464	+0.183	1
4 D COULTHARD	1M30.482	+0.201	7
5 K RAIKKONEN	1M30.558	+0.277	2
6 F ALONSO	1M30.624	+0.343	6
7 R BARRICHELLO	1M30.758	+0.477	5
8 JP MONTOYA	1M31.201	+0.920	3
9 M WEBBER	1M31.305	+1.024	9
10 N HEIDFELD	1M31.783	+1.502	14
11 T SATO	1M31.832	+1.551	20
12 HH FRENTZEN	1M31.892	+1.611	10
13 O PANIS	1M31.908	+1.627	15
14 C DA MATTA	1M32.256	+1.975	13
15 J WILSON	1M32.291	+2.010	17
16 J BUTTON	1M32.374	+2.093	12
17 R FIRMAN	1M33.057	+2.776	16
18 G FISICHELLA	1M33.313	+3.032	11
19 J VERSTAPPEN	1M34.836	+4.555	18
20 N KIESA	1M36.181	+5.900	19

QUALIFYING 2: SATURDAY OCTOBER 11

DRIVER	TIME	GAP	ORDER
1 R BARRICHELLO	1M31.713		14
2 JP MONTOYA	1M32.412	+0.699	13
3 C DA MATTA	1M32.419	+0.706	7
4 O PANIS	1M32.862	+1.149	8
5 F ALONSO	1M33.044	+1.331	15
6 M WEBBER	1M33.106	+1.393	12
7 D COULTHARD	1M33.137	+1.424	17
8 K RAIKKONEN	1M33.272	+1.559	16
9 J BUTTON	1M33.474	+1.761	5
10 J WILSON	1M33.558	+1.845	6
11 N HEIDFELD	1M33.632	+1.919	11
12 HH FRENTZEN	1M33.896	+2.183	9
13 T SATO	1M33.924	+2.211	10
14 M SCHUMACHER	1M34.302	+2.589	18
15 R FIRMAN	1M34.771	+3.058	4
16 G FISICHELLA	1M34.912	+3.199	3
17 J VERSTAPPEN	1M34.975	+3.262	2
18 N KIESA	1M37.226	+5.513	1
19 J TRULLI	NO TIME		19
20 R SCHUMACHER	NO TIME		20

RACE: SUNDAY OCTOBER 12

DRIVER	TEAM	TIM/RET	LAPS
1 R BARRICHELLO	FERRARI	1HR25M11.743	53
2 K RAIKKONEN	MCLAREN MERCEDES	+11.085	53
3 D COULTHARD	MCLAREN MERCEDES	+11.614	53
4 J BUTTON	BAR HONDA	+33.106	53
5 J TRULLI	RENAULT	+34.269	53
6 T SATO	BAR HONDA	+51.692	53
7 C DA MATTA	TOYOTA	+56.794	53
8 M SCHUMACHER	FERRARI	+59.487	53
9 N HEIDFELD	SAUBER PETRONAS	+1M00.159	53
10 O PANIS	TOYOTA	+1M01.844	53
11 M WEBBER	JAGUAR COSWORTH	+1M11.005	53
12 R SCHUMACHER	WILLIAMS BMW	+1 LAP	52
13 J WILSON	JAGUAR COSWORTH	+1 LAP	52
14 R FIRMAN	JORDAN FORD	+2 LAPS	51
15 J VERSTAPPEN	MINARDI COSWORTH	+2 LAPS	51
16 N KIESA	MINARDI COSWORTH	+3 LAPS	50
RET G FISICHELLA	JORDAN FORD	FUEL	33
RET F ALONSO	RENAULT	ENGINE	17
RET HH FRENTZEN	SAUBER PETRONAS	ENGINE	9
RET JP MONTOYA	WILLIAMS BMW	HYDRAULICS	9

FASTEST LAP: R SCHUMACHER WILLIAMS BMW 1M33.408

2003 CHAMPIONSHIP STANDINGS

WORLD DRIVERS' CHAMPIONSHIP

POS	DRIVER	POINTS TOTAL
1	MICHAEL SCHUMACHER	93
2	KIMI RAIKKONEN	91
3	JUAN PABLO MONTOYA	82
4	RUBENS BARRICHELLO	65
5	RALF SCHUMACHER	58
6	FERNANDO ALONSO	55
7	DAVID COULTHARD	51
8	JARNO TRULLI	33
9	JENSON BUTTON	17
10	MARK WEBBER	17
11	HEINZ-HARALD FRENTZEN	13
12	GIANCARLO FISICHELLA	12
13	CRISTIANO DA MATTA	10
14	NICK HEIDFELD	6
15	OLIVIER PANIS	6
16	JACQUES VILLENEUVE	6
17	MARC GENE	4
18	TAKUMA SATO	3
19	RALPH FIRMAN	1
20	JUSTIN WILSON	1
21	ANTONIO PIZZONIA	0
22	JOS VERSTAPPEN	0
23	NICOLAS KIESA	0
24	ZSOLT BAUMGARTNER	0

After a hard fought campaign Michael Schumacher took a Record Breaking sixth World Championship; for the 13th time Ferrari captured the Constuctors' Championship, their fifth consecutive title.

WORLD CONSTRUCTORS' CHAMPIONSHIP

POS	TEAM	POINTS TOTAL
1	SCUDERIA FERRARI MARLBORO	158
2	BMW.WILLIAMSF1 TEAM	144
3	WEST MCLAREN MERCEDES	142
4	MILD SEVEN RENAULT F1 TEAM	88
5	LUCKY STRIKE BAR HONDA	26
6	SAUBER PETRONAS	19
7	JAGUAR RACING	18
8	PANASONIC TOYOTA RACING	16
9	JORDAN FORD	13
10	EUROPEAN MINARDI COSWORTH	0